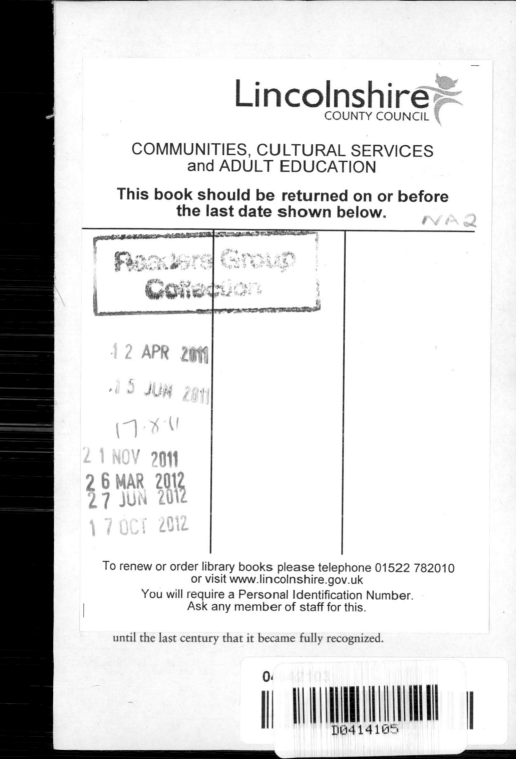

Lincolnshire
COUNTY COUNCIL

COMMUNITIES, CULTURAL SERVICES and ADULT EDUCATION

This book should be returned on or before the last date shown below.

NA2

To renew or order library books please telephone 01522 782010
or visit www.lincolnshire.gov.uk

You will require a Personal Identification Number.
Ask any member of staff for this.

until the last century that it became fully recognized.

JOHN BARNARD is Emeritus Professor of English Literature in the School of English, University of Leeds. He has written extensively on Keats and the Romantics, on seventeenth-century literature and on book history.

JOHN KEATS

Selected Poems

Edited and with an Introduction and Notes by
JOHN BARNARD

PENGUIN BOOKS

PENGUIN CLASSICS

Published by the Penguin Group
Penguin Books Ltd, 80 Strand, London WC2R 0RL, England
Penguin Group (USA) Inc., 375 Hudson Street, New York, New York 10014, USA
Penguin Group (Canada), 90 Eglinton Avenue East, Suite 700, Toronto, Ontario, Canada M4P 2Y3
(a division of Pearson Penguin Canada Inc.)
Penguin Ireland, 25 St Stephen's Green, Dublin 2, Ireland
(a division of Penguin Books Ltd)
Penguin Group (Australia), 250 Camberwell Road, Camberwell, Victoria 3124, Australia
(a division of Pearson Australia Group Pty Ltd)
Penguin Books India Pvt Ltd, 11 Community Centre, Panchsheel Park, New Delhi – 110 017, India
Penguin Group (NZ), 67 Apollo Drive, Rosebank, North Shore 0631, New Zealand
(a division of Pearson New Zealand Ltd)
Penguin Books (South Africa) (Pty) Ltd, 24 Sturdee Avenue, Rosebank, Johannesburg 2196, South Africa

Penguin Books Ltd, Registered Offices: 80 Strand, London WC2R 0RL, England

www.penguin.com

This selection first published 2007

5

Selection, Introduction and Notes, copyright © John Barnard, 2007
All rights reserved

The moral right of the editor has been asserted

Set in 10.25/12.25 pt PostScript Adobe Sabon
Typeset by Rowland Phototypesetting Ltd, Bury St Edmunds, Suffolk
Printed in England by Clays Ltd, St Ives plc

ISBN: 978-0-140-42447-8

www.greenpenguin.co.uk

Penguin Books is committed to a sustainable future
for our business, our readers and our planet.
The book in your hands is made from paper
certified by the Forest Stewardship Council.

Contents

Selected Poems

Chronology

1795 *31 October*: John Keats (K) born at Swan and Hoop Stables, Moorfields, London.

1797 *28 February*: Birth of brother, George.

1799 *18 November*: Birth of brother, Tom.

1801 *28 April*: Birth of brother, Edward, who dies before reaching his first birthday.

1803 *3 June*: Birth of sister, Fanny (Frances Mary).

August: K and George start their education at the Rev. John Clarke's Enfield School as boarders; Tom joins them there later. K befriended by Charles Cowden Clarke, his teacher and son of the headmaster.

1804 *16 April*: Father, Thomas Keats, dies in a riding accident.

27 June: Mother, Frances, marries William Rawlings. The Keats children go to live with their grandparents, John and Alice Jennings, at Ponders End.

1805 *8 March*: Grandfather dies. The family move to Edmonton with Alice Jennings.

21 October: Battle of Trafalgar.

1810 *mid-March*: Mother dies of tuberculosis, watched over by K, and is buried 20 March.

Summer: K leaves Enfield School and is apprenticed to Thomas Hammond, a surgeon and apothecary in Edmonton.

July: Richard Abbey appointed guardian of the Keats children.

1814 Writes 'Imitation of Spenser'.

April: Napoleon abdicates and is exiled to Elba: Louis XVIII proclaimed king of France.

19 December: Death of grandmother. Fanny Keats goes to live with Richard Abbey and his wife.

1815 *2 February*: Writes a sonnet on Leigh Hunt's release from prison.

20 March: Napoleon escapes from Elba, defeated at Waterloo, 18 June.

1 October: Enters Guy's Hospital as a student.

29 October: Appointed dresser (surgeon's assistant) to William Lucas, to start in March 1816 for a year.

1816 *5 May*: 'O Solitude', K's first published poem appears in Leigh Hunt's *Examiner*.

25 July: Passes examination at Apothecaries' Hall; eligible to practise as an apothecary (equivalent to a GP today).

August: Accompanies Tom to Margate, Kent, where K writes verse epistles to George and to Charles Cowden Clarke.

Before 9 October: Joins his brothers in lodgings at 8 Dean Street, Southwark. Resumes duties as a dresser at Guy's Hospital.

October: Meets Leigh Hunt (through Cowden Clarke), Benjamin Robert Haydon and John Hamilton Reynolds. Writes 'On First Looking into Chapman's Homer'.

By 18 November: Has moved with his brothers to 76 Cheapside.

1 December: Hunt includes Chapman sonnet in his *Examiner* article on 'Young Poets' (Keats, Shelley and Reynolds). During December K prepares his first volume for the press.

1817 *16 February*: 'To Kosciusko' printed in the *Examiner*. Hunt shows some of K's poems to Shelley, William Godwin, Basil Montagu, and Hazlitt at a dinner.

1 or 2 March: Sees Elgin Marbles in the British Museum with Haydon.

4 March: Government suspends the Habeas Corpus Act.

7 or 10 March: *Poems* published by C. and J. Ollier.

c. 13 March: Taylor and Hessey agree to publish K's future books.

By 25 March: Has completed work as a dresser and moved to 1 Well Walk, Hampstead, with his brothers.

14 April: Sets out for the Isle of Wight, which he reaches the following day.

18 April: Plans to begin *Endymion*. Reading Shakespeare.

c. *24 April*: Moves to Margate, where Tom joins him.

May: Visits Canterbury, and meets Isabella Jones at Hastings at the end of May or beginning of June.

June: Returns to Hampstead.

c. *21 August*: Has finished *Endymion* Books I and II.

c. *3 September*: Stays in Oxford with Benjamin Bailey where he completes *Endymion* Book III.

5 October: Returns to Hampstead. *Blackwood's Magazine* publishes first attack on the 'Cockney School of Poetry' published this month.

22 November–c. 5 December: Stays at Burford Bridge, Surrey.

28 November: Completes *Endymion*.

28 December: Attends Haydon's 'immortal dinner' at which William Wordsworth and Charles Lamb are present, among others.

1818 *January–February*: Revises *Endymion*. Attends Hazlitt's lectures on the English poets.

23 January: Tom is spitting blood.

March–April: Stays at Teignmouth, Devon, with Tom. Continues preparing *Endymion* for the press.

9–10 April: His original Preface to *Endymion* rejected; writes the published second version.

27 April: About this date *Endymion* published. Has finished *Isabella*.

c. *28 May*: George Keats marries Georgiana Wylie.

June: K's poetry attacked in the *British Critic*.

24 June: Begins walking tour of Scotland with Charles Brown after seeing George and Georgiana Keats set out for America from Liverpool.

1 July: Writes 'On Visiting the Tomb of Burns'.

2 August: Climbs Ben Nevis.

18 August: Returns to Hampstead, having been forced to break off his tour because of a severe chill and sore throat. Finds Tom very ill.

c. *27 September*: Croker's attack on *Endymion* appears in the *Quarterly Review*. Has begun *Hyperion* while nursing Tom.

12 October: The *Examiner* reprints Reynolds's defence of *Endymion*.

24 October: Meets Isabella Jones again.

November: Continues working on *Hyperion*. By the end of this month has probably met Fanny Brawne.

1 December: Death of Tom Keats from tuberculosis. K moves into Charles Brown's house, Wentworth Place, Hampstead.

25 December: Dines with Fanny Brawne, with whom he has reached an 'understanding', and her mother.

1819 *18 or 19 January*: Joins Charles Brown in Chichester, Sussex. Writes *The Eve of St Agnes*.

1 or 2 February: Returns to Wentworth Place, Hampstead, with a sore throat.

13–17 February: Writes 'The Eve of St Mark'.

April–May: Gives up *Hyperion*. Writes 'La Belle Dame sans Merci', experiments with the sonnet form and composes the major odes (except for 'To Autumn').

31 May: Thinks of going to live near Teignmouth or becoming a ship's surgeon: both ideas abandoned on 9 June.

17 June: Asks Haydon and others to return loans.

28 June: Crosses to Isle of Wight and stays at Shanklin, working on *Otho the Great* (a verse tragedy written jointly with Charles Brown) and *Lamia*. Joined there by Brown on about 22 July.

12 August: Moves with Brown to Winchester. Continues work on *Otho the Great* and *Lamia*, and works on *The Fall of Hyperion*.

16 August: Peterloo Massacre, Manchester.

15 September: Returns to Winchester after a five-day trip to London.

19 September: Writes 'To Autumn'.

21 September: Has given up *The Fall of Hyperion*.

8 October: Leaves Winchester for London with Brown, and briefly takes lodgings in Westminster.

Late October: Living with Brown at Wentworth Place, next door to Fanny Brawne.

November: Returns to *The Fall of Hyperion*.

22 December: K is 'rather unwell'. By the end of the month he is engaged to Fanny Brawne.

1820 *9–28 January*: George Keats is visiting London from America in an attempt to sort out the tangled affairs of the Keats children's inheritance. *Otho the Great* rejected by Covent Garden theatre.

29 January: George III dies: the Prince Regent succeeds as George IV.

3 February: After seeing George off to America, K returns to London from Liverpool by stage coach. At 11 p.m. has severe haemorrhage and is confined to house for rest of month.

c. 13 February: Fanny Brawne rejects his offer to end their engagement.

12–13 March: Revising *Lamia*.

27 April: Taylor and Hessey have all of K's manuscripts for his new volume.

4 May: Moves his belongings to Wesleyan Place, Kentish Town, because Brown is renting Wentworth Place.

10 May: 'La Belle Dame sans Merci' printed in the *Examiner*.

c. 11 June: Reads and corrects proofs of *Lamia* volume.

22 June: Has an attack of blood-spitting.

23 June–mid-August: Moves to Leigh Hunt's house in Mortimer Terrace so that he can be better looked after.

July: Taylor and Hessey publish *Lamia, Isabella, The Eve of St Agnes, and Other Poems*.

5 July: His doctor orders him to go to Italy.

August: Shelley invites K to stay with him in Italy. Stays with the Brawnes in their rented half of Wentworth Place and makes an informal will. A belated but sympathetic review of *Endymion* and the *Lamia* volume by Francis Jeffrey appears in the *Edinburgh Review*.

23 August: Richard Abbey refuses to give K money.

13 September: Joseph Severn decides to accompany him to Italy.

18 September: Sails from Gravesend by night on the *Maria Crowther*.

21–31 October: The ship is held in quarantine in Naples.

15 November: Reaches Rome, and takes lodgings in the Piazza di Spagna.

30 November: Writes his last known letter (to Charles Brown).

10 December: Has relapse.

1821 *23 February*: Dies at 11 p.m.

26 February: Buried in the Protestant Cemetery in Rome.

17 March: News of his death reaches London.

Introduction

The three very early poems which open this selection already show the apparently contradictory pressures which characterize Keats's intellectual and artistic life. His earliest known poem, 'Imitation of Spenser', is self-consciously literary in its origins. As its title makes clear, this looks to the literary past for inspiration. The next two, however, are addressed to the immediate political present. The whole of Keats's life (1795–1821) was lived under the shadow of the Napoleonic Wars and their immediate aftermath. It was a period of repressive rule by Tory ministries, which, threatened by social unrest and fearful of revolution, employed spies and the law in an attempt to prevent legitimate protest in print or at public meetings. 'On Peace' celebrates Napoleon's surrender in April 1814 and hopes that Europe's repressive monarchical regimes ('sceptred tyrants', 10) will be replaced by constitutional monarchies. Keats's final plea, 'leave not uncurbed the great' (13), applies as much to Britain as to Europe. 'Lines Written on 29 May' is a contemptuous, impromptu attack on those 'infatuate Britons' who annually celebrated the restoration of Charles II in 1660, an occasion the established church marked with the ringing of church bells across the land. Far from being a cause for celebration, the Restoration, which led to the execution of the true republican patriots, Algernon Sidney, Lord William Russell and Sir Henry Vane, was, according to Keats, the moment of Britain's 'direst, foulest shame' (2). In both poems the eighteen-year-old Keats was echoing the sentiments expressed by the poet and essayist Leigh Hunt (1784–1859) in his liberal weekly periodical, the *Examiner*, which Keats had read since his schooldays. Hunt's political views were common to most of the second-generation Romantics. The last verses Keats is known to have written, 'In after-time, a sage of mickle lore', a mock-Spenserian allegory, depicts the power of a free press overthrowing anti-democratic and tyrannical forces, and demonstrates the consistency of Keats's political beliefs throughout his career. Although the extent to which Keats's liberal politics are expressed in his poetry can be over-stated, there is no doubt, as contemporary reviewers saw, that his poetry is frequently an indirect commentary on the conventional political, religious and sexual attitudes which governed his society.

This is not to say that Keats was a political poet in the way Shelley was. Throughout his life Keats always believed that true poetry was written for posterity, and that its 'realms of gold', whether created by Homer, Dante, Spenser, Shakespeare or Milton, existed in a sphere independent of the accidents of history. Keats is the one great English Romantic poet whose prime belief was in Art and Beauty. 'A thing of beauty is a joy for ever', the opening line of *Endymion: A Poetic Romance*, published in April 1818, is probably Keats's best-known line. It suggests that his poetry belongs to a timeless world of Art, one endorsed by the Grecian Urn's conviction that 'Beauty is Truth, Truth Beauty.' This was certainly how Keats was read by critics in the nineteenth and early to mid-twentieth centuries, yet while his preoccupation in his poetry and letters with the nature of the claims of the imagination and of 'Poesy' is the spur to much of his finest writing, it is also a source of anxiety. In the 'Ode to a Nightingale' the speaker's urge to identify with and merge into the nightingale's song ends in a question, and a move back from imaginative to real time –

> Adieu! the fancy cannot cheat so well
>   As she is famed to do deceiving elf.
> Adieu! adieu! thy plaintive anthem fades
>   Past the near meadows, over the still stream,
>   Up the hill-side; and now 'tis buried deep
>   In the next valley-glades:
>   Was it a vision, or a waking dream?
>   Fled is that music – Do I wake or sleep?

Keats was born in October 1795, son of the manager of a livery stable in Moorfields. His father was killed in a riding accident in 1804, the year after Keats had become a pupil at Enfield School to the north of London. Keats's maternal grandfather, John Jennings, died in 1805, leaving each of the three Keats brothers and their young sister, Fanny, a substantial inheritance, the full extent of which was not revealed until after Keats's death. In 1810 his mother died of tuberculosis, the family disease. By then, Keats had received a good education in the dissenting tradition at Enfield, and had been befriended by the headmaster's son, Charles Cowden Clarke. In 1810 he was apprenticed to the Edmonton apothecary, Thomas Hammond, funded by money drawn against his legacy. Keats continued his medical training at Guy's Hospital, which he entered in October 1815, and ten months later successfully passed the newly rigorous examination to qualify as an apothecary. This allowed him to set up as a medical practitioner. He still had to finish his twelve-month appointment as a dresser, or surgeon's assistant, at Guy's, and completed his time at the hospital in March 1817.

Keats had started writing poetry during his apprenticeship, and his reading in these years was encouraged by Cowden Clarke, but it was not until October 1816, during the final six months of his medical training, that he was introduced to Leigh Hunt, whose *Examiner* had already printed Keats's first published poem, the sonnet 'O Solitude! if I must with thee dwell'. Encouraged by his family and friends, and immediately taken up as a coming poet by Hunt and his circle, which included the painter Benjamin Robert Haydon (1786–1846), and the young poet and journalist John Hamilton Reynolds (1790–1852), Keats published his first volume, *Poems*, in early March 1817, only five months after first meeting Hunt. It is now clear that Keats paid for the printing and publication of *Poems* (1817).[1] This was a remarkably headstrong decision since by this time most of Keats's inheritance had been laid out on his six-and-a-half years of medical training. The volume itself is something of a rag-bag. Its two middle sections are made up of album verse, Spenserian narrative fragments, three verse epistles (to his brother George, Cowden Clarke and the poetaster, George Felton Mathew), and a group of sonnets. Of these, the epistle 'To Charles Cowden Clarke', the 'Imitation of Spenser', 'Specimen of an Induction to a Poem' and several of the sonnets, including 'On First Looking into Chapman's Homer', are reprinted here. In *Poems* (1817) these poems are sandwiched between two longer recently completed poems, 'I stood tip-toe' and 'Sleep and Poetry', the most ambitious poems in the volume, given here in their entirety. 'I stood tip-toe' is a catalogue of characteristic early Keatsian 'luxuries', which begins by drawing on nature ('sweet buds', 'a bush of May flowers', 'a streamlet's rushy banks', 'a tuft of evening primroses'), and ends by invoking mythological stories of the love between gods and humans, notably those of Cupid and Psyche and Diana and Endymion (115–end), the former prefiguring the 'Ode to Psyche' and the latter leading directly to Keats's four-book 'Poetic Romance', *Endymion*. 'Sleep and Poetry' announces Keats's self-dedication to poetry and the pursuit of fame, and includes his assessment of the achievements and shortcomings of contemporary poets. Both works are indebted to Leigh Hunt, a sonnet to whom ('Glory and loveliness have passed away') Keats printed as the dedicatory poem to the volume.

Poems (1817) is a promissory work. It outlines the young poet's ambitions and hopes, but goes little way towards fulfilling them. Despite the high hopes of the Hunt circle and Keats's family and friends, the volume attracted little immediate attention. Its publication did, however, persuade John Taylor and James Hessey, established publishers interested in building up a poetry list, to agree to publish Keats's next volume: Taylor in particular was convinced of Keats's genius, a conviction which continued long after Keats's death and apparent failure.

The extraordinary self-belief and courage with which Keats committed himself to writing a full-scale allegorical work of four thousand lines immediately after the publication of *Poems* (1817) was, on the evidence of his first volume, remarkable. Yet Keats did succeed in drafting *Endymion* between April and November 1817 and discovered himself as a poet in the course of doing so. Without the experience of writing this earlier narrative Keats could not have attempted the epic scale of *Hyperion: A Fragment* the following autumn, and, equally importantly, in the course of composing *Endymion* he began to speculate on the nature of poetry and the imagination in his letters to friends and family.

Keats's preface dismissed *Endymion* as immature even as he published the poem. His 'Poetic Romance' is, however, more substantial than that suggests. Although the poem is loosely structured, and its self-excited dreams of poetry, love and sexual longings can easily be mocked as adolescent fantasizing, *Endymion*'s four books are the most ambitious long poem Keats completed. Its reanimation of Greek mythology is a serious effort to imagine a non-Christian religion based on animism and celebrating human love. At the same time it is an implicit criticism of conventional political and religious beliefs in contemporary England, reacting in particular against the growing forces of prudery. While Regency high society was notable for sexual excess and licence, the middle and lower-middle classes had a strongly demarcated view of male and female roles and a sexual double standard, clearly foreshadowing 'Victorian' attitudes. The notorious *Blackwood's Magazine* review in August 1818 was virulent and personalized. But, seen from a Tory and culturally conservative viewpoint, Keats was, in its words, an 'ignorant and unsettled pretender' as a poet, a vulgarizer of classical mythology, a writer of 'prurient and vulgar lines' unfit for the ladies, a lower-class 'Cockney' imitator of Leigh Hunt, and a 'bantling' who had 'already learned to lisp sedition'. The last charge is based on the invocation to Book III (1–21) of *Endymion*, a savage, if indirectly expressed, attack on Britain's current government, which the reviewer quotes in full. Keats himself said the passage was a clear expression of his attitude to the 'present Ministers'.

One aim of this selection is to emphasize Keats's place as a second-generation Romantic, along with Byron and Shelley, with whom he shares a commitment to the long narrative poem. This has meant annotating the substantial selection from *Endymion* and the two 'Hyperion' fragments more fully than Keats's best known works, partly to explain the allusions to

contemporary events and obscure allegorical passages, partly
to explain what Keats was attempting to make of his material.
In differing ways, Keats's neo-Hellenism is shared by Byron,
Peacock, Leigh Hunt and Shelley, as is his political stance. He
also resembles them in his mixed reaction to Wordsworth.
Wordsworth's achievement was undeniable but his active sup-
port of the Tory government was seen as a betrayal of his earlier
radicalism, and his later poetry seemed to have retreated into a
gloomy subjectivity. It is significant that the older poet rejected
Keats's 'Hymn to Pan' in Book I of *Endymion* as a 'Very pretty
piece of Paganism'.

Keats's final volume, *Lamia, Isabella, The Eve of St Agnes,
and Other Poems*, published two years after the appearance of
Endymion in 1818, contained most of the remainder of Keats's
mature poems written in 1819. The major odes and the three
narrative poems named in the volume's title were accompanied
by some weaker poems. Surprisingly, the volume did not con-
tain either 'La Belle Dame sans Merci' or the strange and power-
ful sonnet, 'A Dream, after reading Dante's Episode of Paolo
and Francesca', both published in Leigh Hunt's new periodical,
the *Indicator*, though over the pseudonym 'Caviare' rather than
Keats's own name. Nor was space found to print any of the
remarkable sonnets Keats had written since 1817: these include,
among others, 'After dark vapours have oppress'd our plains',
the two Elgin Marbles sonnets, 'On the Sea', 'On Sitting Down
to Read *King Lear* Once Again', 'When I have fears that I may
cease to be', 'O thou whose face hath been five years at its slow
ebb', 'The Human Seasons', 'To Ailsa Rock', 'Why did I laugh
tonight? No voice will tell', 'To Sleep', 'If by dull rhymes our
English must be chained' and the two sonnets 'On Fame', while
The Fall of Hyperion was to remain in manuscript until 1857.

In part, the makeup, order, and even the texts of the poems
in Keats's final volume are a result of the editorial work of his
publisher, John Taylor, and the firm's lawyer and Keats's friend,
Richard Woodhouse. They were responsible for revisions in the
wording and punctuation of Keats's manuscript, and for the
ordering of the poems and its title – Keats wanted *The Eve of
St Agnes* to start the volume with the title 'St Agnes' Eve'. Taylor

had, moreover, earlier refused to print Keats's alterations to the same poem, which had made it more sexually explicit, and a note by the publishers told readers that *Hyperion: A Fragment* had been included against the poet's wishes.

The texts printed in *Lamia, Isabella, The Eve of St Agnes, and Other Poems* in 1820 represent a compromise between Taylor's and Woodhouse's judgements on the one hand and Keats's own uncertain critical judgement on the other. Keats's undependable judgement of his own poetry, something evident in the choice of poems for his first volume, reflected the instability of taste evident in the new and growing reading public, of which Keats was himself a representative. The young Keats had shared the 'ladies'' liking for 'romance' as is shown by his attempts to 'revive' Spenserian chivalry, in which Spenserian knights save and serve 'lovely women'. But the Keats who wished to revise *The Eve of St Agnes* or who wrote *Lamia* in 1819 no longer wanted to appeal to the readers of that kind of poem. He told Richard Woodhouse that his changes to *The Eve of St Agnes* were made because 'he does not want ladies to read his poetry: that he writes for men'. The violence of Keats's reaction against what he called 'mawkishness' is because one side of his imagination was strongly attracted by 'romance'. The medieval stories, *Isabella*, *The Eve of St Agnes* and 'La Belle Dame sans Merci', all deal with closely related plots – young lovers whose love is opposed by the real or everyday world. *Isabella* ends in madness and death but asks for the reader's pity. In *The Eve of St Agnes* the lovers escape but into a storm, and La Belle Dame is an ominous, perhaps demonic, lover. Keats's final 'romance' poem, *Lamia*, has a classical setting, and is more self-knowing, ironic and objective. The result is unsettled in tone and unsettling. *Lamia* seems to reject the possibility of romantic love or of the imagination functioning in the real world. These poems can be read very differently, and some readers have seen in *The Eve of St Agnes* an ironic account of its heroine, Madeline, as a foolish virgin, self-deceived by her belief in superstitious rites, instead of a poem celebrating youthful love while perceiving its vulnerability.

Disagreements over the meaning of Keats's romantic narratives reflect his own ambivalences. *Lamia*, a critique of romantic love and fancy, stands at the beginning of the 1820 volume: *Hyperion*, with its faith in evolutionary progress and the triumph of beauty, is placed at the end, an affirmation of what the opening poem attacks. Keats's longing to believe in the consolation offered by poetry and the imagination is matched by a suspicion of their insufficiency as an answer to human suffering. The major odes are invocations of, and powerful meditations upon, the subjects which preoccupy Keats's poetry – love, art, song, sorrow and the natural world. Each poses questions, but only 'To Autumn' implies a resting point. Keats's later re-working of the Hyperion narrative led to the intense self-examination in *The Fall of Hyperion: A Dream*, which describes a rite of passage that initiates the self-conscious modern poet into painful maturity. Keats's poetry does seek to believe in and embody the 'dreams of art', but it also provides a critique of the claims of poetry and the imagination, and questions their capacity to encompass human suffering.

The collaborative way in which the texts and contents of Keats's final publication were settled, and what to a modern reader seems its rather odd inclusions and exclusions, draws attention to a highly unusual feature of Keats's canon – the high proportion of works never published in his lifetime. Of the one hundred and fifty poetic works now included in complete editions of Keats's poetry, only forty-five were published in the three volumes which appeared under his name in 1817, 1818 and 1820. A further eight poems were published in periodicals and two more appeared in Leigh Hunt's *Literary Pocket-Book* for 1819, bringing the total to fifty-five poems. At his death, then, two-thirds of his poetry existed only in manuscript. Scraps from this unpublished manuscript archive first began to reach print very soon after his death, though it was not until Richard Monckton Milnes's *Life, Letters and Literary Remains* (1848) that a serious attempt was made to edit his works. Even so, 'On Peace' remained unpublished until 1905 and 'Lines Written on 29 May' was not printed until 1925. The final addition to the canon was only made in 1939. Keats, that is, would not have wanted his contemporary public to read most of the poems in today's collected editions.

There are interlocking reasons for the curious nature of Keats's canon. In part, the critical failure of *Poems* (1817) and the subsequent virulent attacks on *Endymion*, identifying Keats as a member of Hunt's school of 'Cockney' poets, led him to distrust the reading public. Keats was also more given to self-doubt than is usually allowed. Benjamin Haydon, who was for a time very close to Keats, said 'One day he was full of an epic Poem! another, epic poems were splendid impositions on the world! & never for two days did he know his own intentions.' In addition, he also wrote occasional verse with remarkable facility. This sat awkwardly with his high conception of 'Poesy' and 'Fame'. The alertness to everyday language and life and the sharp sense of humour so evident in Keats's letters are absent from the poems published in his lifetime, which are uniformly 'poetic' and mostly serious. But when Keats put the demands of high art, of 'Poesy' to one side, his poetry has a remarkably wide range of effects, from the light-hearted and playful to the satirical.

Hence this selection includes a large number of poems 'not published by Keats'. Many of these are swiftly written occasional poems addressed to specific readers, or groups of readers, and as such had a limited manuscript circulation. The most obvious examples of these are the charming 'To Mrs Reynolds's Cat' and the extemporaneous 'Character of Charles Brown', a good-natured private joke among friends. While on holiday in Devon Keats amused his male friends with mildly risqué ballads ('Where be ye going, you Devon maid', 'Over the hill and over the dale'). In his letters to his fifteen-year-old sister, Fanny, Keats included sprightly nonsense poems ('Old Meg she was a gypsy', 'A Song about Myself', 'Two or three posies'). The long and elaborate mock conversation between Ben Nevis and the fifty-year-old Scotswoman climbing his side was written to amuse his sick brother Tom. This kind of limited circulation gave Keats space to mock the affectations of fashionable lovers ('And what is love? It is a doll dressed up', 'Pensive they sit, and roll their languid eyes'), to attack the Puritanism

of contemporary religion ('Written in Disgust of Vulgar Super-
stition'), or to satirize the government's ineffectual efforts to
silence the radical publisher and author, William Hone ('Nebu-
chadnezzar's Dream'). At the other extreme are the impromptu
throwaway pieces, 'Give me Women, Wine, and Snuff' and 'I
am as brisk', the first of which was written on the cover of a
fellow student's lecture notebook.

Some of the poems which remained unpublished during
Keats's lifetime were, however, private. 'Read me a lesson,
Muse, and speak it loud' seems to be both self-admonitory and
self-encouraging. 'Lines Written in the Highlands', written in
fourteeners, is an attempt to make up for a 'wretched sonnet'
which Keats felt had failed to do Burns justice. Like his sonnet
'On Visiting the Tomb of Burns' or 'If by dull rhymes our
English must be chained', Keats is using the occasion of writing
to think through his immediate poetic concerns: in that way,
some of these poems are adjuncts to the thinking out loud
which characterizes his letters. 'On Sitting Down to Read *King
Lear* Once Again' at once pays homage to Shakespeare and
asks for his inspiration. The disjointed and disturbed verse
letter to John Hamilton Reynolds, written from Teignmouth
on 25 March 1818, gives a vivid description of a nightmare
in which Keats saw 'too distinct' into nature's 'eternal fierce
destruction', and was clearly not meant to be read by anyone
but Reynolds. Similarly, there is a late group of four poems
written in late 1819 or early 1820 which seem to have been
entirely private in their origin, 'The day is gone, and all its
sweets are gone', 'I cry your mercy, pity, love – ay love', 'What
can I do to drive away' and 'To Fanny', of which the last three
are included here. These distraught and painfully naked poems
were addressed to Fanny Brawne, and meant for her eyes only.
Keats, living next door to Fanny, and, from February 1820,
seriously ill and confined indoors, suffered not only from jeal-
ousy but from an obsessive fear that his love for Fanny was
destroying his poetic abilities.

The penultimate poem in this selection, 'This living hand,
now warm and capable', perhaps a dramatic fragment, seeks to
reach out from the past to the reader's present. Its poignancy is

matched by Keats's final unawareness of what he had achieved. The line which he dictated to Joseph Severn on his deathbed, and which he wished to have inscribed on his tombstone, reads

'Here lies one whose name was writ on water.'

NOTE

1.   See John Barnard, 'First Fruits or "First Blights": A New Account of the Publishing History of Keats's *Poems* (1817)' in *Romanticism*, 12 (2006), 71–101.

Further Reading

EDITIONS

The standard scholarly edition is Jack Stillinger's *The Poems of John Keats* (1978), which contains detailed textual notes: on the transmission of the texts of Keats's poetry, see Stillinger's invaluable *The Texts of Keats's Poems* (1974). Miriam Allott's *The Poems of John Keats* (1970) is the most fully annotated edition available, though the texts of the poems are undependable and the annotation is in some respects out of date. The text of the Penguin *John Keats: The Complete Poems* (1973, 2nd edn. 1977, 3rd edn. 1988), edited by John Barnard, was revised against Stillinger's findings in 1977: it contains extensive annotation, and reprints Wordsworth and Hazlitt on the origins of Greek mythology, Keats's marginalia to *Paradise Lost*, and Keats's review of Edmund Kean's *Richard III*. Elizabeth Cook's Oxford Authors edition, *John Keats* (1990), contains almost all Keats's non-dramatic poetry and a substantial selection of his letters: it is based on a fresh examination of the texts, is well annotated, and reprints Keats's marginalia to Shakespeare's First Folio and *Paradise Lost*, along with Keats's review of Kean.

Photographic facsimiles of Keats's manuscripts accompanied by transcripts and notes are as follows: *John Keats: Poetry Manuscripts at Harvard: A Facsimile Edition*, edited by Jack Stillinger and introduced by Helen Vendler (1990); Stillinger also edited Keats's manuscripts in the seven volumes of *The Manuscripts of the Younger Romantics . . .*, edited by Donald

H. Reiman (1985–9); Robert Gittings edited *The Odes of Keats & Their Earliest Known Manuscripts in Facsimile* (1970).

The Letters of John Keats 1814–1821, 2 vols. (1958), edited by Hyder E. Rollins, is the only complete edition and is annotated. Robert Gittings's generous paperback selection (1970, 1979) makes some corrections to Rollins's edition. The selection edited by Grant F. Scott (2002) is partially modernized, and includes two new letters and the unpublished final page of one of Keats's journal letters to his brother and sister-in-law.

BIOGRAPHY, BIBLIOGRAPHY, SCHOLARLY AIDS

Keats's letters give the most immediate entry to his personality and the development of his mind. These are supplemented by the contemporary letters, records and retrospective accounts made by Keats's family and friends collected in *The Keats Circle*, 2 vols. (2nd edn. 1965), edited by Hyder E. Rollins. Keats's early reception is charted in *Keats: The Critical Heritage* (1971), edited by G. M. Matthews, in Donald H. Reiman's *The Romantics Reviewed: Contemporary Reviews of British Romantic Writers*, Part C, *Shelley, Keats, and London Radical Writers* (1972), and in George H. Ford's *Keats and the Victorians: A Study of his Influence and Rise to Fame 1821–1895* (1944).

The most recent biography is Andrew Motion's *Keats* (1997), which follows recent scholarly writing in emphasizing the political dimensions of Keats's life and work. Robert Gittings's *John Keats* (1968) is based on a re-examination of the archival and other evidence, while Walter Jackson Bate's *John Keats* (1963) concentrates on Keats's poetic development. For an account of Keats's Scottish walking tour with Charles Brown, see Carol Kyros Walker's handsomely produced *Walking North with Keats* (1992), which has excellent photographs and careful annotation.

Bibliographical guides to Keats scholarship and criticism

include Jack Stillinger's chapter in Frank Jordan's *The English Romantics: A Review of Research and Criticism* (4th edn. 1985) and Greg Kucich's chapter in *Literature of the Romantic Period: A Bibliographic Guide* (1998), edited by Michael O'Neill. The *Keats–Shelley Journal* produces an annual bibliography of work published on the second-generation Romantics.

CRITICAL AND SCHOLARLY BOOKS

The critical responses to Keats's poetry are rich, varied and contradictory. The surveys of criticism and scholarship by Jack Stillinger and Greg Kucich, noted above, outline the main trends in recent and current thinking about Keats. Among collections of essays, Hermione de Almeida's *Critical Essays on John Keats* (1990) reprints a number of important essays, along with specially commissioned chapters. Nicholas Roe's *Keats and History* (1994), as its title indicates, locates Keats's poetry in its immediate historical context, and *Keats: Bicentenary Readings* (1997), edited by Michael O'Neill, has, among others, a first-rate chapter on the letters by Timothy Webb. Susan J. Wolfson's *Cambridge Companion to Keats* (2001) gives a good and representative sense of the differing approaches to Keats in the late twentieth century. For compact accounts of Keats's poetry and career, see John Barnard's introductory book, *John Keats* (1987), and Stephen Hebron's generously illustrated outline in the British Library Writers' Lives series (2002).

   John Bayley's 1962 essay on 'Keats and Reality' (reprinted and extended in his *Uses of Division*, 1976) insists on the importance of the early poetry's 'unmisgiving' quality to an understanding of Keats's mature style, while *John Keats's Dream of Truth* (1969) by John Jones is an inward, and individual, account of his poetry of 'feel'. Christopher Ricks's influential *Keats and Embarrassment* (1974) gives an illuminating (and witty) analysis of the way in which the language of the poetry and letters is 'sensitive to, and morally intelligent about, embarrassment'. *The Odes of John Keats* (1983) by Helen

Vendler is a sustained and perceptive close reading of the odes. Other studies of Keats which explicate his ideas and development as a thinker and poet include *Keats and his Poetry* by Morris Dickstein (1971) and Stuart M. Sperry's *Keats the Poet* (1973). See also Susan J. Wolfson's *The Questioning Presence* (1986) on interrogative poetry in Wordsworth, Keats and Romantic poetry.

The title essay of Jack Stillinger's *'The Hoodwinking of Madeline' and Other Essays on Keats's Poems* (1971), which reads the sexual plot of *The Eve of St Agnes* literally, radically challenged previous 'innocent' or aestheticized interpretations. His work on Keats's texts, which revealed *Isabella* to have been written collaboratively, led him to question the Romantics' belief in individual inspiration in his *Multiple Authorship and the Myth of Solitary Genius* (1991).

Jerome McGann's essay, 'Keats and the Historical Method in Literary Criticism', first published in 1979 and reprinted in his *The Beauty of Inflections* (1985), precipitated interest in reading Keats's poetry in relation to, and as a commentary upon, contemporary politics. For a fine study of Keats's education, political attitudes, and their importance for an understanding of Keats's poetry and life, see Nicholas Roe, *Keats and the Culture of Dissent* (1997). Jeffrey Cox explores the sociable nature of Keats's work in *Poetry and Politics in the Cockney School: Keats, Shelley, Hunt and their Circle* (1998).

There is intelligent work on Keats and gender. See, for example, Susan J. Wolfson's chapter in Hermione de Almeida's *Critical Essays*, Anne K. Mellor, 'Ideological Cross-Dressing: John Keats/Emily Brontë' in her *Romanticism and Gender* (1993) and John Whale's compact book, *John Keats* (2005).

On more closely focused topics, Ian Jack's *Keats and the Mirror of Art* (1967) is a full and informative study of the poetry's visual sources, Donald C. Goellnicht's *The Poet-Physician, Keats and Medical Science* (1984) explores Keats's medical education and its effect on his imagery, and Greg Kucich examines *Keats, Shelley, and Romantic Spenserianism* (1991).

A Note on the Texts

The texts in this selection are based on the 1988 edition of *John Keats: The Complete Poems*, in which I give a fuller discussion of some of the dates of composition and choice of textual variants. This was first published in 1973. In 1977 I was able to correct the texts against Jack Stillinger's *The Texts of John Keats* (1974), and made further changes in 1988 from his edition of the poems (1978).

The texts are lightly modernized. Poems published in *Poems* (1817), *Endymion* (1818) and *Lamia, Isabella, The Eve of St Agnes, and Other Poems* (1820) are based on the texts in those volumes. The notes to the poems which did not appear in these three volumes record where and when they were first published and indicate the source of the text adopted.

The chronological ordering follows that of the 1988 edition of *John Keats: The Complete Poems*, with the following exceptions: 'Lines Written on 29 May' was probably written in 1814 not 1815; 'I am as brisk', rather than being undated, was probably written in 1816; and I now think that 'Bright star!' was written in July 1819, rather than later. In addition, Robert Gittings was right to argue that Keats left school and was apprenticed to Thomas Hammond not in 1811, but in the summer of 1810. However, unlike Gittings and some of Keats's other biographers, I believe Keats had to carry out his duties as a dresser at Guy's between autumn 1816 and March 1817.

Selected Poems

Imitation of Spenser

Now Morning from her orient chamber came,
And her first footsteps touched a verdant hill;
Crowning its lawny crest with amber flame,
Silv'ring the untainted gushes of its rill;
Which, pure from mossy beds, did down distill,
And after parting beds of simple flowers,
By many streams a little lake did fill,
Which round its marge reflected woven bowers,
And, in its middle space, a sky that never lowers.

There the king-fisher saw his plumage bright   10
Vying with fish of brilliant dye below;
Whose silken fins and golden scalès light
Cast upward, through the waves, a ruby glow:
There saw the swan his neck of archèd snow,
And oared himself along with majesty;
Sparkled his jetty eyes; his feet did show
Beneath the waves like Afric's ebony,
And on his back a fay reclined voluptuously.

Ah! could I tell the wonders of an isle
That in that fairest lake had placèd been,   20
I could e'en Dido of her grief beguile;
Or rob from aged Lear his bitter teen:
For sure so fair a place was never seen,
Of all that charmed romantic eye:
It seemed an emerald in the silver sheen
Of the bright waters; or as when on high,
Through clouds of fleecy white, laughs the cerulean
      sky.

And all around it dipped luxuriously
Slopings of verdure through the glossy tide,
Which, as it were in gentle amity,   30
Rippled delighted up the flowery side;

As if to glean the ruddy tears, it tried,
Which fell profusely from the rose-tree stem!
Haply it was the workings of its pride,
    In strife to throw upon the shore a gem
Outvying all the buds in Flora's diadem.

On Peace

O Peace! and dost thou with thy presence bless
    The dwellings of this war-surrounded Isle;
Soothing with placid brow our late distress,
    Making the triple kingdom brightly smile?
Joyful I hail thy presence; and I hail
    The sweet companions that await on thee;
Complete my joy – let not my first wish fail,
    Let the sweet mountain nymph thy favourite be,
With England's happiness proclaim Europa's
        liberty.
O Europe! Let not sceptred tyrants see
    That thou must shelter in thy former state;
Keep thy chains burst, and boldly say thou art free;
    Give thy kings law – leave not uncurbed the
        great;
    So with the horrors past thou'lt win thy happier
        fate.

(Not published by Keats)

Lines Written on 29 May,
the Anniversary of the Restoration of Charles II,
on Hearing the Bells Ringing

Infatuate Britons, will you still proclaim
His memory, your direst, foulest shame?
    Nor patriots revere?

Ah! when I hear each traitorous lying bell,
'Tis gallant Sidney's, Russell's, Vane's sad knell,
    That pains my wounded ear.

(Not published by Keats)

'O Solitude! if I must with thee dwell'

O Solitude! if I must with thee dwell,
    Let it not be among the jumbled heap
    Of murky buildings; climb with me the steep –
Nature's observatory – whence the dell,
Its flowery slopes, its river's crystal swell,
    May seem a span; let me thy vigils keep
    'Mongst boughs pavilioned, where the deer's swift
        leap
Startles the wild bee from the foxglove bell.
But though I'll gladly trace these scenes with thee,
    Yet the sweet converse of an innocent mind,   10
    Whose words are images of thought refined,
Is my soul's pleasure; and it sure must be
    Almost the highest bliss of human-kind,
When to thy haunts two kindred spirits flee.

'Give me Women, Wine, and Snuff'

Give me Women, Wine, and Snuff
Until I cry out, 'Hold, enough!'
You may do sans objection
Till the day of resurrection;
For, bless my beard, they aye shall be
My belovèd Trinity.

(Not published by Keats)

'I am as brisk'

I am as brisk
As a bottle of whisk –
Ey and as nimble
As a milliner's thimble.
(Not published by Keats)

Specimen of an Induction to a Poem

Lo! I must tell a tale of chivalry;
For large white plumes are dancing in mine eye,
Not like the formal crest of latter days:
But bending in thousand graceful ways –
So graceful, it seems no mortal hand,
Or e'en the touch of Archimago's wand,
Could charm them into such an attitude.
We must think rather, that in playful mood,
Some mountain breeze had turned its chief delight,
10   To show this wonder of its gentle might.
Lo! I must tell a tale of chivalry;
For while I muse, the lance points slantingly
Athwart the morning air: some lady sweet,
Who cannot feel for cold her tender feet,
From the worn top of some old battlement
Hails it with tears, her stout defender sent:
And from her own pure self no joy dissembling,
Wraps round her ample robe with happy trembling.
Sometimes, when her good Knight his rest would take,
20   It is reflected clearly in a lake,
With the young ashen boughs, 'gainst which it rests,
And th' half-seen mossiness of linnets' nests,
Ah! shall I ever tell its cruelty,
When the fire flashes from a warrior's eye,
And his tremendous hand is grasping it,
And his dark brow for very wrath is knit?

Or when his spirit, with more calm intent,
Leaps to the honours of a tournament,
And makes the gazers round about the ring
Stare at the grandeur of the balancing?   30
No, no! this is far off: – then how shall I
Revive the dying tones of minstrelsy,
Which linger yet about lone gothic arches,
In dark green ivy, and among wild larches?
How sing the splendour of the revelries,
When butts of wine are drunk off to the lees?
And that bright lance against the fretted wall,
Beneath the shade of stately banneral,
Is slung with shining cuirass, sword and shield,
Where ye may see a spur in bloody field?   40
Light-footed damsels move with gentle paces
Round the wide hall, and show their happy faces;
Or stand in courtly talk by fives and sevens,
Like those fair stars that twinkle in the heavens.
Yet must I tell a tale of chivalry –
Or wherefore comes that steed so proudly by?
Wherefore more proudly does the gentle Knight
Rein in the swelling of his ample might?

Spenser! thy brows are archèd, open, kind,
And come like a clear sun-rise to my mind;   50
And always does my heart with pleasure dance,
When I think on thy noble countenance:
Where never yet was aught more earthly seen
Than the pure freshness of thy laurels green.
Therefore, great bard, I not so fearfully
Call on thy spirit to hover nigh
My daring steps: or if thy tender care,
Thus startled unaware,
Be jealous that the foot of other wight
Should madly follow that bright path of light   60
Traced by thy loved Libertas, he will speak,
And tell thee that my prayer is very meek;

That I will follow with due reverence,
And start with awe at mine own strange pretence.
Him thou wilt hear; so I will rest in hope
To see wide plains, fair trees and lawny slope,
The morn, the eve, the light, the shade, the flowers,
Clear streams, smooth lakes, and overlooking towers.

To Charles Cowden Clarke

Oft have you seen a swan superbly frowning,
And with proud breast his own white shadow
    crowning;
He slants his neck beneath the waters bright
So silently, it seems a beam of light
Come from the galaxy: anon he sports –
With outspread winds the Naiad Zephyr courts,
Or ruffles all the surface of the lake
In striving from its crystal face to take
Some diamond water drops, and them to treasure
In milky nest, and sip them off at leisure.
But not a moment can he there insure them,
Nor to such downy rest can he allure them;
For they rush as though they would be free,
And drop like hours into eternity.
Just like that bird am I in loss of time,
Whene'er I venture on the stream of rhyme;
With shattered boat, oar snapped, and canvas rent
I slowly sail, scarce knowing my intent;
Still scooping up water with my fingers,
In which a trembling diamond never lingers.

By this, friend Charles, you may full plainly see
Why I have never penned a line to thee:
Because my thoughts were never free, and clear,
And little fit to please a classic ear;
Because my wine was of too poor a savour
For one whose palate gladdens in the flavour

Of sparkling Helicon – small good it were
To take him to a desert rude, and bare,
Who had on Baiae's shore reclined at ease,
While Tasso's page was floating in a breeze   30
That gave soft music from Armida's bowers,
Mingled with fragrance from her rarest flowers:
Small good to one who had by Mulla's stream
Fondled the maidens with breasts of cream;
Who had beheld Belphoebe in a brook,
And lovely Una in a leafy nook,
And Archimago leaning o'er his book;
Who had of all that's sweet tasted, and seen,
From silvery ripple, up to beauty's queen;
From the sequestered haunts of gay Titania,   40
To the blue dwelling of divine Urania:
One, who of late, had ta'en sweet forest walks
With him who elegantly chats, and talks –
The wronged Libertas – who has told you stories
Of laurel chaplets, and Apollo's glories;
Of troops chivalrous prancing through a city,
And tearful ladies made for love, and pity:
With many else which I have never known.

Thus have I thought; and days on days have flown
Slowly, or rapidly – unwilling still   50
For you to try my dull, unlearned quill.
Nor should I now, but that I've known you long,
That you first taught me all the sweets of song:
The grand, the sweet, the terse, the free, the fine;
What swelled with pathos, and what right divine;
Spenserian vowels that elope with ease,
And float like birds o'er summer seas;
Miltonian storms, and more, Miltonian tenderness;
Michael in arms, and more, meek Eve's slenderness.
Who read for me the sonnet swelling loudly   60
Up to its climax and then dying proudly?
Who found for me the grandeur of the ode,
Growing, like Atlas stronger from its load?

Who let me taste that more than cordial dram,
The sharp, the rapier-pointed epigram?
Showed me that epic was of all the king,
Round, vast, and spanning all like Saturn's ring?
You too upheld the veil from Clio's beauty,
And pointed out the patriot's stern duty;
70 The might of Alfred, and the shaft of Tell;
The hand of Brutus, that so grandly fell
Upon a tyrant's head. Ah! had I never seen,
Or known your kindness, what might I have been?
What my enjoyments in my youthful years,
Bereft of all that now my life endears?
And can I e'er these benefits forget?
And can I e'er repay the friendly debt?
No, doubly no – yet should these rhymings please,
I shall roll on the grass with two-fold ease:
80 For I have long time been my fancy feeding
With hopes that you would one day think the reading
Of my rough verses not an hour misspent;
Should it e'er be so, what a rich content!

Some weeks have passed since last I saw the spires
In lucent Thames reflected – warm desires
To see the sun o'er-peep the eastern dimness,
And morning shadows streaking into slimness
Across the lawny fields, and pebbly water;
To mark the time as they grow broad, and shorter;
90 To feel the air that plays about the hills,
And sips its freshness from the little rills;
To see high, golden corn wave in the light
When Cynthia smiles upon a summer's night,
And peers among the cloudlet's jet and white,
As though she were reclining in a bed
Of bean blossoms, in heaven freshly shed –
No sooner had I stepped into these pleasures
Than I began to think of rhymes and measures:
The air that floated by me seemed to say
100 'Write! thou wilt never have a better day.'

And so I did. When many lines I'd written,
Though with their grace I was not oversmitten,
Yet, as my hand was warm, I thought I'd better
Trust to my feelings, and write you a letter.
Such an attempt required an inspiration
Of a peculiar sort – a consummation –
Which, had I felt, these scribblings might have been
Verses from which the soul would never wean:
But many days have passed since last my heart
Was warmed luxuriously by divine Mozart,   110
By Arne delighted, or by Handel maddened,
Or by the song of Erin pierced and saddened,
What time you were before the music sitting,
And the rich notes to each sensation fitting,
Since I have walked with you through shady lanes
That freshly terminate in open plains,
And revelled in a chat that ceasèd not
When at night-fall among your books we got:
No, nor when supper came, nor after that –
Nor when reluctantly I took my hat;   120
No, nor till cordially you shook my hand
Mid-way between our homes. Your accents bland
Still sounded in my ears, when I no more
Could hear your footsteps touch the gravelly floor.
Sometimes I lost them, and then found again;
You changed the footpath for the grassy plain.
In those still moments I have wished you joys
That well you know to honour – 'Life's very toys
With him,' said I, 'will take a pleasant charm;
It cannot be that aught will work him harm.'   130
These thoughts now come o'er me with all their
    might –
Again I shake your hand – friend Charles, good night.

On First Looking into Chapman's Homer

Much have I travelled in the realms of gold,
   And many goodly states and kingdoms seen;
   Round many western islands have I been
Which bards in fealty to Apollo hold.
Oft of one wide expanse had I been told
   That deep-browed Homer ruled as his demesne;
   Yet did I never breathe its pure serene
Till I heard Chapman speak out loud and bold:
Then felt I like some watcher of the skies
10   When a new planet swims into his ken;
Or like stout Cortez when with eagle eyes
   He stared at the Pacific – and all his men
Looked at each other with a wild surmise –
   Silent, upon a peak in Darien.

To my Brothers

Small, busy flames play through the fresh-laid coals,
   And their faint cracklings o'er our silence creep
   Like whispers of the household gods that keep
A gentle empire o'er fraternal souls.
And while, for rhymes, I search around the poles,
   Your eyes are fixed, as in poetic sleep,
   Upon the lore so voluble and deep,
That aye at fall of night our care condoles.
This is your birth-day Tom, and I rejoice
10   That thus it passes smoothly, quietly.
Many such eves of gently whispering noise
   May we together pass, and calmly try
What are this world's true joys – ere the great voice,
   From its fair face, shall bid our spirits fly.

Addressed to [Haydon]

Great spirits now on earth are sojourning;
  He of the cloud, the cataract, the lake,
  Who on Helvellyn's summit, wide awake,
Catches his freshness from Archangel's wing:
He of the rose, the violet, the spring,
  The social smile, the chain for Freedom's sake:
  And lo! – whose steadfastness would never take
A meaner sound than Raphael's whispering.
And other spirits there are standing apart
  Upon the forehead of the age to come;   10
These, these will give the world another heart,
  And other pulses. Hear ye not the hum
Of mighty workings? –
  Listen awhile ye nations, and be dumb.

'I stood tip-toe upon a little hill'

'Places of nestling green for Poets made.'
            'The Story of Rimini'

I stood tip-toe upon a little hill,
The air was cooling, and so very still,
That the sweet buds which with a modest pride
Pull droopingly, in slanting curve aside,
Their scantly leaved, and finely tapering stems,
Had not yet lost those starry diadems
Caught from the early sobbing of the morn.
The clouds were pure and white as flocks new shorn,
And fresh from the clear brook; sweetly they slept
On the blue fields of heaven, and then there crept 10
A little noiseless noise among the leaves,
Born of the very sigh that silence heaves:
For not the faintest motion could be seen
Of all the shades that slanted o'er the green.

There was wide wandering for the greediest eye,
To peer about upon variety;
Far round the horizon's crystal air to skim,
And trace the dwindled edgings of its brim;
To picture out the quaint, and curious bending
Of a fresh woodland alley, never ending;
Or by the bowery clefts, and leafy shelves,
Guess where the jaunty streams refresh themselves.
I gazed awhile, and felt as light, and free
As though the fanning wings of Mercury
Had played upon my heels: I was light-hearted,
And many pleasures to my vision started;
So I straightway began to pluck a posy
Of luxuries bright, milky, soft and rosy.

A bush of May flowers with the bees about them;
Ah, sure no tasteful nook would be without them;
And let a lush laburnum oversweep them,
And let long grass grow round the roots to keep
        them
Moist, cool and green; and shade the violets,
That they may bind the moss in leafy nets.

A filbert hedge with wild briar overtwined,
And clumps of woodbine taking the soft wind
Upon their summer thrones; there too should be
The frequent chequer of a youngling tree,
That with a score of light green brethren shoots
From the quaint mossiness of agèd roots:
Round which is heard a spring-head of clear waters
Babbling so wildly of its lovely daughters
The spreading blue-bells – it may haply mourn
That such fair clusters should be rudely torn
From their fresh beds, and scattered throughtlessly
By infant hands, left on the path to die.

Open afresh your round of starry folds,
Ye ardent marigolds!
Dry up the moisture from your golden lids,
For great Apollo bids   50
That in these days your praises should be sung
On many harps, which he has lately strung;
And when again your dewiness he kisses,
Tell him, I have you in my world of blisses:
So haply when I rove in some far vale,
His mighty voice may come upon the gale.

Here are sweet peas, on tip-toe for a flight:
With wings of gentle flush o'er delicate white,
And taper fingers catching at all things,
To bind them all about with tiny rings.   60

Linger awhile upon some bending planks
That lean against a streamlet's rushy banks,
And watch intently Nature's gentle doings:
They will be found softer than ring-dove's cooings.
How silent comes the water round that bend;
Not the minutest whisper does it send
To the o'erhanging sallows: blades of grass
Slowly across the chequered shadows pass –
Why, you might read two sonnets, ere they reach
To where the hurrying freshnesses aye preach   70
A natural sermon o'er their pebbly beds;
Where swarms of minnows show their little heads,
Staying their wavy bodies 'gainst the streams,
To taste the luxury of sunny beams
Tempered with coolness. How they ever wrestle
With their own sweet delight, and ever nestle
Their silver bellies on the pebbly sand.
If you but scantily hold out the hand,
That very instant not one will remain;
But turn your eye, and they are there again.   80
The ripples seem right glad to reach those cresses,
And cool themselves among the emerald tresses;

The while they cool themselves, they freshness give,
And moisture, that the bowery green may live:
So keeping up an interchange of favours,
Like good men in the truth of their behaviours.
Sometimes goldfinches one by one will drop
From low-hung branches; little space they stop;
But sip, and twitter, and their feather sleek –
90   Then off at once, as in a wanton freak:
Or perhaps, to show their black, and golden wings,
Pausing upon their yellow flutterings.
Were I in such a place, I sure should pray
That naught less sweet might call my thoughts away,
Than the soft rustle of a maiden's gown
Fanning away the dandelion's down;
Than the light music of her nimble toes
Patting against the sorrel as she goes.
How she would start, and blush, thus to be caught
100 Playing in all her innocence of thought.
O let me lead her gently o'er the brook,
Watch her half-smiling lips, and downward look;
O let me for one moment touch her wrist;
Let me one moment to her breathing list;
And as she leaves me may she often turn
Her fair eyes looking through her locks aubùrn.

    What next? A tuft of evening primroses,
O'er which the mind may hover till it dozes;
O'er which it well might take a pleasant sleep,
110 But that 'tis ever startled by the leap
Of buds into ripe flowers; or by the flitting
Of diverse moths, that aye their rest are quitting;
Or by the moon lifting her silver rim
Above a cloud, and with a gradual swim
Coming into the blue with all her light.
O Maker of sweet poets, dear delight
Of this fair world, and all its gentle livers;
Spangler of clouds, halo of crystal rivers,
Mingler with leaves, and dew and tumbling streams,

Closer of lovely eyes to lovely dreams,   120
Lover of loneliness, and wandering,
Of upcast eye, and tender pondering!
Thee must I praise above all other glories
That smile us on to tell delightful stories.
For what has made the sage or poet write
But the fair paradise of Nature's light?
In the calm grandeur of a sober line,
We see the waving of the mountain pine;
And when a tale is beautifully staid,
We feel the safety of a hawthorn glade: 130
When it is moving on luxurious wings,
The soul is lost in pleasant smotherings:
Fair dewy roses brush against our faces,
And flowering laurels spring from diamond vases;
O'er head we see the jasmine and sweet briar,
And bloomy grapes laughing from green attire;
While at our feet, the voice of crystal bubbles
Charms us at once away from all our troubles:
So that we feel uplifted from the world,
Walking upon the white clouds wreathed and
          curled.   140
So felt he, who first told, how Psyche went
On the smooth wind to realms of wonderment;
What Psyche felt, and Love, when their full lips
First touched; what amorous, and fondling nips
They gave each other's cheeks; with all their sighs,
And how they kissed each other's tremulous eyes;
The silver lamp – the ravishment – the wonder –
The darkness – loneliness – the fearful thunder;
Their woes gone by, and both to heaven upflown,
To bow for gratitude before Jove's throne.   150
So did he feel, who pulled the boughs aside,
That we might look into a forest wide,
To catch a glimpse of Fauns and Dryadès
Coming with softest rustle through the trees,
And garlands woven of flowers wild, and sweet,
Upheld on ivory wrists, or sporting feet:

Telling us how fair, trembling Syrinx fled
Arcadian Pan, with such a fearful dread.
Poor nymph – poor Pan – how he did weep to find,
160   Naught but a lovely sighing of the wind
Along the reedy stream; a half-heard strain,
Full of sweet desolation – balmy pain.

What first inspired a bard of old to sing
Narcissus pining o'er the untainted spring?
In some delicious ramble, he had found
A little space, with boughs all woven round;
And in the midst of all, a clearer pool
Then e'er reflected in its pleasant cool
The blue sky here, and there, serenely peeping
170   Through tendril wreaths fantastically creeping.
And on the bank a lonely flower he spied,
A meek and forlorn flower, with naught of pride,
Drooping its beauty o'er the watery clearness,
To woo its own sad image into nearness:
Deaf to light Zephyrus it would not move;
But still would seem to droop, to pine, to love.
So while the Poet stood in this sweet spot,
Some fainter gleamings o'er his fancy shot;
Nor was it long ere he had told the tale
180   Of young Narcissus, and sad Echo's bale.

Where had he been, from whose warm head
    out-flew
That sweetest of all songs, that ever new,
That aye refreshing, pure deliciousness,
Coming ever to bless
The wanderer by moonlight? to him bringing
Shapes from the invisible world, unearthly singing
From out the middle air, from flowery nests,
And from the pillowy silkiness that rests
Full in the speculation of the stars.
190   Ah! surely he had burst our mortal bars;

Into some wondrous region he had gone,
To search for thee, divine Endymion!

He was a Poet, sure a lover too,
Who stood on Latmos' top, what time there blew
Soft breezes from the myrtle vale below;
And brought in faintness solemn, sweet, and slow
A hymn from Dian's temple; while upswelling,
The incense went to her own starry dwelling.
But though her face was clear as infant's eyes,
Though she stood smiling o'er the sacrifice,   200
The Poet wept at her so piteous fate,
Wept that such beauty should be desolate:
So in fine wrath some golden sounds he won,
And gave meek Cynthia her Endymion.

Queen of the wide air; thou most lovely queen
Of all the brightness that mine eyes have seen!
As thou exceedest all things in thy shine,
So every tale, does this sweet tale of thine.
O for three words of honey, that I might
Tell but one wonder of thy bridal night!   210

Where distant ships do seem to show their keels,
Phoebus awhile delayed his mighty wheels,
And turned to smile upon thy bashful eyes,
Ere he his unseen pomp would solemnize.
The evening weather was so bright and clear,
That men of health were of unusual cheer;
Stepping like Homer at the trumpet's call,
Or young Apollo on the pedestal:
And lovely women were as fair and warm,
As Venus looking sideways in alarm.   220
The breezes were ethereal, and pure,
And crept through half-closed lattices to cure
The languid sick; it cooled their fevered sleep,
And soothed them into slumbers full and deep.

Soon they awoke clear-eyed: nor burnt with thirsting,
Nor with hot fingers, nor with temples bursting:
And springing up, they met the wondering sight
Of their dear friends, nigh foolish with delight;
Who feel their arms, and breasts, and kiss and stare,
And on their placid foreheads part the hair.
Young men, and maidens at each other gazed
With hands held back, and motionless, amazed
To see the brightness in each other's eyes;
And so they stood, filled with a sweet surprise,
Until their tongues were loosed in Poesy.
Therefore no lover did of anguish die:
But the soft numbers, in that moment spoken,
Made silken ties, that never may be broken.
Cynthia! I cannot tell the greater blisses,
That followed thine, and thy dear shepherd's kisses:
Was there a Poet born? – but now no more,
My wandering spirit must no further soar. –

Sleep and Poetry

> *As I lay in my bed slepe full unmete*
> *Was unto me, but why that I ne might*
> *Rest I ne wist, for there n'as earthly wight*
> *[As I suppose] had more of hertis ese*
> *Than I, for I n'ad sicknesse nor disese.*
>
> Chaucer

What is more gentle than a wind in summer?
What is more soothing than the pretty hummer
That stays one moment in an open flower,
And buzzes cheerily from bower to bower?
What is more tranquil than a musk-rose blowing
In a green island, far from all men's knowing?
More healthful than the leafiness of dales?
More secret than a nest of nightingales?

More serene than Cordelia's countenance?
More full of visions than a high romance?   10
What, but thee Sleep? Soft closer of our eyes!
Low murmurer of tender lullabies!
Light hoverer around our happy pillows!
Wreather of poppy buds, and weeping willows!
Silent entangler of a beauty's tresses!
Most happy listener! when the morning blesses
Thee for enlivening all the cheerful eyes
That glance so brightly at the new sun-rise.

    But what is higher beyond thought than thee?
Fresher than berries of a mountain tree?   20
More strange, more beautiful, more smooth, more
        regal,
Than wings of swans, than doves, than dim-seen
        eagle?
What is it? And to what shall I compare it?
It has a glory, and naught else can share it:
The thought thereof is awful, sweet, and holy,
Chasing away all worldliness and folly;
Coming sometimes like fearful claps of thunder,
Or the low rumblings earth's regions under;
And sometimes like a gentle whispering
Of all the secrets of some wondrous thing   30
That breathes about us in the vacant air;
So that we look around with prying stare,
Perhaps to see shapes of light, aërial limning,
And catch soft floatings from a faint-heard
        hymning,
To see the laurel wreath, on high suspended,
That is to crown our name when life is ended.
Sometimes it gives a glory to the voice,
And from the heart up-springs, 'Rejoice! Rejoice!' –
Sounds which will reach the Framer of all things,
And die away in ardent mutterings.   40

No one who once the glorious sun has seen,
And all the clouds, and felt his bosom clean
For his great Maker's presence, but must know
What 'tis I mean, and feel his being glow:
Therefore no insult will I give his spirit,
By telling what he sees from native merit.

O Poesy! for thee I hold my pen
That am not yet a glorious denizen
Of thy wide heaven – Should I rather kneel
50   Upon some mountain-top until I feel
A glowing splendour round about me hung,
And echo back the voice of thine own tongue?
O Poesy! for thee I grasp my pen
That am not yet a glorious denizen
Of thy wide heaven; yet, to my ardent prayer,
Yield from thy sanctuary some clear air,
Smoothed for intoxication by the breath
Of flowering bays, that I may die a death
Of luxury, and my young spirit follow
60   The morning sunbeams to the great Apollo
Like a fresh sacrifice; or, if I can bear
The o'erwhelming sweets, 'twill bring to me the fair
Visions of all places: a bowery nook
Will be elysium – an eternal book
Whence I may copy many a lovely saying
About the leaves, and flowers – about the playing
Of nymphs in woods, and fountains; and the shade
Keeping a silence round a sleeping maid;
And many a verse from so strange influence
70   That we must ever wonder how, and whence
It came. Also imaginings will hover
Round my fire-side, and haply there discover
Vistas of solemn beauty, where I'd wander
In happy silence, like the clear Meander
Through its lone vales; and where I found a spot
Of awfuller shade, or an enchanted grot,

Or a green hill o'erspread with chequered dress
Of flowers, and fearful from its loveliness,
Write on my tablets all that was permitted,
All that was for our human senses fitted.   80
Then the events of this wide world I'd seize
Like a strong giant, and my spirit tease
Till at its shoulders it should proudly see
Wings to find out an immortality.

　　Stop and consider! life is but a day;
A fragile dew-drop on its perilous way
From a tree's summit; a poor Indian's sleep
While his boat hastens to the monstrous steep
Of Montmorenci. Why so sad a moan?
Life is the rose's hope while yet unblown;   90
The reading of an ever-changing tale;
The light uplifting of a maiden's veil;
A pigeon tumbling in clear summer air;
A laughing school-boy, without grief or care,
Riding the springy branches of an elm.

　　O for ten years, that I may overwhelm
Myself in poesy; so I may do the deed
That my own soul has to itself decreed.
Then will I pass the countries that I see
In long perspective, and continually   100
Taste their pure fountains. First the realm I'll
　　pass
Of Flora, and old Pan: sleep in the grass,
Feed upon apples red, and strawberries,
And choose each pleasure that my fancy sees;
Catch the white-handed nymphs in shady places,
To woo sweet kisses from averted faces –
Play with their fingers, touch their shoulders white
Into a pretty shrinking with a bite
As hard as lips can make it, till, agreed,
A lovely tale of human life we'll read.   110

And one will teach a tame dove how it best
May fan the cool air gently o'er my rest;
Another, bending o'er her nimble tread,
Will set a green robe floating round her head,
And still will dance with ever varied ease,
Smiling upon the flowers and the trees:
Another will entice me on, and on
Through almond blossoms and rich cinnamon;
Till in the bosom of a leafy world
120   We rest in silence, like two gems upcurled
In the recesses of a pearly shell.

    And can I ever bid these joys farewell?
Yes, I must pass them for a nobler life,
Where I may find the agonies, the strife
Of human hearts – for lo! I see afar,
O'er-sailing the blue cragginess, a car
And steeds with streamy manes – the charioteer
Looks out upon the winds with glorious fear:
And now the numerous tramplings quiver lightly
130   Along a huge cloud's ridge; and now with sprightly
Wheel downward come they into fresher skies,
Tipped round with silver from the sun's bright eyes.
Still downward with capacious whirl they glide;
And now I see them on a green-hill's side
In breezy rest among the nodding stalks.
The charioteer with wondrous gesture talks
To the trees and mountains; and there soon appear
Shapes of delight, of mystery, and fear,
Passing along before a dusky space
140   Made by some mighty oaks: as they would chase
Some ever-fleeting music on they sweep.
Lo! how they murmur, laugh, and smile, and weep –
Some with upholden hand and mouth severe;
Some with their faces muffled to the ear
Between their arms; some, clear in youthful bloom,
Go glad and smilingly athwart the gloom;

Some looking back, and some with upward gaze;
Yes, thousands in a thousand different ways
Flit onward – now a lovely wreath of girls
Dancing their sleek hair into tangled curls;   150
And now broad wings. Most awfully intent
The driver of those steeds is forward bent,
And seems to listen: O that I might know
All that he writes with such a hurrying glow.

The visions all are fled – the car is fled
Into the light of heaven, and in their stead
A sense of real things comes doubly strong,
And, like a muddy stream, would bear along
My soul to nothingness: but I will strive
Against all doubtings, and will keep alive   160
The thought of that same chariot, and the strange
Journey it went.

                    Is there so small a range
In the present strength of manhood, that the high
Imagination cannot freely fly
As she was wont of old? Prepare her steeds,
Paw up against the light, and do strange deeds
Upon the clouds? Has she not shown us all?
From the clear space of ether, to the small
Breath of new buds unfolding? From the meaning
Of Jove's large eye-brow, to the tender greening   170
Of April meadows? Here her altar shone,
E'en in this isle; and who could paragon
The fervid choir that lifted up a noise
Of harmony, to where it aye will poise
Its mighty self of convoluting sound,
Huge as a planet, and like that roll round,
Eternally around a dizzy void?
Ay, in those days the Muses were nigh cloyed
With honours; nor had any other care
Than to sing out and soothe their wavy hair.   180

Could all this be forgotten? Yes, a schism
Nurtured by foppery and barbarism,
Made great Apollo blush for this his land.
Men were thought wise who could not understand
His glories: with a puling infant's force
They swayed about upon a rocking horse,
And thought it Pegasus. Ah, dismal souled!
The winds of heaven blew, the ocean rolled
Its gathering waves – ye felt it not. The blue
190   Bared its eternal bosom, and the dew
Of summer nights collected still to make
The morning precious: beauty was awake!
Why were ye not awake? But ye were dead
To things ye knew not of – were closely wed
To musty laws lined out with wretched rule
And compass vile: so that ye taught a school
Of dolts to smooth, inlay, and clip, and fit,
Till, like the certain wands of Jacob's wit,
Their verses tallied. Easy was the task:
200   A thousand handicraftsmen wore the mask
Of Poesy. Ill-fated, impious race!
That blasphemed the bright Lyrist to his face,
And did not know it! No, they went about,
Holding a poor, decrepit standard out
Marked with most flimsy mottoes, and in large
The name of one Boileau!

                              O ye whose charge
It is to hover round our pleasant hills!
Whose congregated majesty so fills
My boundly reverence, that I cannot trace
210   Your hallowed names, in this unholy place,
So near those common folk – did not their shames
Affright you? Did our old lamenting Thames
Delight you? Did ye never cluster round
Delicious Avon, with a mournful sound,
And weep? Or did ye wholly bid adieu
To regions where no more the laurel grew?

Or did ye stay to give a welcoming
To some lone spirits who could proudly sing
Their youth away, and die? 'Twas even so.
But let me think away those times of woe: 220
Now 'tis a fairer season; ye have breathed
Rich benedictions o'er us; ye have wreathed
Fresh garlands: for sweet music has been heard
In many places – some has been upstirred
From out its crystal dwelling in a lake,
By a swan's ebon bill; from a thick brake,
Nested and quiet in a valley mild,
Bubbles a pipe – fine sounds are floating wild
About the earth: happy are ye and glad.

    These things are doubtless: yet in truth we've
        had   230
Strange thunders from the potency of song;
Mingled indeed with what is sweet and strong,
From majesty: but in clear truth the themes
Are ugly clubs, the poets Polyphemes
Disturbing the grand sea. A drainless shower
Of light is Poesy; 'tis the supreme of power;
'Tis might half-slumbering on its own right arm.
The very archings of her eye-lids charm
A thousand willing agents to obey,
And still she governs with the mildest sway: 240
But strength alone, though of the Muses born,
Is like a fallen angel: trees uptorn,
Darkness, and worms, and shrouds, and
        sepulchres
Delight it; for it feeds upon the burrs,
And thorns of life; forgetting the great end
Of Poesy, that it should be a friend
To soothe the cares, and lift the thoughts of man.

    Yet I rejoice: a myrtle fairer than
E'er grew in Paphos, from the bitter weeds
Lifts its sweet head into the air, and feeds   250

A silent space with ever sprouting green.
All tenderest birds there find a pleasant screen,
Creep through the shade with jaunty fluttering,
Nibble the little cuppèd flowers and sing.
Then let us clear away the choking thorns
From round its gentle stem; let the young fawns,
Yeaned in after times, when we are flown,
Find a fresh sward beneath it, overgrown
With simple flowers: let there nothing be
260   More boisterous than a lover's bended knee;
Naught more ungentle than the placid look
Of one who leans upon a closèd book;
Naught more untranquil than the grassy slopes
Between two hills. All hail delightful hopes!
As she was wont, th'imagination
Into most lovely labyrinths will be gone,
And they shall be accounted poet-kings
Who simply tell the most heart-easing things.
O may these joys be ripe before I die.

270   Will not some say that I presumptuously
Have spoken? that from hastening disgrace
'Twere better far to hide my foolish face?
That whining boyhood should with reverence bow
Ere the dread thunderbolt could reach? How!
If I do hide myself, it sure shall be
In the very fane, the light of Poesy:
If I do fall, at least I will be laid
Beneath the silence of a poplar shade;
And over me the grass shall be smooth-shaven;
280   And there shall be a kind memorial graven.
But off, Despondence! miserable bane!
They should not know thee, who, athirst to gain
A noble end, are thirsty every hour.
What though I am not wealthy in the dower
Of spanning wisdom; though I do not know
The shiftings of the mighty winds that blow

Hither and thither all the changing thoughts
Of man: though no great minist'ring reason sorts
Out the dark mysteries of human souls
To clear conceiving – yet there ever rolls   290
A vast idea before me, and I glean
Therefrom my liberty; thence too I've seen
The end and aim of Poesy. 'Tis clear
As any thing most true; as that the year
Is made of the four seasons – manifest
As a large cross, some old cathedral's crest,
Lifted to the white clouds. Therefore should I
Be but the essence of deformity,
A coward, did my very eye-lids wink
At speaking out what I have dared to think.   300
Ah! rather let me like a madman run
Over some precipice! let the hot sun
Melt my Dedalian wings, and drive me down
Convulsed and headlong! Stay! an inward frown
Of conscience bids me be more calm awhile.
An ocean dim, sprinkled with many an isle,
Spreads awfully before me. How much toil!
How many days! what desperate turmoil!
Ere I can have explored its widenesses.
Ah, what a task! upon my bended knees,   310
I could unsay those – no, impossible!
Impossible!

　　　　　　For sweet relief I'll dwell
On humbler thoughts, and let this strange assay
Begun in gentleness die so away.
E'en now all tumult from my bosom fades:
I turn full-hearted to the friendly aids
That smooth the path of honour; brotherhood,
And friendliness the nurse of mutual good.
The hearty grasp that sends a pleasant sonnet
Into the brain ere one can think upon it;   320
The silence when some rhymes are coming out;
And when they're come, the very pleasant rout:

The message certain to be done to-morrow –
'Tis perhaps as well that it should be to borrow
Some precious book from out its snug retreat,
To cluster round it when we next shall meet.
Scarce can I scribble on; for lovely airs
Are fluttering round the room like doves in pairs;
Many delights of that glad day recalling,
When first my senses caught their tender falling.
And with these airs come forms of elegance
Stooping their shoulders o'er a horse's prance,
Careless, and grand – fingers soft and round
Parting luxuriant curls – and the swift bound
Of Bacchus from his chariot, when his eye
Made Ariadne's cheek look blushingly.
Thus I remember all the pleasant flow
Of words at opening a portfolio.

    Things such as these are ever harbingers
To trains of peaceful images: the stirs
Of a swan's neck unseen among the rushes;
A linnet starting all about the bushes;
A butterfly, with golden wings broad parted,
Nestling a rose, convulsed as though it smarted
With over-pleasure – many, many more,
Might I indulge at large in all my store
Of luxuries: yet I must not forget
Sleep, quiet with his poppy coronet,
For what there may be worthy in these rhymes
I partly owe to him: and thus, the chimes
Of friendly voices had just given place
To as sweet a silence, when I 'gan retrace
The pleasant day, upon a couch at ease.
It was a poet's house who keeps the keys
Of Pleasure's temple. Round about were hung
The glorious features of the bards who sung
In other ages – cold and sacred busts
Smiled at each other. Happy he who trusts

330

340

350

To clear Futurity his darling fame!
Then there were fauns and satyrs taking aim   360
At swelling apples with a frisky leap
And reaching fingers, 'mid a luscious heap
Of vine leaves. Then there rose to view a fane
Of liny marble, and thereto a train
Of nymphs approaching fairly o'er the sward:
One, loveliest, holding her white hand toward
The dazzling sun-rise: two sisters sweet
Bending their graceful figures till they meet
Over the trippings of a little child:
And some are hearing, eagerly, the wild   370
Thrilling liquidity of dewy piping.
See, in another picture, nymphs are wiping
Cherishingly Diana's timorous limbs –
A fold of lawny mantle dabbling swims
At the bath's edge, and keeps a gentle motion
With the subsiding crystal, as when ocean
Heaves calmly its broad swelling smoothness o'er
Its rocky marge, and balances once more
The patient weeds, that now unshent by foam
Feel all about their undulating home.   380

    Sappho's meek head was there half smiling down
At nothing; just as though the earnest frown
Of over-thinking had that moment gone
From off her brow, and left her all alone.

    Great Alfred's too, with anxious, pitying eyes,
As if he always listened to the sighs
Of the goaded world; and Kosciusko's worn
By horrid sufferance – mightily forlorn.

    Petrarch, outstepping from the shady green,
Starts at the sight of Laura; nor can wean   390
His eyes from her sweet face. Most happy they!
For over them was seen a free display

Of out-spread wings, and from between them shone
The face of Poesy: from off her throne
She overlooked things that I scarce could tell.
The very sense of where I was might well
Keep Sleep aloof: but more than that there came
Thought after thought to nourish up the flame
Within my breast, so that the morning light
400 Surprised me even from a sleepless night;
And up I rose refreshed, and glad, and gay,
Resolving to begin that very day
These lines; and howsoever they be done,
I leave them as a father does his son.

Written in Disgust of Vulgar Superstition

The church bells toll a melancholy round,
   Calling the people to some other prayers,
   Some other gloominess, more dreadful cares,
More hearkening to the sermon's horrid sound.
Surely the mind of man is closely bound
   In some black spell; seeing that each one tears
   Himself from fireside joys, and Lydian airs,
And converse high of those with glory crowned.
Still, still they toll, and I should feel a damp –
10   A chill as from a tomb – did I not know
That they are dying like an outburnt lamp;
   That 'tis their sighing, wailing ere they go
   Into oblivion – that fresh flowers will grow,
And many glories of immortal stamp.

                 (Not published by Keats)

To Kosciusko

Good Kosciusko, thy great name alone
  Is a full harvest whence to reap high feeling;
  It comes upon us like the glorious pealing
Of the wide spheres – an everlasting tone.
And now it tells me, that in worlds unknown,
   The names of heroes burst from clouds concealing,
   And change to harmonies, for ever stealing
Through cloudless blue, and round each silver
      throne.
It tells me too, that on a happy day,
   When some good spirit walks upon the earth,   10
    Thy name with Alfred's and the great of yore
   Gently commingling, gives tremendous birth
To a loud hymn, that sounds far, far away
   To where the great God lives for evermore.

'After dark vapours have oppressed our plains'

After dark vapours have oppressed our plains
  For a long dreary season, comes a day
  Born of the gentle south, and clears away
From the sick heavens all unseemly stains.
The anxious month, relieving from its pains,
  Take as a long-lost right the feel of May,
  The eyelids with the passing coolness play,
Like rose leaves with the drip of summer rains.
And calmest thoughts come round us – as of leaves
  Budding – fruit ripening in stillness – autumn
     suns   10
Smiling at eve upon the quiet sheaves –
Sweet Sappho's cheek – a sleeping infant's breath –
  The gradual sand that through an hour-glass
     runs –
A woodland rivulet – a Poet's death.

To Leigh Hunt, Esq.

Glory and loveliness have passed away;
   For if we wander out in early morn,
   No wreathèd incense do we see upborne
Into the east, to meet the smiling day:
No crowd of nymphs soft voiced and young, and
     gay,
   In woven baskets bringing ears of corn,
   Roses and pinks, and violets, to adorn
The shrine of Flora in her early May.
But there are left delights as high as these,
   And I shall ever bless my destiny,
That in a time, when under pleasant trees
   Pan is no longer sought, I feel a free,
A leafy luxury, seeing I could please
   With these poor offerings, a man like thee.

On Seeing the Elgin Marbles

My spirit is too weak – mortality
   Weighs heavily on me like unwilling sleep,
   And each imagined pinnacle and steep
Of godlike hardship, tells me I must die
Like a sick eagle looking at the sky.
   Yet 'tis a gentle luxury to weep
   That I have not the cloudy winds to keep
Fresh for the opening of the morning's eye.
Such dim-conceivèd glories of the brain
   Bring round the heart an undescribable feud;
So do these wonders a most dizzy pain
   That mingles Grecian grandeur with the rude
Wasting of old Time – with a billowy wave –
   A sun – a shadow of a magnitude.

On the Sea

It keeps eternal whisperings around
   Desolate shores, and with its mighty swell
   Gluts twice ten thousand caverns, till the spell
Of Hecate leaves them their old shadowy sound.
Often 'tis in such gentle temper found,
   That scarcely will the very smallest shell
   Be moved for days from where it sometime fell,
When last the winds of Heaven were unbound.
Oh ye! who have your eye-balls vexed and tired,
   Feast them upon the wideness of the Sea   10
     Oh ye! whose ears are dinned with uproar
       rude,
   Or fed too much with cloying melody –
     Sit ye near some old cavern's mouth and
       brood,
Until ye start, as if the sea-nymphs quired!

'Hither, hither, love –'

Hither, hither, love –
   'Tis a shady mead –
Hither, hither, love,
   Let us feed and feed!

Hither, hither, sweet –
   'Tis a cowslip bed –
Hither, hither, sweet!
   'Tis with dew bespread!

Hither, hither, dear –
   By the breath of life –   10
Hither, hither, dear!
   Be the summer's wife!

Though one moment's pleasure
  In one moment flies,
Though the passion's treasure
  In one moment dies;

Yet it has not passed –
  Think how near, how near! –
And while it doth last,
  Think how dear, how dear!

Hither, hither, hither,
  Love this boon has sent –
If I die and wither
  I shall die content.
            (Not published by Keats)

'The Gothic looks solemn'

The Gothic looks solemn –
  The plain Doric column
Supports an old Bishop and crosier;
  The mouldering arch,
  Shaded o'er by a larch
Stands next door to Wilson the Hosier.

  Vicè – that is, by turns –
  O'er pale faces mourns
The black-tassled trencher and common hat;
  The chantry boy sings,
  The steeple bell rings,
And as for the Chancellor – *dominat.*

  There are plenty of trees,
  And plenty of ease,
And plenty of fat deer for parsons;

And when it is venison,
Short is the benison –
Then each on a leg or thigh fastens.
(Not published by Keats)

Endymion:
A Poetic Romance

'*The stretched metre of an antique song.*'
INSCRIBED TO THE MEMORY OF
THOMAS CHATTERTON

PREFACE

Knowing within myself the manner in which this Poem has
been produced, it is not without a feeling of regret that I make
it public.

What manner I mean, will be quite clear to the reader, who
must soon perceive great inexperience, immaturity, and every
error denoting a feverish attempt, rather than a deed accom-
plished. The two first books, and indeed the two last, I feel
sensible are not of such completion as to warrant their passing
the press; nor should they if I thought a year's castigation would
do them any good; – it will not: the foundations are too sandy.
It is just that this youngster should die away: a sad thought for
me, if I had not some hope that while it is dwindling I may be
plotting, and fitting myself for verses fit to live.

This may be speaking too presumptuously, and may deserve
a punishment: but no feeling man will be forward to inflict it:
he will leave me alone, with the conviction that there is not a
fiercer hell than the failure in a great object. This is not written
with the least atom of purpose to forestall criticisms of course,
but from the desire I have to conciliate men who are competent
to look, and who do look with a zealous eye, to the honour of
English literature.

The imagination of a boy is healthy, and mature imagination
of a man is healthy; but there is a space of life between, in

which the soul is in a ferment, the character undecided, the way
of life uncertain, the ambition thick-sighted: thence proceeds
mawkishness, and all the thousand bitters which those men I
speak of must necessarily taste in going over the following
pages.

I hope I have not in too late a day touched the beautiful
mythology of Greece, and dulled its brightness: for I wish to
try once more, before I bid it farewell.

                                    Teignmouth, 10 April 1818

BOOK I

A thing of beauty is a joy for ever:
Its loveliness increases; it will never
Pass into nothingness; but still will keep
A bower quiet for us, and a sleep
Full of sweet dreams, and health, and quiet breathing.
Therefore, on every morrow, are we wreathing
A flowery band to bind us to the earth,
Spite of despondence, of the inhuman dearth
Of noble natures, of the gloomy days,
Of all the unhealthy and o'er-darkened ways
Made for our searching: yes, in spite of all,
Some shape of beauty moves away the pall
From our dark spirits. Such the sun, the moon,
Trees old, and young, sprouting a shady boon
For simple sheep; and such are daffodils
With the green world they live in; and clear rills
That for themselves a cooling covert make
'Gainst the hot season; the mid forest brake,
Rich with a sprinkling of fair musk-rose blooms:
And such too is the grandeur of the dooms
We have imagined for the mighty dead;
All lovely tales that we have heard or read –
An endless fountain of immortal drink,
Pouring unto us from the heaven's brink.

Nor do we merely feel these essences
For one short hour; no, even as the trees
That whisper round a temple become soon
Dear as the temple's self, so does the moon,
The passion poesy, glories infinite,
Haunt us till they become a cheering light   30
Unto our souls, and bound to us so fast,
That, whether there be shine, or gloom o'ercast,
They alway must be with us, or we die.

Therefore, 'tis with full happiness that I
Will trace the story of Endymion.
The very music of the name has gone
Into my being, and each pleasant scene
Is growing fresh before me as the green
Of our own valleys: so I will begin
Now while I cannot hear the city's din;   40
Now while the early budders are just new,
And run in mazes of the youngest hue
About old forests; while the willow trails
Its delicate amber; and the dairy pails
Bring home increase of milk. And, as the year
Grows lush in juicy stalks, I'll smoothy steer
My little boat, for many quiet hours,
With streams that deepen freshly into bowers.
Many and many a verse I hope to write,
Before the daisies, vermeil-rimmed and white,   50
Hide in deep herbage; and ere yet the bees
Hum about globes of clover and sweet peas,
I must be near the middle of my story.
O may no wintry season, bare and hoary,
See it half finished; but let Autumn bold,
With universal tinge of sober gold,
Be all about me when I make an end.
And now at once, adventuresome, I send
My herald thought into a wilderness –
There let its trumpet blow, and quickly dress   60

My uncertain path with green, that I may speed
Easily onward, thorough flowers and weed.

    Upon the sides of Latmos was outspread
A mighty forest; for the moist earth fed
So plenteously all weed-hidden roots
Into o'er-hanging boughs, and precious fruits.
And it had gloomy shades, sequestered deep,
Where no man went; and if from shepherd's keep
A lamb strayed far a-down those inmost glens,
70   Never again saw he the happy pens
Whither his brethren, bleating with content,
Over the hills at every nightfall went.
Among the shepherds, 'twas believèd ever,
That not one fleecy lamb which thus did sever
From the white flock, but passed unworrièd
By angry wolf, or pard with prying head,
Until it came to some unfooted plains
Where fed the herds of Pan – aye great his gains
Who thus one lamb did lose. Paths there were many,
80   Winding through palmy fern, and rushes fenny,
And ivy banks; all leading pleasantly
To a wide lawn, whence one could only see
Stems thronging all around between the swell
Of turf and slanting branches: who could tell
The freshness of the space of heaven above,
Edged round with dark tree tops? through which a
      dove
Would often beat its wings, and often too
A little cloud would move across the blue.

    Full in the middle of this pleasantness
90   There stood a marble altar, with a tress
Of flowers budded newly; and the dew
Had taken fairy fantasies to strew
Daisies upon the sacred sward last eve,
And so the dawnèd light in pomp receive.

For 'twas the morn: Apollo's upward fire
Made every eastern cloud a silvery pyre
Of brightness so unsullied, that therein
A melancholy spirit well might win
Oblivion, and melt out his essence fine
Into the winds: rain-scented eglantine   100
Gave temperate sweets to that well-wooing sun;
The lark was lost in him; cold springs had run
To warm their chilliest bubbles in the grass;
Man's voice was on the mountains; and the mass
Of nature's lives and wonders pulsed tenfold,
To feel this sun-rise and its glories old.

  Now while the silent workings of the dawn
Were busiest, into that self-same lawn
All suddenly, with joyful cries, there sped
A troop of little children garlanded;   110
Who gathering round the altar, seemed to pry
Earnestly round, as wishing to espy
Some folk of holiday: nor had they waited
For many moments, ere their ears were sated
With a faint breath of music, which even then
Filled out its voice, and died away again.
Within a little space again it gave
Its airy swellings, with a gentle wave,
To light-hung leaves, in smoothest echoes breaking
Through copse-clad valleys – ere their death,
        o'ertaking   120
The surgy murmurs of the lonely sea.

  And now, as deep into the wood as we
Might mark a lynx's eye, there glimmered light
Fair faces and a rush of garments white,
Plainer and plainer showing, till at last
Into the widest alley they all passed,
Making directly for the woodland altar.
O kindly muse! let not my weak tongue falter

In telling of this goodly company,
130   Of their old piety, and of their glee:
But let a portion of ethereal dew
Fall on my head, and presently unmew
My soul – that I may dare, in wayfaring,
To stammer where old Chaucer used to sing.

Leading the way, young damsels danced along,
Bearing the burden of a shepherd song;
Each having a white wicker over-brimmed
With April's tender younglings; next, well trimmed,
A crowd of shepherds with as sunburnt looks
140   As may be read of in Arcadian books,
Such as sat listening round Apollo's pipe,
When the great deity, for earth too ripe,
Let his divinity o'erflowing die
In music, through the vales of Thessaly;
Some idly trailed their sheep-hooks on the ground,
And some kept up a shrilly mellow sound
With ebon-tippèd flutes; close after these,
Now coming from beneath the forest trees,
A venerable priest full soberly,
150   Begirt with ministering looks: alway his eye
Steadfast upon the matted turf he kept,
And after him his sacred vestments swept.
From his right hand there swung a vase, milk-white,
Of mingled wine, out-sparkling generous light;
And in his left he held a basket full
Of all sweet herbs that searching eye could cull:
Wild thyme, and valley-lilies whiter still
Than Leda's love, and cresses from the rill.
His agèd head, crownèd with beechen wreath,
160   Seemed like a poll of ivy in the teeth
Of winter hoar. Then came another crowd
Of shepherds, lifting in due time aloud
Their share of the ditty. After them appeared,
Up-followed by a multitude that reared

Their voices to the clouds, a fair-wrought car,
Easily rolling so as scarce to mar
The freedom of three steeds of dapple brown.
Who stood therein did seem of great renown
Among the throng. His youth was fully blown,
Showing like Ganymede to manhood grown;   170
And, for those simple times, his garments were
A chieftain king's: beneath his breast, half bare,
Was hung a silver bugle, and between
His nervy knees there lay a boar-spear keen.
A smile was on his countenance; he seemed,
To common lookers-on, like one who dreamed
Of idleness in groves Elysian:
But there were some who feelingly could scan
A lurking trouble in his nether lip,
And see that oftentimes the reins would slip   180
Through his forgotten hands: then would they sigh,
And think of yellow leaves, of owlet's cry,
Of logs piled solemnly. Ah, well-a-day.
Why should our young Endymion pine away?

      Soon the assembly, in a circle ranged,
Stood silent round the shrine: each look was changed
To sudden veneration: women meek
Beckoned their sons to silence; while each cheek
Of virgin bloom paled gently for slight fear.
Endymion too, without a forest peer,   190
Stood, wan, and pale, and with an awèd face,
Among his brothers of the mountain chase.
In midst of all, the venerable priest
Eyed them with joy from greatest to the least,
And, after lifting up his agèd hands,
Thus spake he: 'Men of Latmos! shepherd bands!
Whose care it is to guard a thousand flocks:
Whether descended from beneath the rocks
That overtop your mountains; whether come
From valleys where the pipe is never dumb;   200

Or from your swelling downs, where sweet air stirs
Blue hare-bells lightly, and where prickly furze
Buds lavish gold; or ye, whose precious charge
Nibble their fill at ocean's very marge,
Whose mellow reeds are touched with sounds forlorn
By the dim echoes of old Triton's horn;
Mothers and wives! who day by day prepare
The scrip, with needments, for the mountain air;
And all ye gentle girls who foster up
210   Udderless lambs, and in a little cup
Will put choice honey for a favoured youth –
Yea, every one attend! for in good truth
Our vows are wanting to our great god Pan.
Are not our lowing heifers sleeker than
Night-swollen mushrooms? Are not our wide plains
Speckled with countless fleeces? Have not rains
Greened over April's lap? No howling sad
Sickens our fearful ewes; and we have had
Great bounty from Endymion our lord.
220   The earth is glad: the merry lark has poured
His early song against yon breezy sky,
That spreads so clear o'er our solemnity.'

    Thus ending, on the shrine he heaped a spire
Of teeming sweets, enkindling sacred fire;
Anon he stained the thick and spongy sod
With wine, in honour of the shepherd-god.
Now while the earth was drinking it, and while
Bay leaves were crackling in the fragrant pile,
And gummy frankincense was sparkling bright
230   'Neath smothering parsley, and a hazy light
Spread greyly eastward, thus a chorus sang:

    'O thou, whose mighty palace roof doth hang
From jagged trunks, and overshadoweth
Eternal whispers, glooms, the birth, life, death
Of unseen flowers in heavy peacefulness;
Who lov'st to see the hamadryads dress

Their ruffled locks where meeting hazels darken;
And through whole solemn hours dost sit, and
    hearken
The dreary melody of bedded reeds
In desolate places, where dank moisture breeds   240
The pipy hemlock to strange overgrowth;
Bethinking thee, how melancholy loth
Thou wast to lose fair Syrinx – do thou now –
By thy love's milky brow! –
By all the trembling mazes that she ran –
Hear us, great Pan!

  'O thou, for whose soul-soothing quiet, turtles
Passion their voices cooingly 'mong myrtles,
What time thou wanderest at eventide
Through sunny meadows, that outskirt the side   250
Of thine enmossèd realms: O thou, to whom
Broad-leavèd fig trees even now foredoom
Their ripened fruitage; yellow-girted bees
Their golden honeycombs; our village leas
Their fairest-blossomed beans and poppied corn;
The chuckling linnet its five young unborn
To sing for thee; low creeping strawberries
Their summer coolness; pent up butterflies
Their freckled wings; yea, the fresh budding year
All its completions – be quickly near,   260
By every wind that nods the mountain pine,
O forester divine!

  'Thou, to whom every faun and satyr flies
For willing service; whether to surprise
The squatted hare while in half-sleeping fit;
Or upward ragged precipices flit
To save poor lambkins from the eagle's maw;
Or by mysterious enticement draw
Bewildered shepherds to their path again;
Or to tread breathless round the frothy main,   270

And gather up all fancifullest shells
For thee to tumble into Naiads' cells,
And, being hidden, laugh at their out-peeping;
Or to delight thee with fantastic leaping,
The while they pelt each other on the crown
With silvery oak apples, and fir cones brown –
By all the echoes that about thee ring,
Hear us, O satyr king!

'O Hearkener to the loud clapping shears
280   While ever and anon to his shorn peers
A ram goes bleating; Winder of the horn,
When snouted wild-boars routing tender corn
Anger our huntsmen; Breather round our farms,
To keep off mildews, and all weather harms;
Strange ministrant of undescribèd sounds,
That come a-swooning over hollow grounds,
And wither drearily on barren moors;
Dread opener of the mysterious doors
Leading to universal knowledge – see,
290   Great son of Dryope,
The many that are come to pay their vows
With leaves about their brows!

'Be still the unimaginable lodge
For solitary thinkings; such as dodge
Conception to the very bourne of heaven,
Then leave the naked brain; be still the leaven,
That spreading in this dull and clodded earth
Gives it a touch ethereal – a new birth;
Be still a symbol of immensity;
300   A firmament reflected in a sea;
An element filling the space between,
An unknown – but no more! we humbly screen
With uplift hands our foreheads, lowly bending,
And giving out a shout most heaven rending,
Conjure thee to receive our humble paean,
Upon thy Mount Lycean!'

Even while they brought the burden to a close,
A shout from the whole multitude arose,
That lingered in the air like dying rolls
Of abrupt thunder, when Ionian shoals   310
Of dolphins bob their noses through the brine.
Meantime, on shady levels, mossy fine,
Young companies nimbly began dancing
To the swift treble pipe, and humming string.
Ay, those fair living forms swam heavenly
To tunes forgotten – out of memory;
Fair creatures! whose young children's children
      bred
Thermopylae its heroes – not yet dead,
But in old marbles ever beautiful.
High genitors, unconscious did they cull   320
Time's sweet first-fruits – they danced to weariness,
And then in quiet circles did they press
The hillock turf, and caught the latter end
Of some strange history, potent to send
A young mind from its bodily tenement.
Or they might watch the quoit-pitchers, intent
On either side; pitying the sad death
Of Hyacinthus, when the cruel breath
Of Zephyr slew him – Zephyr penitent,
Who now, ere Phoebus mounts the firmament,   330
Fondles the flower amid the sobbing rain.
The archers too, upon a wider plain,
Beside the feathery whizzing of the shaft,
And the dull twanging bowstring, and the raft
Branch down sweeping from a tall ash top,
Called up a thousand thoughts to envelop
Those who would watch. Perhaps, the trembling
      knee
And frantic gape of lonely Niobe –
Poor, lonely Niobe! – when her lovely young
Were dead and gone, and her caressing tongue   340
Lay a lost thing upon her paly lip,
And very, very deadliness did nip

Her motherly cheeks. Aroused from this sad mood
By one, who at a distance loud hallooed,
Uplifting his strong bow into the air,
Many might after brighter visions stare:
After the Argonauts, in blind amaze
Tossing about on Neptune's restless ways,
Until, from the horizon's vaulted side,
350   There shot a golden splendour far and wide,
Spangling those million poutings of the brine
With quivering ore – 'twas even an awful shine
From the exaltation of Apollo's bow;
A heavenly beacon in their dreary woe.
Who thus were ripe for high contemplating,
Might turn their steps towards the sober ring
Where sat Endymion and the agèd priest
'Mong shepherds gone in eld, whose looks increased
The silvery setting of their mortal star.
360   There they discoursed upon the fragile bar
That keeps us from our homes ethereal,
And what our duties there: to nightly call
Vesper, the beauty-crest of summer weather;
To summon all the downiest clouds together
For the sun's purple couch; to emulate
In ministering the potent rule of fate
With speed of fire-tailèd exhalations:
To tint her pallid cheek with bloom, who cons
Sweet poesy by moonlight: besides these,
370   A world of other unguessed offices.
Anon they wandered, by divine converse,
Into Elysium, vying to rehearse
Each one his own anticipated bliss.
One felt heart-certain that he could not miss
His quick-gone love, among fair blossomed boughs,
Where every zephyr-sigh pouts, and endows
Her lips with music for the welcoming.
Another wished, mid that eternal spring,

To meet his rosy child, with feathery sails,
Sweeping, eye-earnestly, through almond vales –   380
Who, suddenly, should stoop through the smooth
        wind,
And with the balmiest leaves his temples bind;
And, ever after, through those regions be
His messenger, his little Mercury.
Some were athirst in soul to see again
Their fellow huntsmen o'er the wide champaign
In times long past; to sit with them, and talk
Of all the chances in their earthly walk;
Comparing, joyfully, their plenteous stores
Of happiness, to when upon the moors,   390
Benighted, close they huddled from the cold,
And shared their famished scrips. Thus all out-told
Their fond-imaginations – saving him
Whose eyelids curtained up their jewels dim,
Endymion: yet hourly had he striven
To hide the cankering venom, that had riven
His fainting recollections. Now indeed
His senses had swooned off; he did not heed
The sudden silence, or the whispers low,
Or the old eyes dissolving at his woe,   400
Or anxious calls, or close of trembling palms,
Or maiden's sigh, that grief itself embalms:
But in the self-same fixèd trance he kept,
Like one who on the earth had never stepped.
Ay, even as dead still as a marble man,
Frozen in that old tale Arabian.

   Who whispers him so pantingly and close?
Peona, his sweet sister – of all those,
His friends, the dearest. Hushing signs she made,
And breathed a sister's sorrow to persuade   410
A yielding up, a cradling on her care.
Her eloquence did breathe away the curse:
She led him, like some midnight spirit-nurse

Of happy changes in emphatic dreams,
Along a path between two little streams –
Guarding his forehead, with her round elbow,
From low-grown branches, and his footsteps slow
From stumbling over stumps and hillocks small –
Until they came to where these streamlets fall,
420   With mingled bubblings and a gentle rush,
Into a river, clear, brimful, and flush
With crystal mocking of the trees and sky.
A little shallop, floating there hard by,
Pointed its beak over the fringèd bank;
And soon it lightly dipped, and rose, and sank,
And dipped again, with the young couple's weight –
Peona guiding, through the water straight,
Towards a bowery island opposite,
Which gaining presently, she steerèd light
430   Into a shady, fresh, and ripply cove,
Where nested was an arbour, overwove
By many a summer's silent fingering;
To whose cool bosom she was used to bring
Her playmates, with their needle broidery,
And minstrel memories of times gone by.

      So she was gently glad to see him laid
Under her favourite bower's quiet shade,
On her own couch, new made of flower leaves,
Dried carefully on the cooler side of sheaves
440   When last the sun his autumn tresses shook,
And the tanned harvesters rich armfuls took.
Soon was he quieted to slumbrous rest:
But, ere it crept upon him, he had pressed
Peona's busy hand against his lips,
And still, a-sleeping, held her finger-tips
In tender pressure. And as a willow keeps
A patient watch over the stream that creeps
Windingly by it, so the quiet maid
Held her in peace: so that a whispering blade

Of grass, a wailful gnat, a bee bustling   450
Down in the blue-bells, or a wren light rustling
Among sere leaves and twigs, might all be heard.

   O magic sleep! O comfortable bird,
That broodest o'er the troubled sea of the mind
Till it is hushed and smooth! O unconfined
Restraint! imprisoned liberty! great key
To golden palaces, strange minstrelsy,
Fountains grotesque, new trees, bespangled caves,
Echoing grottoes, full of tumbling waves
And moonlight; ay, to all the mazy world   460
Of silvery enchantment! Who, upfurled
Beneath thy drowsy wing a triple hour,
But renovates and lives? – Thus, in the bower,
Endymion was calmed to life again.
Opening his eyelids with a healthier brain,
He said: 'I feel this thine endearing love
All through my bosom: thou art as a dove
Trembling its closèd eyes and sleekèd wings
About me; and the pearliest dew not brings
Such morning incense from the fields of May,   470
As do those brighter drops that twinkling stray
From those kind eyes – the very home and haunt
Of sisterly affection. Can I want
Aught else, aught nearer heaven, than such tears?
Yet dry them up, in bidding hence all fears
That, any longer, I will pass my days
Alone and sad. No, I will once more raise
My voice upon the mountain-heights; once more
Make my horn parley from their foreheads hoar;
Again my trooping hounds their tongues shall loll   480
Around the breathèd boar; again I'll poll
The fair-grown yew tree for a chosen bow;
And, when the pleasant sun is getting low,
Again I'll linger in a sloping mead
To hear the speckled thrushes, and see feed

Our idle sheep. So be thou cheerèd, sweet,
And, if thy lute is here, softly entreat
My soul to keep in its resolvèd course.'

Hereat Peona, in their silver source,
490   Shut her pure sorrow-drops with glad exclaim,
And took a lute, from which there pulsing came
A lively prelude, fashioning the way
In which her voice should wander. 'Twas a lay
More subtle cadenced, more forest wild
Than Dryope's lone lulling of her child;
And nothing since has floated in the air
So mournful strange. Surely some influence rare
Went, spiritual, through the damsel's hand;
For still, with Delphic emphasis, she spanned
500   The quick invisible strings, even though she saw
Endymion's spirit melt away and thaw
Before the deep intoxication.
But soon she came, with sudden burst, upon
Her self-possession – swung the lute aside,
And earnestly said: 'Brother, 'tis vain to hide
That thou dost know of things mysterious,
Immortal, starry; such alone could thus
Weigh down thy nature. Hast thou sinned in aught
Offensive to the heavenly powers? Caught
510   A Paphian dove upon a message sent?
Thy deathful bow against some deer-head bent
Sacred to Dian? Haply, thou hast seen
Her naked limbs among the alders green –
And that, alas! is death. No, I can trace
Something more high-perplexing in thy face!'

Endymion looked at her, and pressed her hand,
And said, 'Art thou so pale, who wast so bland
And merry in our meadows? How is this?
Tell me thine ailment – tell me all amiss!

Ah! thou hast been unhappy at the change   520
Wrought suddenly in me. What indeed more
    strange?
Or more complete to overwhelm surmise?
Ambition is no sluggard: 'tis no prize,
That toiling years would put within my grasp,
That I have sighed for; with so deadly gasp
No man e'er panted for a mortal love.
So all have set my heavier grief above
These things which happen. Rightly have they done:
I, who still saw the horizontal sun
Heave his broad shoulder o'er the edge of the
    world,   530
Out-facing Lucifer, and then had hurled
My spear aloft, as signal for the chase –
I, who, for very sport of heart, would race
With my own steed from Araby; pluck down
A vulture from his towery perching; frown
A lion into growling, loth retire –
To lose, at once, all my toil-breeding fire,
And sink thus low! but I will ease my breast
Of secret grief, here in this bowery nest.

    'This river does not see the naked sky,   540
Till it begins to progress silverly
Around the western border of the wood,
Whence, from a certain spot, its winding flood
Seems at the distance like a crescent moon:
And in that nook, the very pride of June,
Had I been used to pass my weary eves;
The rather for the sun unwilling leaves
So dear a picture of his sovereign power,
And I could witness his most kingly hour,
When he doth tighten up the golden reins,   550
And paces leisurely down amber plains
His snorting four. Now when his chariot last
Its beams against the zodiac-lion cast,

There blossomed suddenly a magic bed
Of sacred ditamy, and poppies red:
At which I wondered greatly, knowing well
That but one night had wrought this flowery spell;
And, sitting down close by, began to muse
What it might mean. Perhaps, thought I, Morpheus,
560 In passing here, his owlet pinions shook;
Or, it may be, ere matron Night uptook
Her ebon urn, young Mercury, by stealth,
Had dipped his rod in it: such garland wealth
Came not by common growth. Thus on I thought,
Until my head was dizzy and distraught.
Moreover, through the dancing poppies stole
A breeze, most softly lulling to my soul,
And shaping visions all about my sight
Of colours, wings, and bursts of spangly light;
The which became more strange, and strange, and
570   dim,
And then were gulfed in a tumultuous swim –
And then I fell asleep. Ah, can I tell
The enchantment that afterwards befell?
Yet it was but a dream: yet such a dream
That never tongue, although it overteem
With mellow utterance, like a cavern spring,
Could figure out and to conception bring
All I beheld and felt. Methought I lay
Watching the zenith, where the milky way
580 Among the stars in virgin splendour pours;
And travelling my eye, until the doors
Of heaven appeared to open for my flight,
I became loth and fearful to alight
From such high soaring by a downward glance:
So kept me steadfast in that airy trance,
Spreading imaginary pinions wide.
When, presently, the stars began to glide,
And faint away, before my eager view:
At which I sighed that I could not pursue,

And dropped my vision to the horizon's verge –   590
And lo! from opening clouds, I saw emerge
The loveliest moon, that ever silvered o'er
A shell for Neptune's goblet: she did soar
So passionately bright, my dazzled soul
Commingling with her argent spheres did roll
Through clear and cloudy, even when she went
At last into a dark and vapoury tent –
Whereat, methought, the lidless-eyèd train
Of planets all were in the blue again.
To commune with those orbs, once more I raised   600
My sight right upward: but it was quite dazed
By a bright something, sailing down apace,
Making me quickly veil my eyes and face:
Again I looked, and, O ye deities,
Who from Olympus watch our destinies!
Whence that completed form of all completeness?
Whence came that high perfection of all sweetness?
Speak, stubborn earth, and tell me where, O where
Hast thou a symbol of her golden hair?
Not oat-sheaves drooping in the western sun;   610
Not – thy soft hand, fair sister! let me shun
Such follying before thee – yet she had,
Indeed, locks bright enough to make me mad;
And they were simply gordianed up and braided,
Leaving, in naked comeliness, unshaded,
Her pearl-round ears, white neck, and orbèd brow;
The which were blended in, I know not how,
With such a paradise of lips and eyes,
Blush-tinted cheeks, half smiles, and faintest sighs,
That, when I think thereon, my spirit clings   620
And plays about its fancy, till the stings
Of human neighbourhood envenom all.
Unto what awful power shall I call?
To what high fane? – Ah! see her hovering feet,
More bluely veined, more soft, more whitely sweet
Than those of sea-born Venus, when she rose
From out her cradle shell. The wind out-blows

Her scarf into a fluttering pavilion;
'Tis blue, and over-spangled with a million
Of little eyes, as though thou wert to shed,
Over the darkest, lushest blue-bell bed,
Handfuls of daisies.' – 'Endymion, how strange!
Dream within dream!' – 'She took an airy range,
And then, towards me, like a very maid,
Came blushing, waning, willing, and afraid,
And pressed me by the hand: Ah! 'twas too much;
Methought I fainted at the charmèd touch,
Yet held my recollection, even as one
Who dives three fathoms where the waters run
Gurgling in beds of coral: for anon,
I felt up-mounted in that region
Where falling stars dart their artillery forth,
And eagles struggle with the buffeting north
That balances the heavy meteor-stone –
Felt too, I was not fearful, nor alone,
But lapped and lulled along the dangerous sky.
Soon, as it seemed, we left our journeying high,
And straightway into frightful eddies swooped,
Such as aye muster where grey time has scooped
Huge dens and caverns in a mountain's side:
There hollow sounds aroused me, and I sighed
To faint once more by looking on my bliss –
I was distracted; madly did I kiss
The wooing arms which held me, and did give
My eyes at once to death – but 'twas to live,
To take in draughts of life from the gold fount
Of kind and passionate looks; to count, and count
The moments, by some greedy help that seemed
A second self, that each might be redeemed
And plundered of its load of blessedness.
Ah, desperate mortal! I e'en dared to press
Her very cheek against my crownèd lip,
And, at that moment, felt my body dip
Into a warmer air – a moment more,
Our feet were soft in flowers. There was store

Of newest joys upon that alp. Sometimes
A scent of violets, and blossoming limes,
Loitered around us; then of honey cells,
Made delicate from all white-flower bells;
And once, above the edges of our nest,   670
An arch face peeped – an Oread as I guessed.

      'Why did I dream that sleep o'er-powered me
In midst of all this heaven? Why not see,
Far off, the shadows of his pinions dark,
And stare them from me? But no, like a spark
That needs must die, although its little beam
Reflects upon a diamond, my sweet dream
Fell into nothing – into stupid sleep.
And so it was, until a gentle creep,
A careful moving, caught my waking ears,   680
And up I started. Ah! my sighs, my tears,
My clenchèd hands – for lo! the poppies hung
Dew-dabbled on their stalks, the ouzel sung
A heavy ditty, and the sullen day
Had chidden herald Hesperus away,
With leaden looks: the solitary breeze
Blustered, and slept, and its wild self did tease
With wayward melancholy; and I thought,
Mark me, Peona! that sometimes it brought
Faint fare-thee-wells, and sigh-shrillèd adieus! –   690
Away I wandered – all the pleasant hues
Of heaven and earth had faded: deepest shades
Were deepest dungeons; heaths and sunny glades
Were full of pestilent light; our taintless rills
Seemed sooty, and o'er-spread with upturned gills
Of dying fish; the vermeil rose had blown
In frightful scarlet, and its thorns out-grown
Like spiked aloe. If an innocent bird
Before my heedless footsteps stirred and stirred
In little journeys, I beheld in it   700
A disguised demon, missionèd to knit
My soul with under-darkness, to entice

My stumblings down some monstrous precipice:
Therefore I eager followed, and did curse
The disappointment. Time, that agèd nurse,
Rocked me to patience. Now, thank gentle heaven!
These things, with all their comfortings, are given
To my down-sunken hours, and with thee,
Sweet sister, help to stem the ebbing sea
710   Of weary life.'

              Thus ended he, and both
Sat silent: for the maid was very loth
To answer; feeling well that breathèd words
Would all be lost, unheard, and vain as swords
Against the enchasèd crocodile, or leaps
Of grasshoppers against the sun. She weeps,
And wonders; struggles to devise some blame;
To put on such a look as would say, *Shame
On this poor weakness!* but, for all her strife,
She could as soon have crushed away the life
720   From a sick dove. At length, to break the pause,
She said with trembling chance: 'Is this the cause?
This all? Yet it is strange, and sad, alas!
That one who through this middle earth should pass
Most like a sojourning demi-god, and leave
His name upon the harp-string, should achieve
No higher bard than simple maidenhood,
Singing alone, and fearfully – how the blood
Left his young cheek; and how he used to stray
He knew not where; and how he would say, *nay*,
730   If any said 'twas love – and yet 'twas love;
What could it be but love? How a ring-dove
Let fall a sprig of yew tree in his path;
And how he died; and then, that love doth scathe
The gentle heart, as northern blasts do roses;
And then the ballad of his sad life closes
With sighs, and an 'alas'! – Endymion!
Be rather in the trumpet's mouth – anon

Among the winds at large, that all may hearken!
Although, before the crystal heavens darken,
I watch and dote upon the silver lakes   740
Pictured in western cloudiness, that takes
The semblance of gold rocks and bright gold sands,
Islands, and creeks, and amber-fretted strands
With horses prancing o'er them, palaces
And towers of amethyst – would I so tease
My pleasant days, because I could not mount
Into those regions? The Morphean fount
Of that fine element that visions, dreams,
And fitful whims of sleep are made of, streams
Into its airy channels with so subtle,   750
So thin a breathing, not the spider's shuttle,
Circled a million times within the space
Of a swallow's nest-door, could delay a trace,
A tinting of its quality: how light
Must dreams themselves be, seeing they're more
        slight
Than the mere nothing that engenders them!
Then wherefore sully the entrusted gem
Of high and noble life with thoughts so sick?
Why pierce high-fronted honour to the quick
For nothing but a dream?' Hereat the youth   760
Looked up: a conflicting of shame and ruth
Was in his plaited brow: yet, his eyelids
Widened a little, as when Zephyr bids
A little breeze to creep between the fans
Of careless butterflies. Amid his pains
He seemed to taste a drop of manna-dew,
Full palatable; and a colour grew
Upon his cheek, while thus he lifeful spake.

    'Peona! ever have I longed to slake
My thirst for the world's praises: nothing base,   770
No merely slumbrous phantasm, could unlace
The stubborn canvas for my voyage prepared –
Though now 'tis tattered, leaving my bark bared

And sullenly drifting: yet my higher hope
Is of too wide, too rainbow-large a scope,
To fret at myriads of earthly wrecks.
Wherein lies happiness? In that which becks
Our ready minds to fellowship divine,
A fellowship with essence; till we shine,
780   Full alchemized, and free of space. Behold
The clear religion of heaven! Fold
A rose leaf round thy finger's taperness,
And soothe thy lips; hist, when the airy stress
Of music's kiss impregnates the free winds,
And with a sympathetic touch unbinds
Aeolian magic from their lucid wombs:
Then old songs waken from enclouded tombs;
Old ditties sigh above their father's grave;
Ghosts of melodious prophesyings rave
790   Round every spot where trod Apollo's foot;
Bronze clarions awake, and faintly bruit,
Where long ago a giant battle was;
And, from the turf, a lullaby doth pass
In every place where infant Orpheus slept.
Feel we these things? – that moment have we stepped
Into a sort of oneness, and our state
Is like a floating spirit's. But there are
Richer entanglements, enthralments far
More self-destroying, leading, by degrees,
800   To the chief intensity: the crown of these
Is made of love and friendship, and sits high
Upon the forehead of humanity.
All its more ponderous and bulky worth
Is friendship, whence there ever issues forth
A steady splendour; but at the tip-top,
There hangs by unseen film, an orbèd drop
Of light, and that is love: its influence,
Thrown in our eyes, genders a novel sense,
At which we start and fret; till in the end,
810   Melting into its radiance, we blend,

Mingle, and so become a part of it –
Nor with aught else can our souls interknit
So wingedly. When we combine therewith,
Life's self is nourished by its proper pith,
And we are nurtured like a pelican brood.
Ay, so delicious is the unsating food,
That men, who might have towered in the van
Of all the congregated world, to fan
And winnow from the coming step of time
All chaff of custom, wipe away all slime   820
Left by men-slugs and human serpentry,
Have been content to let occasion die,
Whilst they did sleep in love's elysium.
And, truly, I would rather be struck dumb,
Than speak against this ardent listlessness:
For I have ever thought that it might bless
The world with benefits unknowingly,
As does the nightingale, up-perchèd high,
And cloistered among cool and bunchèd leaves –
She sings but to her love, nor e'er conceives   830
How tip-toe Night holds back her dark-grey hood.
Just so may love, although 'tis understood
The mere commingling of passionate breath,
Produce more than our searching witnesseth –
What I know not: but who, of men, can tell
That flowers would bloom, or that green fruit would
        swell
To melting pulp, that fish would have bright mail,
The earth its dower of river, wood, and vale,
The meadows runnels, runnels pebble-stones,
The seed its harvest, or the lute its tones,   840
Tones ravishment, or ravishment its sweet,
If human souls did never kiss and greet?

    'Now, if this earthly love has power to make
Men's being mortal, immortal; to shake
Ambition from their memories, and brim
Their measure of content; what merest whim,

Seems all this poor endeavour after fame,
To one, who keeps within his steadfast aim
A love immortal, an immortal too.
850   Look not so wildered; for these things are true,
And never can be born of atomies
That buzz about our slumbers, like brain-flies,
Leaving us fancy-sick. No, no, I'm sure,
My restless spirit never could endure
To brood so long upon one luxury,
Unless it did, though fearfully, espy
A hope beyond the shadow of a dream.
My sayings will the less obscurèd seem,
When I have told thee how my waking sight
860   Has made me scruple whether that same night
Was passed in dreaming. Hearken, sweet Peona!
Beyond the matron-temple of Latona,
Which we should see but for these darkening boughs,
Lies a deep hollow, from whose ragged brows
Bushes and trees do lean all round athwart
And meet so nearly, that with wings outraught,
And spreaded tail, a vulture could not glide
Past them, but he must brush on every side.
Some mouldered steps lead into this cool cell,
870   Far as the slabbèd margin of a well,
Whose patient level peeps its crystal eye
Right upward, through the bushes, to the sky.
Oft have I brought thee flowers, on their stalks set
Like vestal primroses, but dark velvet
Edges them round, and they have golden pits:
'Twas there I got them, from the gaps and slits
In a mossy stone, that sometimes was my seat,
When all above was faint with midday heat.
And there in strife no burning thoughts to heed,
880   I'd bubble up the water through a reed;
So reaching back to boyhood; make me ships
Of moulted feathers, touchwood, alder chips,
With leaves stuck in them; and the Neptune be
Of their petty ocean. Oftener, heavily,

When love-lorn hours had left me less a child,
I sat contemplating the figures wild
Of o'er-head clouds melting the mirror through.
Upon a day, while thus I watched, by flew
A cloudy Cupid, with his bow and quiver,
So plainly charactered, no breeze would shiver   890
The happy chance: so happy, I was fain
To follow it upon the open plain,
And, therefore, was just going, when, behold!
A wonder, fair as any I have told –
The same bright face I tasted in my sleep,
Smiling in the clear well. My heart did leap
Through the cool depth. – It moved as if to flee –
I started up – when lo! refreshfully,
There came upon my face in plenteous showers,
Dew-drops, and dewy buds, and leaves, and
          flowers,   900
Wrapping all objects from my smothered sight,
Bathing my spirit in a new delight.
Ay, such a breathless honey-feel of bliss
Alone preserved me from the drear abyss
Of death, for the fair form had gone again.
Pleasure is oft a visitant; but pain
Clings cruelly to us, like the gnawing sloth
On the deer's tender haunches; late, and loth,
'Tis scared away by slow returning pleasure.
How sickening, how dark the dreadful leisure   910
Of weary days, made deeper exquisite,
By a fore-knowledge of unslumbrous night!
Like sorrow came upon me, heavier still,
Than when I wandered from the poppy hill:
And a whole age of lingering moments crept
Sluggishly by, ere more contentment swept
Away at once the deadly yellow spleen.
Yes, thrice have I this fair enchantment seen;
Once more been tortured with renewèd life.
When last the wintry gusts gave over strife   920

With the conquering sun of spring, and left the skies
Warm and serene, but yet with moistened eyes
In pity of the shattered infant buds –
That time thou didst adorn, with amber studs,
My hunting cap, because I laughed and smiled,
Chatted with thee, and many days exiled
All torment from my breast – 'twas even then,
Straying about, yet, cooped up in the den
Of helpless discontent, hurling my lance
930   From place to place, and following at chance,
At last, by hap, through some young trees it struck,
And, plashing among bedded pebbles, stuck
In the middle of a brook, whose silver ramble
Down twenty little falls, through reeds and bramble,
Tracing along, it brought me to a cave,
Whence it ran brightly forth, and white did lave
The nether sides of mossy stones and rock –
'Mong which it gurgled blythe adieus, to mock
Its own sweet grief at parting. Overhead,
940   Hung a lush screen of drooping weeds, and spread
Thick, as to curtain up some wood-nymph's home.
"Ah! impious mortal, whither do I roam?"
Said I, low voiced: "Ah, whither! 'Tis the grot
Of Proserpine, when Hell, obscure and hot,
Doth her resign, and where her tender hands
She dabbles, on the cool and sluicy sands;
Or 'tis the cell of Echo, where she sits,
And babbles thorough silence, till her wits
Are gone in tender madness, and anon,
950   Faints into sleep, with many a dying tone
Of sadness. O that she would take my vows,
And breathe them sighingly among the boughs,
To sue her gentle ears for whose fair head,
Daily, I pluck sweet flowerets from their bed,
And weave them dyingly – send honey-whispers
Round every leaf, that all those gentle lispers
May sigh my love unto her pitying!
O charitable Echo! hear, and sing

This ditty to her! Tell her –" So I stayed
My foolish tongue, and listening, half afraid,   960
Stood stupefied with my own empty folly,
And blushing for the freaks of melancholy.
Salt tears were coming, when I heard my name
Most fondly lipped, and then these accents came:
"Endymion! the cave is secreter
Than the isle of Delos. Echo hence shall stir
No sighs but sigh-warm kisses, or light noise
Of thy combing hand, the while it travelling cloys
And trembles through my labyrinthine hair."
At that oppressed I hurried in. Ah! where   970
Are those swift moments? Whither are they fled?
I'll smile no more, Peona; nor will wed
Sorrow the way to death; but patiently
Bear up against it – so farewell, sad sigh;
And come instead demurest meditation,
To occupy me wholly, and to fashion
My pilgrimage for the world's dusky brink.
No more will I count over, link by link,
My chain of grief: no longer strive to find
A half-forgetfulness in mountain wind   980
Blustering about my ears. Ay, thou shalt see,
Dearest of sisters, what my life shall be;
What a calm round of hours shall make my days.
There is a paly flame of hope that plays
Where'er I look; but yet, I'll say 'tis naught –
And here I bid it die. Have not I caught,
Already, a more healthy countenance?
By this the sun is setting; we may chance
Meet some of our near-dwellers with my car.'

   This said, he rose, faint-smiling like a star   990
Through autumn mists, and took Peona's hand:
They stepped into the boat, and launched from land.

BOOK II

[*Invocation*]

O sovereign power of love! O grief! O balm!
All records, saving thine, come cool, and calm,
And shadowy, through the mist of passèd years:
For others, good or bad, hatred and tears
Have become indolent, but touching thine,
One sigh doth echo, one poor sob doth pine,
One kiss brings honey-dew from buried days.
The woes of Troy, towers smothering o'er their blaze,
Stiff-holden shields, far-piercing spears, keen blades,
Struggling, and blood, and shrieks – all dimly fades
Into some backward corner of the brain:
Yet, in our very souls, we feel amain
The close of Troilus and Cressid sweet.
Hence, pageant history! hence, gilded cheat!
Swart planet in the universe of deeds!
Wide sea, that one continuous murmur breeds
Along the pebbled shore of memory!
Many old rotten-timbered boats there be
Upon thy vaporous bosom, magnified
To goodly vessels; many a sail of pride,
And golden keeled, is left unlaunched and dry.
But wherefore this? What care, though owl did fly
About the great Athenian admiral's mast?
What care, though striding Alexander passed
The Indus with his Macedonian numbers?
Though old Ulysses tortured from his slumbers
The glutted Cyclops, what care? – Juliet leaning
Amid her window-flowers, sighing, weaning
Tenderly her fancy from its maiden snow,
Doth more avail than these. The silver flow
Of Hero's tears, the swoon of Imogen,
Fair Pastorella in the bandit's den,
Are things to brood on with more ardency
Than the death-day of empires. Fearfully

Must such conviction come upon his head,
Who, thus far, discontent, has dared to tread,
Without one muse's smile, or kind behest,
The path of love and poesy. But rest,
In chafing restlessness, is yet more drear
Than to be crushed in striving to uprear   40
Love's standard on the battlements of song.
So once more days and nights aid me along,
Like legioned soldiers.

[*Venus and Adonis*]

After a thousand mazes overgone,
At last, with sudden step, he came upon
A chamber, myrtle walled, embowered high,
Full of light, incense, tender minstrelsy,   390
And more of beautiful and strange beside:
For on a silken couch of rosy pride,
In midst of all, there lay a sleeping youth
Of fondest beauty; fonder, in fair sooth,
Than sighs could fathom, or contentment reach:
And coverlids gold-tinted like the peach,
Or ripe October faded marigolds,
Fell sleek about him in a thousand folds –
Not hiding up an Apollonian curve
Of neck and shoulder, nor the tenting swerve   400
Of knee from knee, nor ankles pointing light;
But rather, giving them to the fillèd sight
Officiously. Sideway his face reposed
On one white arm, and tenderly unclosed,
By tenderest pressure, a faint damask mouth
To slumbery pout; just as the morning south
Disparts a dew-lipped rose. Above his head,
Four lily stalks did their white honours wed
To make a coronal; and round him grew
All tendrils green, of every bloom and hue,   410
Together intertwined and trammelled fresh:
The vine of glossy sprout; the ivy mesh,

Shading its Ethiope berries; and woodbine,
Of velvet leaves and bugle-blooms divine;
Convolvulus in streakèd vases flush;
The creeper, mellowing for an autumn blush;
And virgin's bower, trailing airily;
With others of the sisterhood. Hard by,
Stood serene Cupids watching silently.
420 One, kneeling to a lyre, touched the strings,
Muffling to death the pathos with his wings;
And, ever and anon, uprose to look
At the youth's slumber; while another took
A willow-bough, distilling odorous dew,
And shook it on his hair; another flew
In through the woven roof, and fluttering-wise
Rained violets upon his sleeping eyes.

　　At these enchantments, and yet many more,
The breathless Latmian wondered o'er and o'er;
430 Until, impatient in embarrassment,
He forthright passed, and lightly treading went
To that same feathered lyrist, who straightway,
Smiling, thus whispered: 'Though from upper day
Thou art a wanderer, and thy presence here
Might seem unholy, be of happy cheer!
For 'tis the nicest touch of human honour,
When some ethereal and high-favouring donor
Presents immortal bowers to mortal sense –
As now 'tis done to thee, Endymion. Hence
440 Was I in no wise startled. So recline
Upon these living flowers. Here is wine,
Alive with sparkles – never, I aver,
Since Ariadne was a vintager,
So cool a purple: taste these juicy pears,
Sent me by sad Vertumnus, when his fears
Were high about Pomona: here is cream,
Deepening to richness from a snowy gleam;
Sweeter than that nurse Amalthea skimmed
For the boy Jupiter: and here, undimmed

By any touch, a bunch of blooming plums   450
Ready to melt between an infant's gums:
And here is manna picked from Syrian trees,
In starlight, by the three Hesperides.
Feast on, and meanwhile I will let thee know
Of all these things around us.' He did so,
Still brooding o'er the cadence of his lyre;
And thus: 'I need not any hearing tire
By telling how the sea-born goddess pined
For a mortal youth, and how she strove to bind
Him all in all unto her doting self.   460
Who would not be so prisoned? but, fond elf,
He was content to let her amorous plea
Faint through his careless arms; content to see
An unseized heaven dying at his feet;
Content, O fool! to make a cold retreat,
When on the pleasant grass such love, lovelorn,
Lay sorrowing; when every tear was born
Of diverse passion; when her lips and eyes
Were closed in sullen moisture, and quick sighs
Came vexed and pettish through her nostrils small. 470
Hush! no exclaim – yet, justly mightest thou call
Curses upon his head. – I was half glad,
But my poor mistress went distract and mad,
When the boar tusked him: so away she flew
To Jove's high throne, and by her plainings drew
Immortal tear-drops down the thunderer's beard;
Whereon, it was decreed he should be reared
Each summer-time to life. Lo! this is he,
That same Adonis, safe in the privacy
Of this still region all his winter-sleep.   480
Ay, sleep; for when our love-sick queen did weep
Over his wanèd corse, the tremulous shower
Healed up the wound, and, with a balmy power,
Medicined death to a lengthened drowsiness:
The which she fills with visions, and doth dress
In all this quiet luxury; and hath set
Us young immortals, without any let,

To watch his slumber through. 'Tis well nigh passed,
Even to a moment's filling up, and fast
490   She scuds with summer breezes, to pant through
The first long kiss, warm firstling, to renew
Embowered sports in Cytherea's isle.
Look! how those wingèd listeners all this while
Stand anxious! See! behold!' – This clamant word
Broke through the careful silence; for they heard
A rustling noise of leaves, and out there fluttered
Pigeons and doves: Adonis something muttered
The while one hand, that erst upon his thigh
Lay dormant, moved convulsed and gradually
500   Up to his forehead. Then there was a hum
Of sudden voices, echoing, 'Come! come!
Arise! awake! Clear summer has forth walked
Unto the clover-sward, and she has talked
Full soothingly to every nested finch:
Rise, Cupids! or we'll give the blue-bell pinch
To your dimpled arms. Once more sweet life begin!'
At this, from every side they hurried in,
Rubbing their sleepy eyes with lazy wrists,
And doubling over head their little fists
510   In backward yawns. But all were soon alive:
For as delicious wine doth, sparkling, dive
In nectared clouds and curls through water fair,
So from the arbour roof down swelled an air
Odorous and enlivening; making all
To laugh, and play, and sing, and loudly call
For their sweet queen – when lo! the wreathèd green
Disparted, and far upward could be seen
Blue heaven, and a silver car, air-borne,
Whose silent wheels, fresh wet from clouds of morn,
520   Spun off a drizzling dew, which falling chill
On soft Adonis' shoulders, made him still
Nestle and turn uneasily about.
Soon were the white doves plain, with necks stretched
        out,

And silken traces tightened in descent;
And soon, returning from love's banishment,
Queen Venus leaning downward open-armed.
Her shadow fell upon his breast, and charmed
A tumult to his heart, and a new life
Into his eyes. Ah, miserable strife,
But for her comforting! unhappy sight,   530
But meeting her blue orbs! Who, who can write
Of these first minutes? The unchariest muse
To embracements warm as theirs makes coy excuse.

    O it has ruffled every spirit there,
Saving Love's self, who stands superb to share
The general gladness. Awfully he stands;
A sovereign quell is in his waving hands;
No sight can bear the lightning of his bow;
His quiver is mysterious, none can know
What themselves think of it; from forth his eyes   540
There darts strange light of varied hues and dyes;
A scowl is sometimes on his brow, but who
Look full upon it feel anon the blue
Of his fair eyes run liquid through their souls.
Endymion feels it, and no more controls
The burning prayer within him; so, bent low,
He had begun a plaining of his woe.
But Venus, bending forward, said: 'My child,
Favour this gentle youth; his days are wild
With love – he – but alas! too well I see   550
Thou know'st the deepness of his misery.
Ah, smile not so, my son: I tell thee true,
That when through heavy hours I used to rue,
The endless sleep of this new-born Adon',
This stranger aye I pitied. For upon
A dreary morning once I fled away
Into the breezy clouds, to weep and pray
For this my love, for vexing Mars had teased
Me even to tears. Thence, when a little eased,

560   Down-looking, vacant, through a hazy wood,
       I saw this youth as he despairing stood:
       Those same dark curls blown vagrant in the wind;
       Those same full-fringèd lids a constant blind
       Over his sullen eyes. I saw him throw
       Himself on withered leaves, even as though
       Death had come sudden; for no jot he moved,
       Yet muttered wildly. I could hear he loved
       Some fair immortal, and that his embrace
       Had zoned her through the night. There is no trace
570   Of this in heaven: I have marked each cheek,
       And find it is the vainest thing to seek;
       And that of all things 'tis kept secretest.
       Endymion! one day thou wilt be blest:
       So still obey the guiding hand that fends
       Thee safely through these wonders for sweet ends.
       'Tis a concealment needful in extreme,
       And if I guessed not so, the sunny beam
       Thou shouldst mount up to with me. Now adieu!
       Here must we leave thee.' – At these words up-flew
580   The impatient doves, up-rose the floating car,
       Up went the hum celestial. High afar
       The Latmian saw them minish into naught;
       And, when all were clear vanished, still he caught
       A vivid lightning from that dreadful bow.
       When all was darkened, with Aetnean throe
       The earth closed – gave a solitary moan –
       And left him once again in twilight lone.

                      [*End of Book II*]

                                 Ye who have yearned
       With too much passion, will here stay and pity
       For the mere sake of truth, as 'tis a ditty
830   Not of these days, but long ago 'twas told
       By a cavern wind unto a forest old;
       And then the forest told it in a dream
       To a sleeping lake, whose cool and level gleam

A poet caught as he was journeying
To Phoebus' shrine; and in it he did fling
His weary limbs, bathing an hour's space,
And after, straight in that inspirèd place
He sang the story up into the air,
Giving it universal freedom. There
Has it been ever sounding for those ears   840
Whose tips are glowing hot. The legend cheers
You sentinel stars; and he who listens to it
Must surely be self-doomed or he will rue it:
For quenchless burnings come upon the heart,
Made fiercer by a fear lest any part
Should be engulfèd in the eddying wind.
As much as here is penned doth always find
A resting place, thus much comes clear and plain.
Anon the strange voice is upon the wane –
And 'tis but echoed from departing sound,   850
That the fair visitant at last unwound
Her gentle limbs, and left the youth asleep. –
Thus the tradition of the gusty deep.

      Now turn we to our former chroniclers. –
Endymion awoke, that grief of hers
Sweet-paining on his ear: he sickly guessed
How lone he was once more, and sadly pressed
His empty arms together, hung his head,
And most forlorn upon that widowed bed
Sat silently. Love's madness he had known: 860
Often with more than tortured lion's groan
Moanings had burst from him; but now that rage
Had passed away. No longer did he wage
A rough-voiced war against the dooming stars.
No, he had felt too much for such harsh jars.
The lyre of his soul Aeolian-tuned
Forgot all violence, and but communed
With melancholy thought. O he had swooned
Drunken from Pleasure's nipple; and his love
Henceforth was dove-like. Loth was he to move   870

From the imprinted couch, and when he did,
'Twas with slow, languid paces, and face hid
In muffling hands. So tempered, out he strayed
Half seeing visions that might have dismayed
Alecto's serpents; ravishments more keen
Than Hermes' pipe, when anxious he did lean
Over eclipsing eyes; and at the last
It was a sounding grotto, vaulted vast,
O'er-studded with a thousand, thousand pearls,
880   And crimson-mouthèd shells with stubborn curls,
Of every shape and size, even to the bulk
In which whales arbour close, to brood and sulk
Against an endless storm. Moreover too,
Fish-semblances, of green and azure hue,
Ready to snort their streams. In this cool wonder
Endymion sat down, and 'gan to ponder
On all his life: his youth, up to the day
When 'mid acclaim, and feasts, and garlands gay,
He stepped upon his shepherd throne; the look
890   Of his white palace in wild forest nook,
And all the revels he had lorded there;
Each tender maiden whom he once thought fair,
With every friend and fellow-woodlander –
Passed like a dream before him. Then the spur
Of the old bards to mighty deeds; his plans
To nurse the golden age 'mong shepherd clans;
That wondrous night; the great Pan-festival;
His sister's sorrow; and his wanderings all,
Until into the earth's deep maw he rushed;
900   Then all its buried magic, till it flushed
High with excessive love. 'And now', thought he,
'How long must I remain in jeopardy
Of blank amazements that amaze no more?
Now I have tasted her sweet soul to the core
All other depths are shallow: essences,
Once spiritual, are like muddy lees,
Meant but to fertilize my earthly root,
And make my branches lift a golden fruit

Into the bloom of heaven. Other light,
Though it be quick and sharp enough to blight   910
The Olympian eagle's vision, is dark,
Dark as the parentage of chaos. Hark!
My silent thoughts are echoing from these shells;
Or they are but the ghosts, the dying swells
Of noises far away? – list!' – Hereupon
He kept an anxious ear. The humming tone
Came louder, and behold, there as he lay,
On either side out-gushed, with misty spray,
A copious spring; and both together dashed
Swift, mad, fantastic round the rocks, and lashed   920
Among the conches and shells of the lofty grot,
Leaving a trickling dew. At last they shot
Down from the ceiling's height, pouring a noise
As of some breathless racers whose hopes poise
Upon the last few steps, and with spent force
Along the ground they took a winding course.
Endymion followed – for it seemed that one
Ever pursued, the other strove to shun –
Followed their languid mazes, till well nigh
He had left thinking of the mystery,   930
And was now rapt in tender hoverings
Over the vanished bliss. Ah! what is it sings
His dream away? What melodies are these?
They sound as through the whispering of trees,
Not native in such barren vaults. Give ear!

'O Arethusa, peerless nymph! why fear
Such tenderness as mine? Great Dian, why,
Why didst thou hear her prayer? O that I
Were rippling round her dainty fairness now,
Circling about her waist, and striving how   940
To entice her to a dive! then stealing in
Between her luscious lips and eyelids thin!
O that her shining hair was in the sun,
And I distilling from it thence to run

In amorous rillets down her shrinking form!
To linger on her lily shoulders, warm
Between her kissing breasts, and every charm
Touch-raptured! – See how painfully I flow;
Fair maid, be pitiful to my great woe.
950 Stay, stay thy weary course, and let me lead,
A happy wooer, to the flowery mead
Where all that beauty snared me.' – 'Cruel god,
Desist! or my offended mistress' nod
Will stagnate all thy fountains – tease me not
With siren words – Ah, have I really got
Such power to madden thee? And is it true –
Away, away, or I shall dearly rue
My very thoughts: in mercy then away,
Kindest Alpheus, for should I obey
960 My own dear will, 'twould be a deadly bane.
O, Oread-Queen! would that thou hadst a pain
Like this of mine, then would I fearless turn
And be a criminal. Alas, I burn,
I shudder – gentle river, get thee hence.
Alpheus! thou enchanter! every sense
Of mine was once made perfect in these woods.
Fresh breezes, bowery lawns, and innocent floods,
Ripe fruits, and lonely couch, contentment gave;
But ever since I heedlessly did lave
970 In thy deceitful stream, a panting glow
Grew strong within me: wherefore serve me so,
And call it love? Alas, 'twas cruelty.
Not once more did I close my happy eye
Amid the thrushes' song. Away! Avaunt!
O 'twas a cruel thing.' – 'Now thou dost taunt
So softly, Arethusa, that I think
If thou wast playing on my shady brink,
Thou wouldst bathe once again. Innocent maid!
Stifle thine heart no more; nor be afraid
980 Of angry powers – there are deities
Will shade us with their wings. Those fitful sighs

'Tis almost death to hear. O let me pour
A dewy balm upon them! – fear no more,
Sweet Arethusa! Dian's self must feel
Sometimes these very pangs. Dear maiden, steal
Blushing into my soul, and let us fly
These dreary caverns for the open sky.
I will delight thee all my winding course,
From the green sea up to my hidden source
About Arcadian forests; and will show   990
The channels where my coolest waters flow
Through mossy rocks; where, 'mid exuberant green,
I roam in pleasant darkness, more unseen
Than Saturn in his exile; where I brim
Round flowery islands, and take thence a skim
Of mealy sweets, which myriads of bees
Buzz from their honeyed wings: and thou shouldst
      please
Thyself to choose the richest, where we might
Be incense-pillowed every summer night.
Doff all sad fears, thou white deliciousness,   1000
And let us be thus comforted; unless
Thou couldst rejoice to see my hopeless stream
Hurry distracted from Sol's temperate beam,
And pour to death along some hungry sands.' –
'What can I do, Alpheus? Dian stands
Severe before me. Persecuting fate!
Unhappy Arethusa! thou wast late
A huntress free in –' At this, sudden fell
Those two sad streams adown a fearful dell.
The Latmian listened, but he heard no more,   1010
Save echo, faint repeating o'er and o'er
The name of Arethusa. On the verge
Of that dark gulf he wept, and said: 'I urge
Thee, gentle Goddess of my pilgrimage,
By our eternal hopes, to soothe, to assuage,
If thou art powerful, these lovers' pains;
And make them happy in some happy plains.'

He turned – there was a whelming sound – he
    stepped –
There was a cooler light; and so he kept
1020 Towards it by a sandy path, and lo!
More suddenly than doth a moment go,
The visions of the earth were gone and fled –
He saw the giant sea above his head.

BOOK III

There are who lord it o'er their fellow-men
With most prevailing tinsel: who unpen
Their baaing vanities, to browse away
The comfortable green and juicy hay
From human pastures; or – O torturing fact! –
Who, through an idiot blink, will see unpacked
Fire-branded foxes to sear up and singe
Our gold and ripe-eared hopes. With not one tinge
Of sanctuary splendour, not a sight
10   Able to face an owl's, they still are dight
By the blear-eyed nations in empurpled vests,
And crowns, and turbans. With unladen breasts,
Save of blown self-applause, they proudly mount
To their spirit's perch, their being's high account,
Their tip-top nothings, their dull skies, their thrones –
Amid the fierce intoxicating tones
Of trumpets, shoutings, and belaboured drums,
And sudden cannon. Ah! how all this hums,
In wakeful ears, like uproar passed and gone –
20   Like thunder clouds that spake to Babylon,
And set those old Chaldeans to their tasks. –
Are then regalities all gilded masks?
No, there are thronèd seats unscalable
But by a patient wing, a constant spell,
Or by ethereal things that, unconfined,
Can make a ladder of the eternal wind,
And poise about in cloudy thunder-tents
To watch the abysm-birth of elements.

Ay, 'bove the withering of old-lipped Fate
A thousand Powers keep religious state,   30
In water, fiery realm, and airy bourne,
And, silent as a consecrated urn,
Hold sphery sessions for a season due.
Yet few of these far majesties – ah, few! –
Have bared their operations to this globe –
Few, who with gorgeous pageantry enrobe
Our piece of heaven – whose benevolence
Shakes hand with our own Ceres, every sense
Filling with spiritual sweets to plenitude,
As bees gorge full their cells. And, by the feud   40
'Twixt Nothing and Creation, I here swear,
Eterne Apollo! that thy Sister fair
Is of all these the gentlier-mightiest.
When thy gold breath is misting in the west,
She unobservèd steals unto her throne,
And there she sits most meek and most alone;
As if she had not pomp subservient;
As if thine eye, high Poet, was not bent
Towards her with the Muses in thine heart;
As if the ministering stars kept not apart,   50
Waiting for silver-footed messages.
O Moon! the oldest shades 'mong oldest trees
Feel palpitations when thou lookest in:
O Moon! old boughs lisp forth a holier din
The while they feel thine airy fellowship.
Thou dost bless everywhere, with silver lip
Kissing dead things to life. The sleeping kine,
Couched in thy brightness, dream of fields divine:
Innumerable mountains rise, and rise,
Ambitious for the hallowing of thine eyes;   60
And yet thy benediction passeth not
One obscure hiding-place, one little spot
Where pleasure may be sent. The nested wren
Has thy fair face within its tranquil ken,
And from beneath a sheltering ivy leaf
Takes glimpses of thee; thou art a relief

To the poor patient oyster, where it sleeps
Within its pearly house. The mighty deeps,
The monstrous sea is thine – the myriad sea!
70   O Moon! far-spooming Ocean bows to thee,
And Tellus feels his forehead's cumbrous load.

[*Glaucus's Story*]

                      'My soul stands
Now past the midway from mortality,
And so I can prepare without a sigh
To tell thee briefly all my joy and pain.
I was a fisher once, upon this main,
And my boat danced in every creek and bay.
320   Rough billows were my home by night and day –
The sea-gulls not more constant – for I had
No housing from the storm and tempests mad,
But hollow rocks – and they were palaces
Of silent happiness, of slumbrous ease:
Long years of misery have told me so.
Ay, thus it was one thousand years ago.
One thousand years! – Is it then possible
To look so plainly through them? to dispel
A thousand years with backward glance sublime?
330   To breathe away as 'twere all scummy slime
From off a crystal pool, to see its deep,
And one's own image from the bottom peep?
Yes: now I am no longer wretched thrall,
My long captivity and moanings all
Are but a slime, a thin-pervading scum,
The which I breathe away, and thronging come
Like things of yesterday my youthful pleasures.

    'I touched no lute, I sang not, trod no measures:
I was a lonely youth on desert shores.
340   My sports were lonely, 'mid continuous roars,
And craggy isles, and sea-mew's plaintive cry
Plaining discrepant between sea and sky.

Dolphins were still my playmates; shapes unseen
Would let me feel their scales of gold and green,
Nor be my desolation; and, full oft,
When a dread waterspout had reared aloft
Its hungry hugeness, seeming ready-ripe
To burst with hoarsest thunderings, and wipe
My life away like a vast sponge of fate,
Some friendly monster, pitying my sad state,   350
Has dived to its foundations, gulfed it down,
And left me tossing safely. But the crown
Of all my life was utmost quietude:
More did I love to lie in cavern rude,
Keeping in wait whole days for Neptune's voice,
And if it came at last, hark, and rejoice!
There blushed no summer eve but I would steer
My skiff along green shelving coasts, to hear
The shepherd's pipe come clear from aery steep,
Mingled with ceaseless bleatings of his sheep: 360
And never was a day of summer shine,
But I beheld its birth upon the brine,
For I would watch all night to see unfold
Heaven's gates, and Aethon snort his morning gold
Wide o'er the swelling streams: and constantly
At brim of day-tide, on some grassy lea,
My nets would be spread out, and I at rest.
The poor folk of the sea-country I blessed
With daily boon of fish most delicate:
They knew not whence this bounty, and elate   370
Would strew sweet flowers on a sterile beach.

   'Why was I not contented? Wherefore reach
At things which, but for thee, O Latmian!
Had been my dreary death? Fool! I began
To feel distempered longings: to desire
The utmost privilege that ocean's sire
Could grant in benediction – to be free
Of all his kingdom. Long in misery

I wasted, ere in one extremest fit
380   I plunged for life or death. To interknit
One's senses with so dense a breathing stuff
Might seem a work of pain; so not enough
Can I admire how crystal-smooth it felt,
And buoyant round my limbs. At first I dwelt
Whole days and days in sheer astonishment,
Forgetful utterly of self-intent,
Moving but with the mighty ebb and flow.
Then, like a new-fledged bird that first doth show
His spreaded feathers to the morrow chill,
390   I tried in fear the pinions of my will.
'Twas freedom! and at once I visited
The ceaseless wonders of this ocean-bed.
No need to tell thee of them, for I see
That thou hast been a witness – it must be –
For these I know thou canst not feel a drouth,
By the melancholy corners of that mouth.
So I will in my story straightway pass
To more immediate matter. Woe, alas!
That love should be my bane! Ah, Scylla fair!
400   Why did poor Glaucus ever, ever dare
To sue thee to his heart? Kind stranger-youth!
I loved her to the very white of truth,
And she would not conceive it. Timid thing!
She fled me swift as sea-bird on the wing,
Round every isle, and point, and promontory,
From where large Hercules wound up his story
Far as Egyptian Nile. My passion grew
The more, the more I saw her dainty hue
Gleam delicately through the azure clear,
410   Until 'twas too fierce agony to bear;
And in that agony, across my grief
It flashed, that Circe might find some relief –
Cruel enchantress! So above the water
I reared my head, and looked for Phoebus' daughter.

Aeaea's isle was wondering at the moon: –
It seemed to whirl around me, and a swoon
Left me dead-drifting to that fatal power.

'When I awoke, 'twas in a twilight bower;
Just when the light of morn, with hum of bees,
Stole through its verdurous matting of fresh trees.   420
How sweet, and sweeter! for I heard a lyre,
And over it a sighing voice expire.
It ceased – I caught light footsteps; and anon
The fairest face that morn e'er looked upon
Pushed through a screen of roses. Starry Jove!
With tears, and smiles, and honey-words she wove
A net whose thraldom was more bliss than all
The range of flowered Elysium. Thus did fall
The dew of her rich speech: "Ah! Art awake?
O let me hear thee speak, for Cupid's sake!   430
I am so oppressed with joy! Why, I have shed
An urn of tears, as though thou wert cold-dead.
And now I find thee living, I will pour
From these devoted eyes their silver store,
Until exhausted of the latest drop,
So it will pleasure thee, and force thee stop
Here, that I too may live: but if beyond
Such cool and sorrowful offerings, thou art fond
Of soothing warmth, of dalliance supreme;
If thou art ripe to taste a long love-dream;   440
If smiles, if dimples, tongues for ardour mute,
Hang in thy vision like a tempting fruit,
O let me pluck it for thee." Thus she linked
Her charming syllables, till indistinct
Their music came to my o'er-sweetened soul;
And then she hovered over me, and stole
So near, that if no nearer it had been
This furrowed visage thou hadst never seen.

'Young man of Latmos! thus particular
450   Am I, that thou mayst plainly see how far
This fierce temptation went: and thou mayst not
Exclaim, "How then, was Scylla quite forgot?"

'Who could resist? Who in this universe?
She did so breathe ambrosia; so immerse
My fine existence in a golden clime.
She took me like a child of suckling time,
And cradled me in roses. Thus condemned,
The current of my former life was stemmed,
And to this arbitrary queen of sense
460   I bowed a trancèd vassal: nor would thence
Have moved, even though Amphion's harp had
          wooed
Me back to Scylla o'er the billows rude.
For as Apollo each eve doth devise
A new apparelling for western skies,
So every eve, nay, every spendthrift hour,
Shed balmy consciousness within that bower.
And I was free of haunts umbrageous;
Could wander in the mazy forest-house
Of squirrels, foxes shy, and antlered deer,
470   And birds from coverts innermost and drear
Warbling for very joy mellifluous sorrow –
To me new born delights!

                              'Now let me borrow,
For moments few, a temperament as stern
As Pluto's sceptre, that my words not burn
These uttering lips, while I in calm speech tell
How specious heaven was changed to real hell.

'One morn she left me sleeping: half awake
I sought for her smooth arms and lips, to slake
My greedy thirst with nectarous camel-draughts;
480   But she was gone. Whereat the barbèd shafts

Of disappointment stuck in me so sore,
That out I ran and searched the forest o'er.
Wandering about in pine and cedar gloom
Damp awe assailed me; for there 'gan to boom
A sound of moan, an agony of sound,
Sepulchral from the distance all around.
Then came a conquering earth-thunder, and
    rumbled
That fierce complain to silence, while I stumbled
Down a precipitous path, as if impelled.
I came to a dark valley. – Groanings swelled   490
Poisonous about my ears, and louder grew,
The nearer I approached a flame's gaunt blue,
That glared before me through a thorny brake.
This fire, like the eye of gordian snake,
Bewitched me towards, and I soon was near
A sight too fearful for the feel of fear:
In thicket hid I cursed the haggard scene –
The banquet of my arms, my arbour queen,
Seated upon an up-torn forest root;
And all around her shapes, wizard and brute,   500
Laughing, and wailing, grovelling, serpenting,
Showing tooth, tusk, and venom-bag, and sting!
O such deformities! Old Charon's self,
Should he give up awhile his penny pelf,
And take a dream 'mong rushes Stygian,
It could not be so phantasied. Fierce, wan,
And tyrannizing was the lady's look,
As over them a gnarlèd staff she shook.
Oft-times upon the sudden she laughed out,
And from a basket emptied to the rout   510
Clusters of grapes, the which they ravened quick
And roared for more; with many a hungry lick
About their shaggy jaws. Avenging, slow,
Anon she took a branch of mistletoe,
And emptied on't a black dull-gurgling phial –
Groaned one and all, as if some piercing trial

Was sharpening for their pitiable bones.
She lifted up the charm: appealing groans
From their poor breasts went sueing to her ear
520   In vain; remorseless as an infant's bier
She whisked against their eyes the sooty oil.
Whereat was heard a noise of painful toil,
Increasing gradual to a tempest rage,
Shrieks, yells, and groans of torture-pilgrimage;
Until their grievèd bodies 'gan to bloat
And puff from the tail's end to stiflèd throat.
Then was appalling silence: then a sight
More wildering than all that hoarse affright;
For the whole herd, as by a whirlwind writhen,
530   Went through the dismal air like one huge Python
Antagonizing Boreas – and so vanished.
Yet there was not a breath of wind: she banished
These phantoms with a nod. Lo! from the dark
Came waggish fauns, and nymphs, and satyrs stark,
With dancing and loud revelry – and went
Swifter than centaurs after rapine bent.
Sighing an elephant appeared and bowed
Before the fierce witch, speaking thus aloud
In human accent: "Potent goddess! chief
540   Of pains resistless! make my being brief,
Or let me from this heavy prison fly –
Or give me to the air, or let me die!
I sue not for my happy crown again;
I sue not for my phalanx on the plain;
I sue not for my lone, my widowed wife;
I sue not for my ruddy drops of life,
My children fair, my lovely girls and boys!
I will forget them; I will pass these joys;
Ask naught so heavenward, so too, too high:
550   Only I pray, as fairest boon, to die,
Or be delivered from this cumbrous flesh,
From this gross, detestable, filthy mesh,
And merely given to the cold bleak air.
Have mercy, Goddess! Circe, feel my prayer!"

   'That cursed magician's name fell icy numb
Upon my wild conjecturing: truth had come
Naked and sabre-like against my heart.
I saw a fury whetting a death-dart;
And my slain spirit, overwrought with fright,
Fainted away in that dark lair of night.   560
Think, my deliverer, how desolate
My waking must have been! disgust, and hate,
And terrors manifold divided me
A spoil amongst them. I prepared to flee
Into the dungeon core of that wild wood:
I fled three days – when lo! before me stood
Glaring the angry witch. O Dis! even now,
A clammy dew is beading on my brow,
At mere remembering her pale laugh, and curse.
"Ha! ha! Sir Dainty! there must be a nurse   570
Made of rose leaves and thistledown, express,
To cradle thee my sweet, and lull thee – yes,
I am too flinty-hard for thy nice touch:
My tenderest squeeze is but a giant's clutch.
So, fairy-thing, it shall have lullabies
Unheard of yet: and it shall still its cries
Upon some breast more lily-feminine.
Oh, no – it shall not pine, and pine, and pine
More than one pretty, trifling thousand years;
And then 'twere pity, but fate's gentle shears   580
Cut short its immortality. Sea-flirt!
Young dove of the waters! truly I'll not hurt
One hair of thine: see how I weep and sigh,
That our heart-broken parting is so nigh.
And must we part? Ah, yes, it must be so.
Yet ere thou leavest me in utter woe,
Let me sob over thee my last adieus,
And speak a blessing. Mark me! Thou hast thews
Immortal, for thou art of heavenly race:
But such a love is mine, that here I chase   590
Eternally away from thee all bloom
Of youth, and destine thee towards a tomb.

Hence shalt thou quickly to the watery vast;
And there, ere many days be overpassed,
Disabled age shall seize thee; and even then
Thou shalt not go the way of agèd men;
But live and wither, cripple and still breathe
Ten hundred years – which gone, I then bequeath
Thy fragile bones to unknown burial.
600   Adieu, sweet love, adieu!" – As shot stars fall,
She fled ere I could groan for mercy. Stung
And poisoned was my spirit; despair sung
A war-song of defiance 'gainst all hell.
A hand was at my shoulder to compel
My sullen steps; another 'fore my eyes
Moved on with pointed finger. In this guise
Enforcèd, at the last by ocean's foam
I found me – by my fresh, my native home.
Its tempering coolness, to my life akin,
610   Came salutary as I waded in;
And, with a blind voluptuous rage, I gave
Battle to the swollen billow-ridge, and drave
Large froth before me, while there yet remained
Hale strength, nor from my bones all marrow drained.

   'Young lover, I must weep – such hellish spite
With dry cheek who can tell? While thus my might
Proving upon this element, dismayed,
Upon a dead thing's face my hand I laid.
I looked – 'twas Scylla! Cursèd, cursèd Circe!
620   O vulture-witch, hast never heard of mercy?
Could not thy harshest vengeance be content,
But thou must nip this tender innocent
Because I loved her? – Cold, O cold indeed
Were her fair limbs, and like a common weed
The sea-swell took her hair. Dead as she was
I clung about her waist, nor ceased to pass
Fleet as an arrow through unfathomed brine,
Until there shone a fabric crystalline,

Ribbed and inlaid with coral, pebble, and pearl.
Headlong I darted; at one eager swirl   630
Gained its bright portal, entered, and behold!
'Twas vast, and desolate, and icy-cold;
And all around – But wherefore this to thee
Who in few minutes more thyself shalt see? –
I left poor Scylla in a niche and fled.
My fevered parchings up, my scathing dread
Met palsy half-way: soon these limbs became
Gaunt, withered, sapless, feeble, cramped, and
        lame . . .'

BOOK IV

[*Invocation*]

Muse of my native land! loftiest Muse!
O first-born on the mountains! by the hues
Of heaven on the spiritual air begot!
Long didst thou sit alone in northern grot,
While yet our England was a wolfish den;
Before our forests heard the talk of men;
Before the first of Druids was a child,
Long didst thou sit amid our regions wild
Rapt in a deep prophetic solitude.
There came an eastern voice of solemn mood –   10
Yet was thou patient. Then sang forth the Nine,
Apollo's garland – yet didst thou divine
Such home-bred glory, that they cried in vain,
'Come hither, Sister of the Island!' Plain
Spake fair Ausonia; and once more she spake
A higher summons – still didst thou betake
Thee to thy native hopes. O thou hast won
A full accomplishment! The thing is done,
Which undone, these our latter days had risen
On barren souls. Great Muse, thou know'st what
        prison,   20
Of flesh and bone, curbs, and confines, and frets
Our spirit's wings. Despondency besets

Our pillows, and the fresh tomorrow morn
Seems to give forth its light in very scorn
Of our dull, uninspired, snail-pacèd lives.
Long have I said, how happy he who shrives
To thee! But then I thought on poets gone,
And could not pray – nor could I now – so on
I move to the end in lowliness of heart.

[*Indian Maid's Roundelay*]
                              Then she,
Sitting beneath the midmost forest tree,
For pity sang this roundelay:

    'O Sorrow,
    Why dost borrow
The natural hue of health, from vermeil lips? –
    To give maiden blushes
150   To the white rose bushes?
Or is't thy dewy hand the daisy tips?

    'O Sorrow
    Why dost borrow
The lustrous passion from a falcon-eye? –
    To give the glow-worm light?
    Or, on a moonless night,
To tinge, on syren shores, the salt sea-spry?

    'O Sorrow,
    Why dost borrow
160 The mellow ditties from a mourning tongue? –
    To give at evening pale
    Unto the nightingale,
That thou mayst listen the cold dews among?

'O Sorrow,
  Why dost borrow
Heart's lightness from the merriment of May? –
    A lover would not tread
    A cowslip on the head,
Though he should dance from eve till peep of day –
    Nor any drooping flower   170
    Held sacred for thy bower,
Wherever he may sport himself and play.

'To Sorrow,
  I bade good-morrow,
And thought to leave her far away behind.
    But cheerly, cheerly,
    She loves me dearly;
She is so constant to me, and so kind:
    I would deceive her
    And so leave her,   180
But ah! she is so constant and so kind.

'Beneath my palm trees, by the river side,
I sat a-weeping: in the whole world wide
There was no one to ask me why I wept –
    And so I kept
Brimming the water lily cups with tears
    Cold as my fears.

'Beneath my palm trees, by the river side,
I sat a-weeping: what enamoured bride,
Cheated by shadowy wooer from the clouds,   190
    But hides and shrouds
Beneath dark palm trees by a river-side?

'And as I sat, over the light blue hills
There came a noise of revellers: the rills
Into the wide stream came of purple hue –
    'Twas Bacchus and his crew!
The earnest trumpet spake, and silver thrills

From kissing cymbals made a merry din –
    'Twas Bacchus and his kin!
200   Like to a moving vintage down they came,
Crowned with green leaves, and faces all on flame –
All madly dancing through the pleasant valley,
    To scare thee, Melancholy!
O then, O then, thou wast a simple name!
And I forgot thee, as the berried holly
By shepherds is forgotten, when, in June,
Tall chestnuts keep away the sun and moon –
    I rushed into the folly!

'Within his car, aloft, young Bacchus stood,
210   Trifling his ivy-dart, in dancing mood,
    With sidelong laughing;
And little rills of crimson wine imbrued
His plump white arms, and shoulders, enough white
    For Venus' pearly bite;
And near him rode Silenus on his ass,
Pelted with flowers as he on did pass
    Tipsily quaffing.

'Whence came ye, merry Damsels! whence came ye!
So many, and so many, and such glee?
220   Why have ye left your bowers desolate,
    Your lutes and gentler fate? –
"We follow Bacchus! Bacchus on the wing,
    A-conquering!
Bacchus, young Bacchus! good or ill betide,
We dance before him thorough kingdoms wide –
Come hither, lady fair, and joinèd be
    To our wild minstrelsy!"

'Whence came ye, jolly Satyrs! whence came ye!
So many, and so many, and such glee?
230   Why have ye left your forest haunts, why left
    Your nuts in oak-tree cleft? –
"For wine, for wine we left our kernel tree;

For wine we left our heath, and yellow brooms,
    And cold mushrooms;
For wine we follow Bacchus through the earth –
Great God of breathless cups and chirping mirth!
Come hither, lady fair, and joinèd be
    To our mad minstrelsy!"

'Over wide streams and mountains great we went,
And, save when Bacchus kept his ivy tent,   240
Onward the tiger and the leopard pants,
    With Asian elephants:
Onward these myriads – with song and dance,
With zebras striped, and sleek Arabians' prance,
Web-footed alligators, crocodiles,
Bearing upon their scaly backs, in files,
Plump infant laughers mimicking the coil
Of seamen, and stout galley-rowers' toil –
With toying oars and silken sails they glide,
    Nor care for wind and tide.   250

'Mounted on panthers' furs and lions' manes,
From rear to van they scour about the plains;
A three days' journey in a moment done:
And always, at the rising of the sun,
About the wilds they hunt with spear and horn,
    On spleenful unicorn.

'I saw Osirian Egypt kneel adown
    Before the vine-wreath crown!
I saw parched Abyssinia rouse and sing
    To the silver cymbals' ring!   260
I saw the whelming vintage hotly pierce
    Old Tartary the fierce!
The kings of Ind their jewel-sceptres vail,
And from their treasures scatter pearlèd hail.
Great Brahma from his mystic heaven groans,
    And all his priesthood moans;
Before young Bacchus' eye-wink turning pale. –

Into these regions came I following him,
Sick hearted, weary – so I took a whim
270   To stray away into these forests drear
            Alone, without a peer:
And I have told thee all thou mayest hear.

            'Young stranger!
            I've been a ranger
In search of pleasure throughout every clime:
            Alas, 'tis not for me!
            Bewitched I sure must be,
To lose in grieving all my maiden prime.

            'Come then, Sorrow!
280   Sweetest Sorrow!
Like an own babe I nurse thee on my breast:
            I thought to leave thee
            And deceive thee,
But now of all the world I love thee best.

            'There is not one,
            No, no, not one
But thee to comfort a poor lonely maid:
            Thou art her mother,
            And her brother,
290   Her playmate, and her wooer in the shade.'

                    [*Conclusion*]

900   ... At the last
Endymion said: 'Are not our fates all cast?
Why stand we here? Adieu, ye tender pair!
Adieu!' Whereat those maidens, with wild stare,
Walked dizzily away. Painèd and hot
His eyes went after them, until they got
Near to a cypress grove, whose deadly maw,
In one swift moment, would what then he saw
Engulf for ever. 'Stay!' he cried, 'ah, stay!
Turn, damsels! hist! one word I have to say.

Sweet Indian, I would see thee once again.   910
It is a thing I dote on: so I'd fain,
Peona, ye should hand in hand repair
Into those holy groves, that silent are
Behind great Dian's temple. I'll be yon,
At Vesper's earliest twinkle – they are gone –
But once, once, once again –' At this he pressed
His hands against his face, and then did rest
His head upon a mossy hillock green,
And so remained as he a corpse had been
All the long day, save when he scantly lifted   920
His eyes abroad, to see how shadows shifted
With the slow move of time – sluggish and weary
Until the poplar tops, in journey dreary,
Had reached the river's brim. Then up he rose,
And, slowly as that very river flows,
Walked towards the temple grove with this lament:
'Why such a golden eve? The breeze is sent
Careful and soft, that not a leaf may fall
Before the serene father of them all
Bows down his summer head below the west.   930
Now am I of breath, speech, and speed possessed,
But at the setting I must bid adieu
To her for the last time. Night will strew
On the damp grass myriads of lingering leaves,
And with them shall I die; nor much it grieves
To die, when summer dies on the cold sward.
Why, I have been a butterfly, a lord
Of flowers, garlands, love-knots, silly posies,
Groves, meadows, melodies, and arbour roses.
My kingdom's at its death, and just it is   940
That I should die with it: so in all this
We miscall grief, bale, sorrow, heartbreak, woe,
What is there to plain of? By Titan's foe
I am but rightly served.' So saying, he
Tripped lightly on, in sort of deathful glee,
Laughing at the clear stream and setting sun,
As though they jests had been: nor had he done

His laugh at nature's holy countenance,
Until that grove appeared, as if perchance,
950   And then his tongue with sober seemlihed
Gave utterance as he entered: 'Ha! I said,
"King of the butterflies", but by this gloom,
And by old Rhadamanthus' tongue of doom,
This dusk religion, pomp of solitude,
And the Promethean clay by thief endued,
By old Saturnus' forelock, by his head
Shook with eternal palsy, I did wed
Myself to things of light from infancy;
And thus to be cast out, thus lorn to die,
960   Is sure enough to make a mortal man
Grow impious.' So he inwardly began
On things for which no wording can be found,
Deeper and deeper sinking, until drowned
Beyond the reach of music: for the choir
Of Cynthia he heard not, though rough briar
Nor muffling thicket interposed to dull
The vesper hymn, far swollen, soft and full,
Through the dark pillars of those sylvan aisles.
He saw not the two maidens, nor their smiles,
970   Wan as primroses gathered at midnight
By chilly-fingered spring. 'Unhappy wight!
Endymion!' said Peona, 'we are here!
What wouldst thou ere we all are laid on bier?'
Then he embraced her, and his lady's hand
Pressed, saying: 'Sister, I would have command,
If it were heaven's will, on our sad fate.'
At which that dark-eyed stranger stood elate
And said, in a new voice, but sweet as love,
To Endymion's amaze: 'By Cupid's dove,
980   And so thou shalt! and by the lily truth
Of my own breast thou shalt, belovèd youth!'
And as she spake, into her face there came
Light, as reflected from a silver flame:
Her long black hair swelled ampler, in display
Full golden; in her eyes a brighter day

Dawned blue and full of love. Ay, he beheld
Phoebe, his passion! Joyous she upheld
Her lucid bow, continuing thus: 'Drear, drear
Has our delaying been; but foolish fear
Withheld me first; and then decrees of fate;   990
And then 'twas fit that from this mortal state
Thou shouldst, my love, by some unlooked for
        change
Be spiritualized. Peona, we shall range
These forests, and to thee they safe shall be
As was thy cradle; hither shalt thou flee
To meet us many a time.' Next Cynthia bright
Peona kissed, and blessed with fair good-night:
Her brother kissed her too, and knelt adown
Before his goddess, in a blissful swoon.
She gave her fair hands to him, and behold,   1000
Before three swiftest kisses he had told,
They vanished far away! – Peona went
Home through the gloomy wood in wonderment.

'In drear-nighted December'

I

In drear-nighted December,
        Too happy, happy tree,
Thy branches ne'er remember
        Their green felicity:
    The north cannot undo them,
    With a sleety whistle through them,
    Nor frozen thawing glue them
        From budding at the prime.

II

In drear-nighted December,
        Too happy, happy brook,   10
Thy bubblings can ne'er remember
        Apollo's summer look;

But with a sweet forgetting,
They stay their crystal fretting,
Never, never petting
    About the frozen time.

III
Ah! would 'twere so with many
    A gentle girl and boy!
But were there ever any
        Writhed not of passèd joy?
The feel of not to feel it,
When there is none to heal it,
Nor numbèd sense to steal it,
    Was never said in rhyme.
                    (Not published by Keats)

Nebuchadnezzar's Dream

Before he went to live with owls and bats
    Nebuchadnezzar had an ugly dream,
    Worse than a housewife's when she thinks her cream
Made a naumachia for mice and rats.
So scared she sent for that 'Good King of Cats',
    Young Daniel, who straightway did pluck the beam
    From out his eye, and said 'I do not deem
Your sceptre worth a straw – your cushion old
                    door-mats.'
A horrid nightmare similar somewhat
    Of late has haunted a most valiant crew
        Of loggerheads and chapmen – we are told
That any Daniel though he be a sot
    Can make their lying lips turn pale of hue
        By drawling out, 'Ye are that head of Gold.'
                    (Not published by Keats)

To Mrs Reynolds's Cat

Cat! who hast passed thy grand climacteric,
 How many mice and rats hast in thy days
 Destroyed? How many tit-bits stolen? Gaze
With those bright languid segments green, and prick
Those velvet ears – but prithee do not stick
 Thy latent talons in me, and up-raise
 Thy gentle mew, and tell me all thy frays
Of fish and mice, and rats and tender chick.
Nay, look not down, nor lick thy dainty wrists –
 For all the wheezy asthma, and for all   10
Thy tail's tip is nicked off, and though the fists
 Of many a maid have given thee many a maul,
Still is that fur as soft as when the lists
 In youth thou enteredst on glass-bottled wall.

                                    (Not published by Keats)

On Sitting Down to Read King Lear Once Again

O golden-tongued Romance, with serene lute!
 Fair plumèd Syren, Queen of far-away!
 Leave melodizing on this wintry day,
Shut up thine olden pages, and be mute:
Adieu! for, once again, the fierce dispute
 Betwixt damnation and impassioned clay
 Must I burn through, once more humbly assay
The bitter-sweet of this Shakespearian fruit:
Chief Poet! and ye clouds of Albion,
 Begetters of our deep eternal theme!   10
When through the old oak forest I am gone,
 Let me not wander in a barren dream,
But, when I am consumèd in the fire,
Give me new Phoenix wings to fly at my desire.

                                    (Not published by Keats)

'When I have fears that I may cease to be'

When I have fears that I may cease to be
   Before my pen has gleaned my teeming brain,
Before high-pilèd books, in charactery,
   Hold like rich garners the full-ripened grain;
When I behold, upon the night's starred face,
   Huge cloudy symbols of a high romance,
And think that I may never live to trace
   Their shadows, with the magic hand of chance;
And when I feel, fair creature of an hour!
   That I shall never look upon thee more,
Never have relish in the faery power
   Of unreflecting love! – then on the shore
Of the wide world I stand alone, and think
Till love and fame to nothingness do sink.

(Not published by Keats)

'O blush not so! O blush not so!'

I

O blush not so! O blush not so!
   Or I shall think you knowing;
And if you smile the blushing while,
   The maidenheads are going.

II

There's a blush for won't, and a blush for shan't,
   And a blush for having done it:
There's a blush for thought, and a blush for naught,
   And a blush for just begun it.

III

O sigh not so! O sigh not so!
   For it sounds of Eve's sweet pippin;
By those loosened hips you have tasted the pips
   And fought in an amorous nipping.

IV

Will you play once more at nice-cut-core,
　　For it only will last our youth out?
And we have the prime of the kissing time,
　　We have not one sweet tooth out.

V

There's a sigh for yes, and a sigh for no,
　　And a sigh for I can't bear it!
O what can be done, shall we stay or run?
　　O, cut the sweet apple and share it!　　20
　　　　　　(Not published by Keats)

To –*

Time's sea hath been five years at its slow ebb,
　　Long hours have to and fro let creep the sand,
Since I was tangled in thy beauty's web,
　　And snared by the ungloving of thy hand.
And yet I never look on midnight sky,
　　But I behold thine eyes' well-memoried light;
I cannot look upon the rose's dye,
　　But to thy cheek my soul doth take its flight,
I cannot look on any budding flower,
　　But my fond ear, in fancy at thy lips,　　10
And hearkening for a love-sound, doth devour
　　Its sweets in the wrong sense:– Thou dost eclipse
Every delight with sweet remembering,
And grief unto my darling joys dost bring.
　　　　　　(Not published by Keats)

*A lady he saw for some few moments at Vauxhall.

'O *thou whose face hath felt the Winter's wind*'

['. . . I had no Idea but of the Morning and the Thrush said I
was right – seeming to say . . .'
                    (letter to J. H. Reynolds, 19 February 1816)]

'O thou whose face hath felt the Winter's wind,
    Whose eye has seen the snow-clouds hung in mist,
    And the black elm tops, 'mong the freezing stars,
    To thee the spring will be a harvest-time.
O thou, whose only book has been the light
    Of supreme darkness which thou feddest on
    Night after night when Phoebus was away,
    To thee the Spring shall be a triple morn.
O fret not after knowledge – I have none,
    And yet my song comes native with the warmth.
O fret not after knowledge – I have none,
    And yet the Evening listens. He who saddens
At thought of idleness cannot be idle,
And he's awake who thinks himself asleep.'
                            (Not published by Keats)

The Human Seasons

Four seasons fill the measure of the year;
    There are four seasons in the mind of man.
He has his lusty Spring, when fancy clear
    Takes in all beauty with an easy span.
He has his Summer, when luxuriously
    Spring's honeyed cud of youthful thought he loves
To ruminate, and by such dreaming nigh
    His nearest unto heaven. Quiet coves
His soul hath in its Autumn, when his wings
    He furleth close; contented so to look
On mists in idleness – to let fair things
    Pass by unheeded as a threshold brook.

He has his Winter too of pale misfeature,
Or else he would forego his mortal nature.

'For there's Bishop's Teign'

I

For there's Bishop's Teign
And King's Teign
And Coomb at the clear Teign head –
Where close by the stream
You may have your cream
All spread upon barley bread.

II

There's Arch Brook
And there's Larch Brook
Both turning many a mill;
And cooling the drouth
Of the salmon's mouth,
And fattening his silver gill.

10

III

There is Wild Wood,
A mild hood
To the sheep on the lea o' the down,
Where the golden furze,
With its green, thin spurs,
Doth catch at the maiden's gown.

IV

There is Newton Marsh
With its spear grass harsh –
A pleasant summer level
Where the maidens sweet
Of the Market Street
Do meet in the grass to revel.

20

V

There's the barton rich
With dyke and ditch
And hedge for the thrush to live in,
And the hollow tree
For the buzzing bee
30   And a bank for the wasp to hive in.

VI

And O, and O,
The daisies blow
And the primroses are wakened,
And violet white
Sits in silver plight,
And the green bud's as long the spike end.

VII

Then who would go
Into dark Soho,
And chatter with dack-haired critics,
40   When he can stay
For the new-mown hay,
And startle the dappled prickets?

(Not published by Keats)

'Where be ye going, you Devon maid?'

I

Where be ye going, you Devon maid?
What have ye there i' the basket?
Ye tight little fairy, just fresh from the dairy,
Will ye give me some cream if I ask it?

II

I love your meads, and I love your flowers,
    And I loved your junkets mainly,
But 'hind the door I love kissing more,
    O look not so disdainly.

III

I love your hills, and I love your dales,
    And I love your flocks a-bleating –   10
But O, on the heather to lie together,
    With both our hearts a-beating!

IV

I'll put your basket all safe in a *nook*,
    And your shawl I hang up *on this willow*,
And we will sigh in the daisy's eye
    And kiss on a grass-green pillow.

                   (Not published by Keats)

'Over the hill and over the dale'

Over the hill and over the dale,
And over the bourn to Dawlish –
Where gingerbread wives have a scanty sale
And gingerbread nuts are smallish.

Rantipole Betty she ran down a hill
And kicked up her petticoats fairly.
Says I, 'I'll be Jack if you will be Jill.'
So she sat on the grass debonairly.

'Here's somebody coming, here's somebody
    coming!'
Says I, ' 'Tis the wind at a parley.'   10
So without any fuss, any hawing and humming,
She lay on the grass debonairly.

'Here's somebody here, here's somebody *there*!'
Says I, 'Hold your tongue, you young gypsy.'
So she held her tongue and lay plump and fair,
And dead as a Venus tipsy.

O who wouldn't hie to Dawlish fair,
O who wouldn't stop in a meadow?
O [who] would not rumple the daisies there,
20   And make the wild fern for a bed do?

(Not published by Keats)

To J. H. Reynolds, Esq.

Dear Reynolds, as last night I lay in bed,
There came before my eyes that wonted thread
Of shapes, and shadows, and remembrances,
That every other minute vex and please:
Things all disjointed come from North and South –
Two witch's eyes above a cherub's mouth,
Voltaire with casque and shield and habergeon,
And Alexander with his nightcap on,
Old Socrates a-tying his cravat,
10   And Hazlitt playing with Miss Edgeworth's cat,
And Junius Brutus, pretty well so so,
Making the best of's way towards Soho.

Few are there who escape these visitings –
Perhaps one or two whose lives have patient wings,
And through whose curtains peeps no hellish nose,
No wild-boar tushes, and no mermaid's toes;
But flowers bursting out with lusty pride,
And young Aeolian harps personified,
Some, Titian colours touched into real life –
20   The sacrifice goes on; the pontiff knife
Gloams in the sun, the milk-white heifer lows,
The pipes go shrilly, the libation flows;

A white sail shows above the green-head cliff,
Moves round the point, and throws her anchor stiff.
The mariners join hymn with those on land.

You know the Enchanted Castle – it doth stand
Upon a rock, on the border of a lake,
Nested in trees, which all do seem to shake
From some old magic like Urganda's sword.
O Phoebus! that I had thy sacred word   30
To show this castle, in fair dreaming wise,
Unto my friend, while sick and ill he lies!

You know it well enough, where it doth seem
A mossy place, a Merlin's Hall, a dream.
You know the clear lake, and the little isles,
The mountains blue, and cold near-neighbour rills,
All which elsewhere are but half animate;
Here do they look alive to love and hate,
To smiles and frowns; they seem a lifted mound
Above some giant, pulsing underground.   40

Part of the building was a chosen see,
Built by a banished santon of Chaldee;
The other part, two thousand years from him,
Was built by Cuthbert de Saint Aldebrim;
Then there's a little wing, far from the sun,
Built by a Lapland witch turned maudlin nun;
And many other juts of agèd stone
Founded with many a mason-devil's groan.

The doors all look as if they oped themselves,
The windows as if latched by fays and elves,   50
And from them comes a silver flash of light,
As from the westward of a summer's night;
Or like a beauteous woman's large blue eyes
Gone mad through olden songs and poesies –

See! what is coming from the distance dim!
A golden galley all in silken trim!
Three rows of oars are lightening, moment-whiles,
Into the verdurous bosoms of those isles.
Towards the shade, under the castle wall,
60   It comes in silence – now 'tis hidden all.
The clarion sounds, and from a postern-grate
An echo of sweet music doth create
A fear in the poor herdsman, who doth bring
His beasts to trouble the enchanted spring.
He tells of the sweet music, and the spot,
To all his friends – and they believe him not.

O that our dreamings all, of sleep or wake,
Would all their colours from the sunset take,
From something of material sublime,
70   Rather than shadow our own soul's daytime
In the dark void of night. For in the world
We jostle – but my flag is not unfurled
On the admiral staff – and to philosophize
I dare not yet! O, never will the prize,
High reason, and the lore of good and ill,
Be my award! Things cannot to the will
Be settled, but they tease us out of thought.
Or is it that imagination brought
Beyond its proper bound, yet still confined,
80   Lost in a sort of purgatory blind,
Cannot refer to any standard law
Of either earth or heaven? It is a flaw
In happiness, to see beyond our bourne –
It forces us in summer skies to mourn;
It spoils the singing of the nightingale.

Dear Reynolds, I have a mysterious tale,
And cannot speak it. The first page I read
Upon a lampit rock of green seaweed
Among the breakers. 'Twas a quiet eve;
90   The rocks were silent, the wide sea did weave

An untumultuous fringe of silver foam
Along the flat brown sand. I was at home
And should have been most happy – but I saw
Too far into the sea, where every maw
The greater on the less feeds evermore. –
But I saw too distinct into the core
Of an eternal fierce destruction,
And so from happiness I far was gone.
Still am I sick of it; and though, today,
I've gathered young spring-leaves, and flowers gay   100
Of periwinkle and wild strawberry,
Still do I that most fierce destruction see –
The shark at savage prey, the hawk at pounce,
The gentle robin, like a pard or ounce,
Ravening a worm. – Away, ye horrid moods!
Moods of one's mind! You know I hate them well,
You know I'd sooner be a clapping bell
To some Kamchatkan missionary church,
Than with these horrid moods be left in lurch.
Do you get health – and Tom the same – I'll dance,   110
And from detested moods in new romance
Take refuge. Of bad lines a centaine dose
Is sure enough – and so 'here follows prose' . . .

(Not published by Keats)

Isabella; or, The Pot of Basil

I

Fair Isabel, poor simple Isabel!
   Lorenzo, a young palmer in Love's eye!
They could not in the self-same mansion dwell
   Without some stir of heart, some malady;
They could not sit at meals but feel how well
   It soothed each to be the other by;
They could not, sure, beneath the same roof sleep
But to each other dream, and nightly weep.

II

With every morn their love grew tenderer,
    With every eve deeper and tenderer still;
He might not in house, field, or garden stir,
    But her full shape would all his seeing fill;
And his continual voice was pleasanter
    To her than noise of trees or hidden rill;
Her lute-string gave an echo of his name,
She spoilt her half-done broidery with the same.

III

He knew whose gentle hand was at the latch
    Before the door had given her to his eyes;
And from her chamber-window he would catch
    Her beauty farther than the falcon spies;
And constant as her vespers would he watch,
    Because her face was turned to the same skies;
And with sick longing all the night outwear,
To hear her morning-step upon the stair.

IV

A whole long month of May in this sad plight
    Made their cheeks paler by the break of June:
'To-morrow will I bow to my delight,
    To-morrow will I ask my lady's boon.'
'O may I never see another night,
    Lorenzo, if thy lips breathe not love's tune.'
So spake they to their pillows; but, alas,
Honeyless days and days did he let pass –

V

Until sweet Isabella's untouched cheek
    Fell sick within the rose's just domain,
Fell thin as a young mother's, who doth seek
    By every lull to cool her infant's pain:

'How ill she is,' said he, 'I may not speak,
   And yet I will, and tell my love all plain:
If looks speak love-laws, I will drink her tears,
   And at the least 'twill startle off her cares.'   40

VI

So said he one fair morning, and all day
   His heart beat awfully against his side;
And to his heart he inwardly did pray
   For power to speak; but still the ruddy tide
Stifled his voice, and pulsed resolve away –
   Fevered his high conceit of such a bride,
Yet brought him to the meekness of a child:
Alas! when passion is both meek and wild!

VII

So once more he had waked and anguishèd
   A dreary night of love and misery,   50
If Isabel's quick eye had not been wed
   To every symbol on his forehead high.
She saw it waxing very pale and dead,
   And straight all flushed; so, lispèd tenderly,
'Lorenzo!' – here she ceased her timid quest,
But in her tone and look he read the rest.

VIII

'O Isabella, I can half-perceive
   That I may speak my grief into thine ear.
If thou didst ever anything believe,
   Believe how I love thee, believe how near   60
My soul is to its doom: I would not grieve
   Thy hand by unwelcome pressing, would not fear
Thine eyes by gazing; but I cannot live
Another night, and not my passion shrive.

IX

'Love! thou art leading me from wintry cold,
    Lady! thou leadest me to summer clime,
And I must taste the blossoms that unfold
    In its ripe warmth this gracious morning time.'
So said, his erewhile timid lips grew bold,
    And poesied with hers in dewy rhyme:
Great bliss was with them, and great happiness
Grew, like a lusty flower, in June's caress.

70

X

Parting they seemed to tread upon the air,
    Twin roses by the zephyr blown apart
Only to meet again more close, and share
    The inward fragrance of each other's heart.
She, to her chamber gone, a ditty fair
    Sang, of delicious love and honeyed dart;
He with light steps went up a western hill,
And bade the sun farewell, and joyed his fill.

80

XI

All close they met again, before the dusk
    Had taken from the stars its pleasant veil,
All close they met, all eves, before the dusk
    Had taken from the stars its pleasant veil,
Close in a bower of hyacinth and musk,
    Unknown of any, free from whispering tale.
Ah! better had it been for ever so,
Than idle ears should pleasure in their woe.

XII

Were they unhappy then? – It cannot be –
    Too many tears for lovers have been shed,
Too many sighs give we to them in fee,
    Too much of pity after they are dead,

90

Too many doleful stories do we see,
    Whose matter in bright gold were best be read;
Except in such a page where Theseus' spouse
Over the pathless waves towards him bows.

XIII

But, for the general award of love,
    The little sweet doth kill much bitterness;
Though Dido silent is in under-grove,
    And Isabella's was a great distress,   100
Though young Lorenzo in warm Indian clove
    Was not embalmed, this truth is not the less –
Even bees, the little almsmen of spring-bowers,
Know there is richest juice in poison-flowers.

XIV

With her two brothers this fair lady dwelt,
    Enrichèd from ancestral merchandise,
And for them many a weary hand did swelt
    In torchèd mines and noisy factories,
And many once proud-quivered loins did melt
    In blood from stinging whip – with hollow eyes   110
Many all day in dazzling river stood,
To take the rich-ored driftings of the flood.

XV

For them the Ceylon diver held his breath,
    And went all naked to the hungry shark;
For them his ears gushed blood; for them in death
    The seal on the cold ice with piteous bark
Lay full of darts; for them alone did seethe
    A thousand men in troubles wide and dark:
Half-ignorant, they turned an easy wheel,
That set sharp racks at work to pinch and peel.   120

XVI

Why were they proud? Because their marble founts
    Gushed with more pride than do a wretch's tears? –
Why were they proud? Because fair orange-mounts
    Were of more soft ascent than lazar stairs? –
Why were they proud? Because red-lined accounts
    Were richer than the songs of Grecian years? –
Why were they proud? again we ask aloud,
Why in the name of Glory were they proud?

XVII

Yet were these Florentines as self-retired
    In hungry pride and gainful cowardice,
As two close Hebrews in that land inspired,
    Paled in and vineyarded from beggar-spies –
The hawks of ship-mast forests – the untired
    And panniered mules for ducats and old lies –
Quick cat's-paws on the generous stray-away –
Great wits in Spanish, Tuscan, and Malay.

XVIII

How was it these same ledger-men could spy
    Fair Isabella in her downy nest?
How could they find out in Lorenzo's eye
    A straying from his toil? Hot Egypt's pest
Into their vision covetous and sly!
    How could these money-bags see east and west? –
Yet so they did – and every dealer fair
Must see behind, as doth the hunted hare.

XIX

O eloquent and famed Boccaccio!
    Of thee we now should ask forgiving boon,
And of thy spicy myrtles as they blow,
    And of thy roses amorous of the moon,

And of thy lilies, that do paler grow
    Now they can no more hear thy gittern's tune,   150
For venturing syllables that ill beseem
The quiet glooms of such a piteous theme.

XX

Grant thou a pardon here, and then the tale
    Shall move on soberly, as it is meet;
There is no other crime, no mad assail
    To make old prose in modern rhyme more sweet:
But it is done – succeed the verse or fail –
    To honour thee, and thy gone spirit greet,
To stead thee as a verse in English tongue,
An echo of thee in the north wind sung.   160

XXI

These brethren having found by many signs
    What love Lorenzo for their sister had,
And how she loved him too, each unconfines
    His bitter thoughts to other, well nigh mad
That he, the servant of their trade designs,
    Should in their sister's love be blithe and glad,
When 'twas their plan to coax her by degrees
To some high noble and his olive-trees.

XXII

And many a jealous conference had they,
    And many times they bit their lips alone,   170
Before they fixed upon a surest way
    To make the youngster for his crime atone;
And at the last, these men of cruel clay
    Cut Mercy with a sharp knife to the bone,
For they resolvèd in some forest dim
To kill Lorenzo, and there bury him.

XXIII

So on a pleasant morning, as he leant
   Into the sunrise, o'er the balustrade
Of the garden-terrace, towards him they bent
180   Their footing through the dews; and to him said,
'You seem there in the quiet of content,
   Lorenzo, and we are most loth to invade
Calm speculation; but if you are wise,
Bestride your steed while cold is in the skies.

XXIV

'Today we purpose, ay, this hour we mount
   To spur three leagues towards the Apennine;
Come down, we pray thee, ere the hot sun count
   His dewy rosary on the eglantine.'
Lorenzo, courteously as he was wont,
190   Bowed a fair greeting to these serpents' whine;
And went in haste, to get in readiness,
With belt, and spur, and bracing huntsman's dress.

XXV

And as he to the court-yard passed along,
   Each third step did he pause, and listened oft
If he could hear his lady's matin-song,
   Or the light whisper of her footstep soft;
And as he thus over his passion hung,
   He heard a laugh full musical aloft,
When, looking up, he saw her features bright
200   Smile through an in-door lattice, all delight.

XXVI

'Love, Isabel!' said he, 'I was in pain
   Lest I should miss to bid thee a good morrow:
Ah! what if I should lose thee, when so fain
   I am to stifle all the heavy sorrow

Of a poor three hours' absence? but we'll gain
   Out of the amorous dark what day doth borrow.
Good bye! I'll soon be back.' 'Good bye!' said she –
And as he went she chanted merrily.

XXVII

So the two brothers and their murdered man
   Rode past fair Florence, to where Arno's stream   210
Gurgles through straitened banks, and still doth fan
   Itself with dancing bulrush, and the bream
Keeps head against the freshets. Sick and wan
   The brothers' faces in the ford did seem,
Lorenzo's flush with love. – They passed the water
Into a forest quiet for the slaughter.

XXVIII

There was Lorenzo slain and buried in,
   There in that forest did his great love cease.
Ah! when a soul doth thus its freedom win,
   It aches in loneliness – is ill at peace   220
As the break-covert blood-hounds of such sin.
   They dipped their swords in the water, and did
      tease
Their horses homeward, with convulsèd spur,
Each richer by his being a murderer.

XXIX

They told their sister how, with sudden speed,
   Lorenzo had ta'en ship for foreign lands,
Because of some great urgency and need
   In their affairs, requiring trusty hands.
Poor girl! put on thy stifling widow's weed,
   And 'scape at once from Hope's accursèd bands;   230
Today thou wilt not see him, nor tomorrow,
And the next day will be a day of sorrow.

XXX

She weeps alone for pleasures not to be;
    Sorely she wept until the night came on,
And then, instead of love, O misery!
    She brooded o'er the luxury alone:
His image in the dusk she seemed to see,
    And to the silence made a gentle moan,
Spreading her perfect arms upon the air,
240 And on her couch low murmuring 'Where? O where?'

XXXI

But Selfishness, Love's cousin, held not long
    Its fiery vigil in her single breast.
She fretted for the golden hour, and hung
    Upon the time with feverish unrest –
Not long – for soon into her heart a throng
    Of higher occupants, a richer zest,
Came tragic – passion not to be subdued,
And sorrow for her love in travels rude.

XXXII

In the mid days of autumn, on their eves
250   The breath of Winter comes from far away,
And the sick west continually bereaves
    Of some gold tinge, and plays a roundelay
Of death among the bushes and the leaves,
    To make all bare before he dares to stray
From his north cavern. So sweet Isabel
By gradual decay from beauty fell,

XXXIII

Because Lorenzo came not. Oftentimes
    She asked her brothers, with an eye all pale,
Striving to be itself, what dungeon climes
260   Could keep him off so long? They spake a tale

Time after time, to quiet her. Their crimes
   Came on them, like a smoke from Hinnom's vale;
And every night in dreams they groaned aloud,
To see their sister in her snowy shroud.

XXXIV

And she had died in drowsy ignorance,
   But for a thing more deadly dark than all.
It came like a fierce potion, drunk by chance,
   Which saves a sick man from the feathered pall
For some few gasping moments; like a lance,
   Waking an Indian from his cloudy hall   270
With cruel pierce, and bringing him again
Sense of the gnawing fire at heart and brain.

XXXV

It was a vision. – In the drowsy gloom,
   The dull of midnight, at her couch's foot
Lorenzo stood, and wept: the forest tomb
   Had marred his glossy hair which once could shoot
Lustre into the sun, and put cold doom
   Upon his lips, and taken the soft lute
From his lorn voice, and past his loamèd ears
Had made a miry channel for his tears.   280

XXXVI

Strange sound it was, when the pale shadow spake;
   For there was striving, in its piteous tongue,
To speak as when on earth it was awake,
   And Isabella on its music hung.
Languor there was in it, and tremulous shake,
   As in a palsied Druid's harp unstrung;
And through it moaned a ghostly under-song,
Like hoarse night-gusts sepulchral briars among.

XXXVII

Its eyes, though wild, were still all dewy bright
290   With love, and kept all phantom fear aloof
From the poor girl by magic of their light,
    The while it did unthread the horrid woof
Of the late darkened time – the murderous spite
    Of pride and avarice, the dark pine roof
In the forest, and the sodden turfèd dell,
Where, without any word, from stabs he fell.

XXXVIII

Saying moreover, 'Isabel, my sweet!
    Red whortle-berries droop above my head,
And a large flint-stone weighs upon my feet;
300   Around me beeches and high chestnuts shed
Their leaves and prickly nuts; a sheep-fold bleat
    Comes from beyond the river to my bed:
Go, shed one tear upon my heather-bloom,
And it shall comfort me within the tomb.

XXXIX

'I am a shadow now, alas! alas!
    Upon the skirts of human-nature dwelling
Alone. I chant alone the holy mass,
    While little sounds of life are round me knelling,
And glossy bees at noon do fieldward pass,
310   And many a chapel bell the hour is telling,
Paining me through: those sounds grow strange to me,
And thou art distant in humanity.

XL

'I know what was, I feel full well what is,
    And I should rage, if spirits could go mad;
Though I forget the taste of earthly bliss,
    That paleness warms my grave, as though I had

A seraph chosen from the bright abyss
   To be my spouse: thy paleness makes me glad;
Thy beauty grows upon me, and I feel
A greater love through all my essence steal.'   320

XLI

The Spirit mourn'd 'Adieu!' – dissolved, and left
   The atom darkness in a slow turmoil;
As when of healthful midnight sleep bereft,
   Thinking on rugged hours and fruitless toil,
We put our eyes into a pillowy cleft,
   And see the spangly gloom froth up and boil:
It made sad Isabella's eyelids ache,
And in the dawn she started up awake –

XLII

'Ha! ha!' said she, 'I knew not this hard life,
   I thought the worst was simple misery;   330
I thought some Fate with pleasure or with strife
   Portioned us – happy days, or else to die;
But there is crime – a brother's bloody knife!
   Sweet Spirit, thou hast schooled my infancy:
I'll visit thee for this, and kiss thine eyes,
And greet thee morn and even in the skies.'

XLIII

When the full morning came, she had devised
   How she might secret to the forest hie;
How she might find the clay, so dearly prized,
   And sing to it one latest lullaby;   340
How her short absence might be unsurmised,
   While she the inmost of the dream would try.
Resolved, she took with her an agèd nurse,
And went into that dismal forest-hearse.

XLIV

See, as they creep along the river side,
   How she doth whisper to that agèd dame,
And, after looking round the champaign wide,
   Shows her a knife. – 'What feverous hectic flame
Burns in thee, child? – What good can thee betide,
350   That thou shouldst smile again?' The evening came,
And they had found Lorenzo's earthy bed –
The flint was there, the berries at his head.

XLV

Who hath not loitered in a green church-yard,
   And let his spirit, like a demon-mole,
Work through the clayey soil and gravel hard,
   To see skull, coffined bones, and funeral stole;
Pitying each form that hungry Death hath marred
   And filling it once more with human soul?
Ah! this is holiday to what was felt
360 When Isabella by Lorenzo knelt.

XLVI

She gazed into the fresh-thrown mould, as though
   One glance did fully all its secrets tell;
Clearly she saw, as other eyes would know
   Pale limbs at bottom of a crystal well;
Upon the murderous spot she seemed to grow,
   Like to a native lily of the dell –
Then with her knife, all sudden, she began
To dig more fervently than misers can.

XLVII

Soon she turned up a soilèd glove, whereon
370   Her silk had played in purple phantasies,
She kissed it with a lip more chill than stone,
   And put it in her bosom, where it dries

And freezes utterly unto the bone
   Those dainties made to still an infant's cries:
Then 'gan she work again, nor stayed her care,
But to throw back at times her veiling hair.

XLVIII

That old nurse stood beside her wondering,
   Until her heart felt pity to the core
At sight of such a dismal labouring,
   And so she kneelèd, with her locks all hoar,   380
And put her lean hands to the horrid thing.
   Three hours they laboured at this travail sore –
At last they felt the kernel of the grave,
And Isabella did not stamp and rave.

XLIX

Ah! wherefore all this wormy circumstance?
   Why linger at the yawning tomb so long?
O for the gentleness of old Romance,
   The simple plaining of a minstrel's song!
Fair reader, at the old tale take a glance,
   For here, in truth, it doth not well belong   390
To speak – O turn thee to the very tale,
And taste the music of that vision pale.

L

With duller steel than the Persèan sword
   They cut away no formless monster's head,
But one, whose gentleness did well accord
   With death, as life. The ancient harps have said,
Love never dies, but lives, immortal Lord:
   If Love impersonate was ever dead,
Pale Isabella kissed it, and low moaned.
'Twas Love – cold, dead indeed, but not dethroned.   400

LI

In anxious secrecy they took it home,
 And then the prize was all for Isabel.
She calmed its wild hair with a golden comb,
 And all around each eye's sepulchral cell
Pointed each fringèd lash; the smearèd loam
 With tears, as chilly as a dripping well,
She drenched away – and still she combed, and kept
Sighing all day – and still she kissed, and wept.

LII

Then in a silken scarf – sweet with the dews
410 Of precious flowers plucked in Araby,
And divine liquids come with odorous ooze
 Through the cold serpent-pipe refreshfully –
She wrapped it up; and for its tomb did choose
 A garden-pot, wherein she laid it by,
And covered it with mould, and o'er it set
Sweet basil, which her tears kept ever wet.

LIII

And she forgot the stars, the moon, and sun,
 And she forgot the blue above the trees,
And she forgot the dells where waters run,
420 And she forgot the chilly autumn breeze;
She had no knowledge when the day was done,
 And the new morn she saw not, but in peace
Hung over her sweet basil evermore,
And moistened it with tears unto the core.

LIV

And so she ever fed it with thin tears,
 Whence thick, and green, and beautiful it grew,
So that it smelt more balmy than its peers
 Of basil-tufts in Florence; for it drew

Nurture besides, and life, from human fears,
  From the fast mouldering head there shut from
      view: 430
So that the jewel, safely casketed,
Came forth, and in perfumèd leafits spread.

LV

O Melancholy, linger here awhile!
  O Music, Music, breathe despondingly!
O Echo, Echo, from some sombre isle,
  Unknown, Lethean, sigh to us – O sigh!
Spirits in grief, lift up your heads, and smile.
  Lift up your heads, sweet Spirits, heavily,
And make a pale light in your cypress glooms,
Tinting with silver wan your marble tombs.   440

LVI

Moan hither, all ye syllables of woe,
  From the deep throat of sad Melpomene!
Through bronzèd lyre in tragic order go,
  And touch the strings into a mystery;
Sound mournfully upon the winds and low;
  For simple Isabel is soon to be
Among the dead. She withers, like a palm
Cut by an Indian for its juicy balm.

LVII

O leave the palm to wither by itself;
  Let not quick Winter chill its dying hour! –   450
It may not be – those Baälites of pelf,
  Her brethren, noted the continual shower
From her dead eyes; and many a curious elf,
  Among her kindred, wondered that such dower
Of youth and beauty should be thrown aside
By one marked out to be a noble's bride.

LVIII

And, furthermore, her brethren wondered much
    Why she sat drooping by the basil green,
And why it flourished, as by magic touch.
460   Greatly they wondered what the thing might mean:
They could not surely give belief, that such
    A very nothing would have power to wean
Her from her own fair youth, and pleasures gay,
And even remembrance of her love's delay.

LIX

Therefore they watched a time when they might sift
    This hidden whim; and long they watched in vain:
For seldom did she go to chapel-shrift,
    And seldom felt she any hunger-pain;
And when she left, she hurried back, as swift
470   As bird on wing to breast its eggs again;
And, patient as a hen-bird, sat her there
Beside her basil, weeping through her hair.

LX

Yet they contrived to steal the basil-pot,
    And to examine it in secret place.
The thing was vile with green and livid spot,
    And yet they knew it was Lorenzo's face:
The guerdon of their murder they had got,
    And so left Florence in a moment's space,
Never to turn again. Away they went,
480 With blood upon their heads, to banishment.

LXI

O Melancholy, turn thine eyes away!
    O Music, Music, breathe despondingly!
O Echo, Echo, on some other day,
    From isles Lethean, sigh to us – O sigh!

Spirits of grief, sing not your 'Well-a-way!'
    For Isabel, sweet Isabel, will die –
Will die a death too lone and incomplete,
Now they have ta'en away her basil sweet.

LXII

Piteous she looked on dead and senseless things,
    Asking for her lost basil amorously;
And with melodious chuckle in the strings
    Of her lorn voice, she oftentimes would cry
After the pilgrim in his wanderings,
    To ask him where her basil was, and why
'Twas hid from her: 'For cruel 'tis,' said she,
'To steal my basil-pot away from me.'

LXIII

And so she pined, and so she died forlorn,
    Imploring for her basil to the last.
No heart was there in Florence but did mourn
    In pity of her love, so overcast.
And a sad ditty on this story born
    From mouth to mouth through all the country
        passed:
Still is the burthen sung – 'O cruelty,
To steal my basil-pot away from me!'

On Visiting the Tomb of Burns

The town, the churchyard, and the setting sun,
    The clouds, the trees, the rounded hills all seem,
    Though beautiful, cold – strange – as in a dream
I dreamèd long ago. Now new begun
The short-lived, paly summer is but won
    From winter's ague, for one hour's gleam;
    Through sapphire-warm, their stars do never beam –
All is cold Beauty; pain is never done

For who has mind to relish, Minos-wise,
10   The real of Beauty, free from that dead hue
            Fickly imagination and sick pride
        Cast wan upon it! Burns! with honour due
            I have oft honoured thee. Great shadow, hide
Thy face! I sin against thy native skies.

                                        (Not published by Keats)

'Old Meg she was a gypsy'

Old Meg she was a gypsy,
    And lived upon the moors,
Her bed it was the brown heath turf,
    And her house was out of doors.

Her apples were swart blackberries,
    Her currants pods o' broom,
Her wine was dew o' the wild white rose,
    Her book a churchyard tomb.

Her brothers were the craggy hills,
10   Her sisters larchen trees –
Alone with her great family
    She lived as she did please.

No breakfast had she many a morn,
    No dinner many a noon,
And 'stead of supper she would stare
    Full hard against the moon.

But every morn of woodbine fresh
    She made her garlanding,
And every night the dark glen yew
20   She wove, and she would sing.

And with her fingers old and brown
  She plaited mats o' rushes,
And gave them to the cottagers
  She met among the bushes.

Old Meg was brave as Margaret Queen
  And tall as Amazon,
An old red blanket cloak she wore,
  A chip-hat she had on.
God rest her bones somewhere –
  She died full long agone!   30
          (Not published by Keats)

A Song about Myself

I

There was a naughty boy,
  A naughty boy was he,
He would not stop at home,
  He could not quiet be
    He took
    In his knapsack
    A book
    Full of vowels
    And a shirt
    With some towels –   10
    A slight cap
    For night-cap –
    A hair brush,
    Comb ditto,
    New stockings,
    For old ones
    Would split O!
    This knapsack
    Tight at's back
    He rivetted close   20
And followed his nose

To the North,
To the North,
And followed his nose
To the North.

II
There was a naughty boy
     And a naughty boy was he,
For nothing would he do
     But scribble poetry –
30   He took
          An inkstand
          In his hand
          And a pen
          Big as ten
          In the other
          And away
          In a pother
          He ran
          To the mountains
40   And fountains
          And ghostès
          And postès
          And witches
          And ditches,
          And wrote
          In his coat
          When the weather
          Was cool –
          Fear of gout –
50   And without
          When the weather
          Was warm.
          Och, the charm
          When we choose
To follow one's nose

            To the North,
            To the North,
        To follow one's nose
            To the North!

                    III
There was a naughty boy   60
    And a naughty boy was he,
He kept little fishes
    In washing tubs three
        In spite
        Of the might
        Of the maid,
        Nor afraid
        Of his granny-good,
        He often would
        Hurly burly   70
        Get up early
        And go,
        By hook or crook,
        To the brook
        And bring home
        Miller's thumb,
        Tittlebat
        Not over fat,
        Minnows small
        As the stall   80
        Of a glove,
        Not above
        The size
        Of a nice
        Little baby's
        Little finger –
        O he made
        ('Twas his trade)
    Of fish a pretty kettle,

90   A kettle –
                A kettle,
             Of fish a pretty kettle,
                A kettle!

                    IV
           There was a naughty boy,
              And a naughty boy was he,
           He ran away to Scotland
              The people for to see –
                 There he found
                 That the ground
100   Was as hard,
                 That a yard
                 Was as long,
                 That a song
                 Was as merry,
                 That a cherry
                 Was as red,
                 That lead
                 Was as weighty,
                 That fourscore
110   Was as eighty,
                 That a door
                 Was as wooden
                 As in England –
           So he stood in his shoes
                 And he wondered,
                 He wondered,
           He stood in his
                 Shoes and he wondered.
                    (Not published by Keats)

To Ailsa Rock

Hearken, thou craggy ocean pyramid!
　　Give answer by the voice, the sea-fowls' screams!
　　When were thy shoulders mantled in huge streams?
When from the sun was thy broad forehead hid?
How long is't since the mighty power bid
　　Thee heave to airy sleep from fathom dreams?
　　Sleep in the lap of thunder or sunbeams,
Or when grey clouds are thy cold coverlid?
Thou answer'st not; for thou art dead asleep.
　　Thy life is but two dead eternities –　　　　　　　　10
The last in air, the former in the deep,
　　First with the whales, last with the eagle-skies.
Drowned wast thou till an earthquake made thee steep,
　　Another cannot wake thy giant size!

Lines Written in the Highlands
after a Visit to Burns's Country

There is a joy in footing slow across a silent plain,
Where patriot battle has been fought when glory had the
　　gain;
There is a pleasure on the heath where Druids old have
　　been,
Where mantles grey have rustled by and swept the nettles
　　green;
There is a joy in every spot made known by times of old,
New to the feet, although the tale a hundred times be told;
There is a deeper joy than all, more solemn in the heart,
More parching to the tongue than all, of more divine a
　　smart,
When weary steps forget themselves upon a pleasant turf,
Upon hot sand, or flinty road, or sea-shore iron scurf,　　10

Toward the castle or the cot, where long ago was born
One who was great through mortal days, and died of
    fame unshorn.
Light heather-bells may tremble then, but they are far
    away;
Wood-lark may sing from sandy fern, the sun may hear
    his lay;
Runnels may kiss the grass on shelves and shallows
    clear,
But their low voices are not heard, though come on
    travels drear;
Blood-red the sun may set behind black mountain
    peaks;
Blue tides may sluice and drench their time in caves and
    weedy creeks;
Eagles may seem to sleep wide-wing upon the air;
Ring-doves may fly convulsed across to some
20   high-cedared lair;
But the forgotten eye is still fast wedded to the ground,
As palmer's that, with weariness, mid-desert shrine hath
    found.
At such a time the soul's a child, in childhood is the
    brain;
Forgotten is the worldly heart – alone it beats in vain.
Ay, if a madman could have leave to pass a healthful
    day
To tell his forehead's swoon and faint when first began
    decay,
He might make tremble many a man whose spirit had
    gone forth
To find a bard's low cradle-place about the silent
    North!
Scanty the hour and few the steps beyond the bourn of
    care,
30 Beyond the sweet and bitter world – beyond it unaware;
Scanty the hour and few the steps, because a longer stay
Would bar return, and make a mortal man forget his
    mortal way.

O horrible! to lose the sight of well-remembered face,
Of brother's eyes, of sister's brow, constant to every
    place,
Filling the air, as on we move, with portraiture intense,
More warm than those heroic tints that fill a painter's
    sense,
When shapes of old come striding by, and visages of old,
Locks shining black, hair scanty grey, and passions
    manifold.
No, no, that horror cannot be, for at the cable's length
Man feels the gentle anchor pull and gladdens in its
    strength –   40
One hour, half-idiot, he stands by mossy waterfall,
But in the very next he reads his soul's memorial.
He reads it on the mountain's height, where chance he
    may sit down
Upon rough marble diadem, that hill's eternal crown,
Yet be the anchor e'er so fast, room is there for a prayer.
That man may never lose his mind on mountains bleak
    and bare;
That he may stray league after league some great
    birth-place to find,
And keep his vision clear from speck, his inward sight
    unblind.

(Not published by Keats)

'Read me a lesson, Muse, and speak it loud'

Read me a lesson, Muse, and speak it loud
    Upon the top of Nevis, blind in mist!
I look into the chasms, and a shroud
    Vaporous doth hide them; just so much I wist
Mankind do know of Hell. I look o'erhead,
    And there is sullen mist; even so much
Mankind can tell of Heaven. Mist is spread
    Before the earth, beneath me – even such,

Even so vague is man's sight of himself.
10   Here are the craggy stones beneath my feet –
Thus much I know, that, a poor witless elf,
    I tread on them, that all my eye doth meet
Is mist and crag, not only on this height,
    But in the world of thought and mental might.

(Not published by Keats)

'Upon my life, Sir Nevis, I am piqued'

MRS C.
Upon my life, Sir Nevis, I am piqued
That I have so far panted, tugged and reeked
To do an honour to your bald old pate
And now am sitting on you just to bate,
Without your paying me one compliment.
Alas, 'tis so with all, when our intent
Is plain, and in the eye of all mankind
We fair ones show a preference, too blind!
You gentlemen immediately turn tail –
10   O let me then my helpless fate bewail!
Ungrateful baldpate, have I not disdained
The pleasant vallies, have I not, mad-brained,
Deserted all my pickles and preserves,
My china-closet too – with wretched nerves
To boot – say, wretched ingrate, have I not
Left my soft cushion chair and caudle pot?
'Tis true I had no corns – no! thank the fates,
My shoemaker was always Mr Bates.
And if not Mr Bates, why I'm not old!
20   Still dumb, ungrateful Nevis – still so cold!

(Here the lady took some more whiskey and was putting even more to her lips when she dashed [it] to the ground for the mountain began to grumble – which continued for a few minutes, before he thus began,)

BEN NEVIS

What whining bit of tongue and mouth thus dares
Disturb my slumber of a thousand years?
Even so long my sleep has been secure –
And to be so awaked I'll not endure.
O pain! – for since the eagle's earliest scream
I've had a damned confounded ugly dream,
A nightmare sure. What, Madam, was it you?
It cannot be! My old eyes are not true!
Red Crag, my spectacles! Now let me see!
Good Heavens, Lady, how the Gemini   30
Did you get here? O I shall split my sides!
I shall earthquake –

MRS C.

Sweet Nevis, do not quake, for though I love
Your honest Countenance all things above,
Truly I should not like to be conveyed
So far into your bosom – gentle maid
Loves not too rough a treatment, gentle Sir –
Pray thee be calm, and do not quake nor stir,
No, not a stone, or I shall go in fits –

BEN NEVIS

I must – I shall! I meet not such tit-bits –   40
I meet not such sweet creatures every day!
By my old night-cap, night-cap day and night,
I must have one sweet buss – I must and shall!
Red Crag! – What, Madam, can you then repent
Of all the toil and vigour you have spent
To see Ben Nevis and to touch his nose?
Red Crag, I say! O I must have you close!
Red Crag, there lies beneath my farthest toe
A vein of sulphur – go, dear Red Crag, go –
And rub your flinty back against it. Budge!   50
Dear Madam, I must kiss you, faith I must!
I must embrace you with my dearest gust!

Blockhead, d'ye hear – Blockhead, I'll make her feel –
There lies beneath my east leg's northern heel
A cave of young earth dragons – well, my boy,
Go thither quick and so complete my joy.
Take you a bundle of the largest pines
And, where the sun on fiercest phosphor shines,
Fire them and ram them in the dragons' nest,
60   Then will the dragons fry and fizz their best,
Until ten thousand times no bigger than
Poor alligators – poor things of one span –
Will each one swell to twice ten times the size
Of northern whale. Then for the tender prize –
The moment then – for then will Red Crag rub
His flinty back – and I shall kiss and snub
And press my dainty morsel to my breast.
Blockhead, make haste!

        O Muses weep the rest –
The lady fainted, and he thought her dead,
70   So pulled the clouds again about his head,
And went to sleep again – soon she was roused
By her affrighted servants. Next day housed
Safe on the lowly ground she blessed her fate
That fainting fit was not delayed too late.

              (Not published by Keats)

Fragment: 'Where's the Poet? Show him, show him'

Where's the Poet? Show him, show him,
Muses nine, that I may know him!
'Tis the man who with a man
   Is an equal, be he king,
Or poorest of the beggar-clan,
   Or any other wondrous thing

A man may be 'twixt ape and Plato.
  'Tis the man who with a bird,
Wren or eagle, finds his way to
  All his instincts. He hath heard   10
The lion's roaring, and can tell
  What his horny throat expresseth,
And to him the tiger's yell
  Comes articulate and presseth
On his ear like mother-tongue . . .

            (Not published by Keats)

'And what is love? It is a doll dressed up'

And what is love? It is a doll dressed up
For idleness to cosset, nurse, and dandle;
A thing of soft misnomers, so divine
That silly youth doth think to make itself
Divine by loving, and so goes on
Yawning and doting a whole summer long,
Till Miss's comb is made a pearl tiara,
And common Wellingtons turn Romeo boots;
Till Cleopatra lives at Number Seven,
And Antony resides in Brunswick Square.   10
Fools! if some passions high have warmed the
    world,
If queens and soldiers have played deep for hearts,
It is no reason why such agonies
Should be more common than the growth of weeds.
Fools! make me whole again that weighty pearl
The queen of Egypt melted, and I'll say
That ye may love in spite of beaver hats.

            (Not published by Keats)

Hyperion. A Fragment

BOOK I

Deep in the shady sadness of a vale
Far sunken from the healthy breath of morn,
Far from the fiery noon, and eve's one star,
Sat grey-haired Saturn, quiet as a stone,
Still as the silence round about his lair;
Forest on forest hung above his head
Like cloud on cloud. No stir of air was there,
Not so much life as on a summer's day
Robs not one light seed from the feathered grass,
But where the dead leaf fell, there did it rest.
A stream went voiceless by, still deadened more
By reason of his fallen divinity
Spreading a shade: the Naiad 'mid her reeds
Pressed her cold finger closer to her lips.

Along the margin-sand large foot-marks went,
No further than to where his feet had strayed,
And slept there since. Upon the sodden ground
His old right hand lay nerveless, listless, dead,
Unsceptred; and his realmless eyes were closed;
While his bowed head seemed listening to the Earth,
His ancient mother, for some comfort yet.

It seemed no force could wake him from his place;
But there came one, who with a kindred hand
Touched his wide shoulders, after bending low
With reverence, though to one who knew it not.
She was a Goddess of the infant world;
By her in stature the tall Amazon
Had stood a pigmy's height: she would have ta'en
Achilles by the hair and bent his neck;
Or with a finger stayed Ixion's wheel.
Her face was large as that of Memphian sphinx,

10

20

30

Pedestalled haply in a palace court,
When sages looked to Egypt for their lore.
But O! how unlike marble was that face,
How beautiful, if sorrow had not made
Sorrow more beautiful than Beauty's self.
There was a listening fear in her regard,
As if calamity had but begun;
As if the vanward clouds of evil days
Had spent their malice, and the sullen rear   40
Was with its storèd thunder labouring up.
One hand she pressed upon that aching spot
Where beats the human heart, as if just there,
Though an immortal, she felt cruel pain;
The other upon Saturn's bended neck
She laid, and to the level of his ear
Leaning with parted lips, some words she spake
In solemn tenor and deep organ tone –
Some mourning words, which in our feeble tongue
Would come in these like accents (O how frail   50
To that large utterance of the early Gods!):
'Saturn, look up! – though wherefore, poor old
        King?
I have no comfort for thee, no, not one:
I cannot say, "O wherefore sleepest thou?"
For heaven is parted from thee, and the earth
Knows thee not, thus afflicted, for a God;
And ocean too, with all its solemn noise,
Has from thy sceptre passed; and all the air
Is emptied of thine hoary majesty.
Thy thunder, conscious of the new command,   60
Rumbles reluctant o'er our fallen house;
And thy sharp lightning in unpractised hands
Scorches and burns our once serene domain.
O aching time! O moments big as years!
All as ye pass swell out the monstrous truth,
And press it so upon our weary griefs
That unbelief has not a space to breathe.
Saturn, sleep on – O thoughtless, why did I

Thus violate thy slumbrous solitude?
70   Why should I ope thy melancholy eyes?
Saturn, sleep on, while at thy feet I weep!'

    As when, upon a trancèd summer-night,
Those green-robed senators of mighty woods,
Tall oaks, branch-charmèd by the earnest stars,
Dream, and so dream all night without a stir,
Save from one gradual solitary gust
Which comes upon the silence, and dies off,
As if the ebbing air had but one wave;
So came these words and went; the while in tears
80   She touched her fair large forehead to the ground,
Just where her falling hair might be outspread
A soft and silken mat for Saturn's feet.
One moon, with alteration slow, had shed
Her silver seasons four upon the night,
And still these two were postured motionless,
Like natural sculpture in cathedral cavern;
The frozen God still couchant on the earth,
And the sad Goddess weeping at his feet:
Until at length old Saturn lifted up
90   His faded eyes, and saw his kingdom gone,
And all the gloom and sorrow of the place,
And that fair kneeling Goddess; and then spake,
As with a palsied tongue, and while his beard
Shook horrid with such aspen-malady:
'O tender spouse of gold Hyperion,
Thea, I feel thee ere I see thy face;
Look up, and let me see our doom in it;
Look up, and tell me if this feeble shape
Is Saturn's; tell me, if thou hear'st the voice
100   Of Saturn; tell me, if this wrinkling brow,
Naked and bare of its great diadem,
Peers like the front of Saturn. Who had power
To make me desolate? whence came the strength?
How was it nurtured to such bursting forth,
While Fate seemed strangled in my nervous grasp?

But it is so; and I am smothered up,
And buried from all godlike exercise
Of influence benign on planets pale,
Of admonitions to the winds and seas,
Of peaceful sway above man's harvesting,   110
And all those acts which Deity supreme
Doth ease its heart of love in. – I am gone
Away from my own bosom; I have left
My strong identity, my real self,
Somewhere between the throne and where I sit
Here on this spot of earth. Search, Thea, search!
Open thine eyes eterne, and sphere them round
Upon all space – space starred, and lorn of light;
Space regioned with life-air; and barren void;
Spaces of fire, and all the yawn of hell.   120
Search, Thea, search! and tell me, if thou seest
A certain shape or shadow, making way
With wings or chariot fierce to repossess
A heaven he lost erewhile: it must – it must
Be of ripe progress: Saturn must be King.
Yes, there must be a golden victory;
There must be Gods thrown down, and trumpets
      blown
Of triumph calm, and hymns of festival
Upon the gold clouds metropolitan,
Voices of soft proclaim, and silver stir   130
Of strings in hollow shells; and there shall be
Beautiful things made new, for the surprise
Of the sky-children. I will give command:
Thea! Thea! Thea! where is Saturn?'

    This passion lifted him upon his feet,
And made his hands to struggle in the air,
His Druid locks to shake and ooze with sweat,
His eyes to fever out, his voice to cease.
He stood, and heard not Thea's sobbing deep;
A little time, and then again he snatched   140
Utterance thus: 'But cannot I create?

Cannot I form? Cannot I fashion forth
Another world, another universe,
To overbear and crumble this to naught?
Where is another Chaos? Where?' – That word
Found way unto Olympus, and made quake
The rebel three. Thea was startled up,
And in her bearing was a sort of hope,
As thus she quick-voiced spake, yet full of awe.

150   'This cheers out fallen house: come to our friends,
O Saturn! come away, and give them heart.
I know the covert, for thence came I hither.'
Thus brief; then with beseeching eyes she went
With backward footing through the shade a space:
He followed, and she turned to lead the way
Through agèd boughs, that yielded like the mist
Which eagles cleave up-mounting from their nest.

Meanwhile in other realms big tears were shed,
More sorrow like to this, and such like woe,
160   Too huge for mortal tongue or pen of scribe.
The Titans fierce, self-hid, or prison-bound,
Groaned for the old allegiance once more,
And listened in sharp pain for Saturn's voice.
But one of the whole mammoth-brood still kept
His sovereignty, and rule, and majesty –
Blazing Hyperion on his orbèd fire
Still sat, still snuffed the incense, teeming up
From man to the sun's God – yet unsecure:
For as among us mortals omens drear
170   Fright and perplex, so also shuddered he –
Not at dog's howl, or gloom-bird's hated screech,
Or the familiar visiting of one
Upon the first toll of his passing-bell,
Or prophesyings of the midnight lamp;
But horrors, portioned to a giant nerve,
Oft made Hyperion ache. His palace bright

Bastioned with pyramids of glowing gold,
And touched with shade of bronzèd obelisks,
Glared a blood-red through all its thousand courts,
Arches, and domes, and fiery galleries;   180
And all its curtains of Aurorian clouds
Flushed angerly, while sometimes eagle's wings,
Unseen before by Gods or wondering men,
Darkened the place, and neighing steeds were heard,
Not heard before by Gods or wondering men.
Also, when he would taste the spicy wreaths
Of incense, breathed aloft from sacred hills,
Instead of sweets, his ample palate took
Savour of poisonous brass and metal sick:
And so, when harboured in the sleepy west,   190
After the full completion of fair day,
For rest divine upon exalted couch
And slumber in the arms of melody,
He paced away the pleasant hours of ease
With stride colossal, on from hall to hall;
While far within each aisle and deep recess,
His wingèd minions in close clusters stood,
Amazed and full of fear; like anxious men
Who on wide plains gather in panting troops,
When earthquakes jar their battlements and
          towers.   200
Even now, while Saturn, roused from icy trance,
Went step for step with Thea through the woods,
Hyperion, leaving twilight in the rear,
Came slope upon the threshold of the west;
Then, as was wont, his palace-door flew ope
In smoothest silence, save what solemn tubes,
Blown by the serious Zephyrs, gave of sweet
And wandering sounds, slow-breathèd melodies –
And like a rose in vermeil tint and shape,
In fragrance soft, and coolness to the eye,   210
That inlet to severe magnificence
Stood full blown, for the God to enter in.

He entered, but he entered full of wrath;
His flaming robes streamed out beyond his heels,
And gave a roar, as if of earthly fire,
That scared away the meek ethereal Hours
And made their dove-wings tremble. On he flared,
From stately nave to nave, from vault to vault,
Through bowers of fragrant and enwreathèd light,
220   And diamond-pavèd lustrous long arcades,
Until he reached the great main cupola.
There standing fierce beneath, he stamped his foot,
And from the basement deep to the high towers
Jarred his own golden region; and before
The quavering thunder thereupon had ceased,
His voice leapt out, despite of god-like curb,
To this result: 'O dreams of day and night!
O monstrous forms! O effigies of pain!
O spectres busy in a cold, cold gloom!
230   O lank-eared Phantoms of black-weeded pools!
Why do I know ye? Why have I seen ye? Why
Is my eternal essence thus distraught
To see and to behold these horrors new?
Saturn is fallen, am I too to fall?
Am I to leave this haven of my rest,
This cradle of my glory, this soft clime,
This calm luxuriance of blissful light,
These crystalline pavilions, and pure fanes,
Of all my lucent empire? It is left
240   Deserted, void, nor any haunt of mine.
The blaze, the splendour, and the symmetry,
I cannot see – but darkness, death and darkness.
Even here, into my centre of repose,
The shady visions come to domineer,
Insult, and blind, and stifle up my pomp. –
Fall! – No, by Tellus and her briny robes!
Over the fiery frontier of my realms
I will advance a terrible right-arm
Shall scare that infant thunderer, rebel Jove,

And bid old Saturn take his throne again.' – 250
He spake, and ceased, the while a heavier threat
Held struggle with his throat but came not forth;
For as in theatres of crowded men
Hubbub increases more they call out 'Hush!',
So at Hyperion's words the Phantoms pale
Bestirred themselves, thrice horrible and cold;
And from the mirrored level where he stood
A mist arose, as from a scummy marsh.
At this, through all his bulk an agony
Crept gradual, from the feet unto the crown, 260
Like a lithe serpent vast and muscular
Making slow way, with head and neck convulsed
From over-strainèd might. Released, he fled
To the eastern gates, and full six dewy hours
Before the dawn in season due should blush,
He breathed fierce breath against the sleepy portals,
Cleared them of heavy vapours, burst them wide
Suddenly on the ocean's chilly streams.
The planet orb of fire, whereon he rode
Each day from east to west the heavens through, 270
Spun round in sable curtaining of clouds;
Not therefore veilèd quite, blindfold, and hid,
But ever and anon the glancing spheres,
Circles, and arcs, and broad-belting colure,
Glowed through, and wrought upon the muffling dark
Sweet-shapèd lightnings from the nadir deep
Up to the zenith – hieroglyphics old
Which sages and keen-eyed astrologers
Then living on the earth, with labouring thought
Won from the gaze of many centuries – 280
Now lost, save what we find on remnants huge
Of stone, or marble swart, their import gone,
Their wisdom long since fled. Two wings this orb
Possessed for glory, two fair argent wings,
Ever exalted at the God's approach:
And now, from forth the gloom their plumes immense

Rose, one by one, till all outspreaded were;
While still the dazzling globe maintained eclipse,
Awaiting for Hyperion's command.
290 Fain would he have commanded, fain took throne
And bid the day begin, if but for change.
He might not. – No, though a primeval God:
The sacred seasons might not be disturbed.
Therefore the operations of the dawn
Stayed in their birth, even as here 'tis told.
Those silver wings expanded sisterly,
Eager to sail their orb; the porches wide
Opened upon the dusk demesnes of night;
And the bright Titan, frenzied with new woes,
300 Unused to bend, by hard compulsion bent
His spirit to the sorrow of the time;
And all along a dismal rack of clouds,
Upon the boundaries of day and night,
He stretched himself in grief and radiance faint.
There as he lay, the Heaven with its stars
Looked down on him with pity, and the voice
Of Coelus, from the universal space,
Thus whispered low and solemn in his ear:
'O brightest of my children dear, earth-born
310 And sky-engendered, Son of Mysteries
All unrevealèd even to the powers
Which met at thy creating; at whose joys
And palpitations sweet, and pleasures soft,
I, Coelus, wonder how they came and whence;
And at the fruits thereof what shapes they be,
Distinct, and visible – symbols divine,
Manifestations of that beauteous life
Diffused unseen throughout eternal space:
Of these new-formed art thou, O brightest child!
320 Of these, thy brethren and the Goddesses!
There is sad feud among ye, and rebellion
Of son against his sire. I saw him fall,
I saw my first-born tumbled from his throne!
To me his arms were spread, to me his voice

Found way from forth the thunders round his head!
Pale wox I, and in vapours hid my face.
Art thou, too, near such doom? Vague fear there is:
For I have seen my sons most unlike Gods.
Divine ye were created, and divine
In sad demeanour, solemn, undisturbed, 330
Unrufflèd, like high Gods, ye lived and ruled:
Now I behold in you fear, hope, and wrath;
Actions of rage and passion – even as
I see them, on the mortal world beneath,
In men who die. This is the grief, O Son!
Sad sign of ruin, sudden dismay, and fall!
Yet do thou strive; as thou art capable,
As thou canst move about, an evident God;
And canst oppose to each malignant hour
Ethereal presence. I am but a voice; 340
My life is but the life of winds and tides,
No more than winds and tides can I avail. –
But thou canst. – Be thou therefore in the van
Of circumstance; yea, seize the arrow's barb
Before the tense string murmur. – To the earth!
For there thou wilt find Saturn, and his woes.
Meantime I will keep watch on thy bright sun,
And of thy seasons be a careful nurse.' –
Ere half this region-whisper had come down,
Hyperion arose, and on the stars 350
Lifted his curvèd lids, and kept them wide
Until it ceased; and still he kept them wide;
And still they were the same bright, patient stars.
Then with a slow incline of his broad breast,
Like to a diver in the pearly seas,
Forward he stooped over the airy shore,
And plunged all noiseless into the deep night.

BOOK II

Just at the self-same beat of Time's wide wings,
Hyperion slid into the rustled air
And Saturn gained with Thea that sad place
Where Cybele and the bruised Titans mourned.
It was a den where no insulting light
Could glimmer on their tears; where their own groans
They felt, but heard not, for the solid roar
Of thunderous waterfalls and torrents hoarse,
Pouring a constant bulk, uncertain where.
Crag jutting forth to crag, and rocks that seemed
Ever as if just rising from a sleep,
Forehead to forehead held their monstrous horns;
And thus in thousand hugest fantasies
Made a fit roofing to this nest of woe.
Instead of thrones, hard flint they sat upon,
Couches of rugged stone, and slaty ridge
Stubborned with iron. All were not assembled:
Some chained in torture, and some wandering.
Coeus, and Gyges, and Briareüs,
Typhon, and Dolor, and Porphyrion,
With many more, the brawniest in assault,
Were pent in regions of laborious breath;
Dungeoned in opaque element, to keep
Their clenchèd teeth still clenched, and all their limbs
Locked up like veins of metal, cramped and screwed;
Without a motion, save of their big hearts
Heaving in pain, and horribly convulsed
With sanguine fev'rous boiling gurge of pulse.
Mnemosyne was straying in the world;
Far from her moon had Phoebe wanderèd;
And many else were free to roam abroad,
But for the main, here found they covert drear.
Scarce images of life, one here, one there,
Lay vast and edgeways; like a dismal cirque
Of Druid stones, upon a forlorn moor,
When the chill rain begins at shut of eve,

In dull November, and their chancel vault,
The Heaven itself, is blinded throughout night.
Each one kept shroud, nor to his neighbour gave
Or word, or look, or action of despair.   40
Creüs was one; his ponderous iron mace
Lay by him, and a shattered rib of rock
Told of his rage, ere he thus sank and pined.
Iäpetus another; in his grasp,
A serpent's plashy neck; its barbèd tongue
Squeezed from the gorge, and all its uncurled length
Dead – and because the creature could not spit
Its poison in the eyes of conquering Jove.
Next Cottus; prone he lay, chin uppermost,
As though in pain, for still upon the flint   50
He ground severe his skull, with open mouth
And eyes at horrid working. Nearest him
Asia, born of most enormous Caf,
Who cost her mother Tellus keener pangs,
Though feminine, than any of her sons:
More thought than woe was in her dusky face,
For she was prophesying of her glory;
And in her wide imagination stood
Palm-shaded temples, and high rival fanes,
By Oxus or in Ganges' sacred isles.   60
Even as Hope upon her anchor leans,
So leant she, not so fair, upon a tusk
Shed from the broadest of her elephants.
Above her, on a crag's uneasy shelve,
Upon his elbow raised, all prostrate else,
Shadowed Enceladus – once tame and mild
As grazing ox unworried in the meads;
Now tiger-passioned, lion-thoughted, wroth,
He meditated, plotted, and even now
Was hurling mountains in that second war,   70
Not long delayed, that scared the younger Gods
To hide themselves in forms of beast and bird.
Not far hence Atlas; and beside him prone
Phorcus, the sire of Gorgons. Neighboured close

Oceanus, and Tethys, in whose lap
Sobbed Clymene among her tangled hair.
In midst of all lay Themis, at the feet
Of Ops the queen all clouded round from sight;
No shape distinguishable, more than when
80   Thick night confounds the pine-tops with the clouds –
And many else whose names may not be told.
For when the Muse's wings are air-ward spread,
Who shall delay her flight? And she must chant
Of Saturn, and his guide, who now had climbed
With damp and slippery footing from a depth
More horrid still. Above a sombre cliff
Their heads appeared, and up their stature grew
Till on the level height their steps found ease:
Then Thea spread abroad her trembling arms
90   Upon the precincts of this nest of pain,
And sidelong fixed her eye on Saturn's face.
There saw she direst strife – the supreme God
At war with all the frailty of grief,
Of rage, of fear, anxiety, revenge,
Remorse, spleen, hope, but most of all despair.
Against these plagues he strove in vain; for Fate
Had poured a mortal oil upon his head,
A disanointing poison, so that Thea,
Affrighted, kept her still, and let him pass
100   First onwards in, among the fallen tribe.

       As with us mortal men, the laden heart
Is persecuted more, and fevered more,
When it is nighing to the mournful house
Where other hearts are sick of the same bruise;
So Saturn, as he walked into the midst,
Felt faint, and would have sunk among the rest,
But that he met Enceladus's eye,
Whose mightiness, and awe of him, at once
Came like an inspiration; and he shouted,
110   'Titans, behold your God!' At which some groaned;
Some started on their feet; some also shouted;

Some wept, some wailed, all bowed with reverence;
And Ops, uplifting her black folded veil,
Showed her pale cheeks, and all her forehead wan,
Her eye-brows thin and jet, and hollow eyes.
There is a roaring in the bleak-grown pines
When Winter lifts his voice; there is a noise
Among immortals when a God gives sign,
With hushing finger, how he means to load
His tongue with the full weight of utterless thought,   120
With thunder, and with music, and with pomp:
Such noise is like the roar of bleak-grown pines,
Which, when it ceases in this mountained world,
No other sound succeeds; but ceasing here,
Among these fallen, Saturn's voice therefrom
Grew up like organ, that begins anew
Its strain, when other harmonies, stopped short,
Leave the dinned air vibrating silverly.
Thus grew it up: 'Not in my own sad breast,
Which is its own great judge and searcher-out,   130
Can I find reason why ye should be thus:
Not in the legends of the first of days,
Studied from that old spirit-leavèd book
Which starry Uranus with finger bright
Saved from the shores of darkness, when the waves
Low-ebbed still hid it up in shallow gloom –
And the which book ye know I ever kept
For my firm-basèd footstool – Ah, infirm!
Not there, nor in sign, symbol, or portent
Of element, earth, water, air, and fire –   140
At war, at peace, or inter-quarrelling
One against one, or two, or three, or all
Each several one against the other three,
As fire with air loud warring when rain-floods
Drown both, and press them both against earth's face,
Where, finding sulphur, a quadruple wrath
Unhinges the poor world – not in that strife,
Wherefrom I take strange lore, and read it deep,
Can I find reason why ye should be thus –

150　　No, nowhere can unriddle, though I search,
And pore on Nature's universal scroll
Even to swooning, why ye, Divinities,
The first-born of all shaped and palpable Gods,
Should cower beneath what, in comparison,
Is untremendous might. Yet ye are here,
O'erwhelmed, and spurned, and battered, ye are here!
O Titans, shall I say, "Arise!"? – Ye groan:
Shall I say "Crouch!"? – Ye groan. What can I then?
O Heaven wide! O unseen parent dear!
160　　What can I? Tell me, all ye brethren Gods,
How we can war, how engine our great wrath!
O speak your counsel now, for Saturn's ear
Is all a-hungered. Thou, Oceanus,
Ponderest high and deep, and in thy face
I see, astonied, that severe content
Which comes of thought and musing. Give us help!'

　　So ended Saturn; and the God of the Sea,
Sophist and sage from no Athenian grove,
But cogitation in his watery shades,
170　　Arose, with locks not oozy, and began,
In murmurs which his first-endeavouring tongue
Caught infant-like from the far-foamèd sands.
'O ye, whom wrath consumes! who, passion-stung,
Writhe at defeat, and nurse your agonies!
Shut up your senses, stifle up your ears,
My voice is not a bellows unto ire.
Yet listen, ye who will, whilst I bring proof
How ye, perforce, must be content to stoop;
And in the proof much comfort will I give,
180　　If ye will take that comfort in its truth.
We fall by course of Nature's law, not force
Of thunder, or of Jove. Great Saturn, thou
Hast sifted well the atom-universe;
But for this reason, that thou art the King,
And only blind from sheer supremacy,
One avenue was shaded from thine eyes,

Through which I wandered to eternal truth.
And first, as thou wast not the first of powers,
So art thou not the last; it cannot be:
Thou art not the beginning nor the end.   190
From Chaos and parental Darkness came
Light, the first fruits of that intestine broil,
That sullen ferment, which for wondrous ends
Was ripening in itself. The ripe hour came,
And with it Light, and Light, engendering
Upon its own producer, forthwith touched
The whole enormous matter into life.
Upon that very hour, our parentage,
The Heavens, and the Earth, were manifest:
Then thou first born, and we the giant race,   200
Found ourselves ruling new and beauteous realms.
Now comes the pain of truth, to whom 'tis pain –
O folly! for to bear all naked truths,
And to envisage circumstance, all calm,
That is the top of sovereignty. Mark well!
As Heaven and Earth are fairer, fairer far
Than Chaos and blank Darkness, though once chiefs;
And as we show beyond that Heaven and Earth
In form and shape compact and beautiful,
In will, in action free, companionship,   210
And thousand other signs of purer life;
So on our heels a fresh perfection treads,
A power more strong in beauty, born of us
And fated to excel us, as we pass
In glory that old Darkness: nor are we
Thereby more conquered, than by us the rule
Of shapeless Chaos. Say, doth the dull soil
Quarrel with the proud forests it hath fed,
And feedeth still, more comely than itself?
Can it deny the chiefdom of green groves?   220
Or shall the tree be envious of the dove
Because it cooeth, and hath snowy wings
To wander wherewithal and find its joys?
We are such forest-trees, and our fair boughs

Have bred forth, not pale solitary doves,
But eagles golden-feathered, who do tower
Above us in their beauty, and must reign
In right thereof. For 'tis the eternal law
That first in beauty should be first in might.
230 Yea, by that law, another race may drive
Our conquerors to mourn as we do now.
Have ye beheld the young God of the Seas,
My dispossessor? Have ye seen his face?
Have ye beheld his chariot, foamed along
By noble wingèd creatures he hath made?
I saw him on the calmèd waters scud,
With such a glow of beauty in his eyes,
That it enforced me to bid sad farewell
To all my empire: farewell sad I took,
240 And hither came, to see how dolorous fate
Had wrought upon ye; and how I might best
Give consolation in this woe extreme.
Receive the truth, and let it be your balm.'

Whether through posed conviction, or disdain,
They guarded silence, when Oceanus
Left murmuring, what deepest thought can tell?
But so it was; none answered for a space,
Save one whom none regarded, Clymene;
And yet she answered not, only complained,
250 With hectic lips, and eyes up-looking mild,
Thus wording timidly among the fierce:
'O Father, I am here the simplest voice,
And all my knowledge is that joy is gone,
And this thing woe crept in among our hearts,
There to remain for ever, as I fear.
I would not bode of evil, if I thought
So weak a creature could turn off the help
Which by just right should come of mighty Gods;
Yet let me tell my sorrow, let me tell
260 Of what I heard, and how it made me weep,
And know that we had parted from all hope.

I stood upon a shore, a pleasant shore,
Where a sweet clime was breathèd from a land
Of fragrance, quietness, and trees, and flowers.
Full of calm joy it was, as I of grief;
Too full of joy and soft delicious warmth;
So that I felt a movement in my heart
To chide, and to reproach that solitude
With songs of misery, music of our woes;
And sat me down, and took a mouthèd shell   270
And murmured into it, and made melody –
O melody no more! for while I sang,
And with poor skill let pass into the breeze
The dull shell's echo, from a bowery strand
Just opposite, an island of the sea,
There came enchantment with the shifting wind,
That did both drown and keep alive my ears.
I threw my shell away upon the sand,
And a wave filled it, as my sense was filled
With that new blissful golden melody.   280
A living death was in each gush of sounds,
Each family of rapturous hurried notes,
That fell, one after one, yet all at once,
Like pearl beads dropping sudden from their string;
And then another, then another strain,
Each like a dove leaving its olive perch,
With music winged instead of silent plumes,
To hover round my head, and make me sick
Of joy and grief at once. Grief overcame,
And I was stopping up my frantic ears,   290
When, past all hindrance of my trembling hands,
A voice came sweeter, sweeter than all tune,
And still it cried, "Apollo! young Apollo!
The morning-bright Apollo! young Apollo!"
I fled, it followed me, and cried "Apollo!"
O Father, and O Brethren, had ye felt
Those pains of mine – O Saturn, hadst thou felt,
Ye would not call this too indulgèd tongue
Presumptuous, in thus venturing to be heard.'

300   So far her voice flowed on, like timorous brook
         That, lingering along a pebbled coast,
         Doth fear to meet the sea: but sea it met,
         And shuddered; for the overwhelming voice
         Of huge Enceladus swallowed it in wrath:
         The ponderous syllables, like sullen waves
         In the half-glutted hollows of reef-rocks,
         Came booming thus, while still upon his arm
         He leaned – not rising, from supreme contempt:
         'Or shall we listen to the over-wise,
310   Or to the over-foolish, Giant-Gods?
         Not thunderbolt on thunderbolt, till all
         That rebel Jove's whole armoury were spent,
         Not world on world upon these shoulders piled
         Could agonize me more than baby-words
         In midst of this dethronement horrible.
         Speak! Roar! Shout! Yell! ye sleepy Titans all.
         Do ye forget the blows, the buffets vile?
         Are ye not smitten by a youngling arm?
         Dost thou forget, sham Monarch of the Waves,
320   Thy scalding in the seas? What, have I roused
         Your spleens with so few simple words as these?
         O joy! for now I see ye are not lost:
         O joy! for now I see a thousand eyes
         Wide-glaring for revenge!' – As this he said,
         He lifted up his stature vast, and stood,
         Still without intermission speaking thus:
         'Now ye are flames, I'll tell you how to burn,
         And purge the ether of our enemies;
         How to feed fierce the crooked stings of fire,
330   And singe away the swollen clouds of Jove,
         Stifling that puny essence in its tent.
         O let him feel the evil he hath done;
         For though I scorn Oceanus's lore,
         Much pain have I for more than loss of realms:
         The days of peace and slumbrous calm are fled;
         Those days, all innocent of scathing war,
         When all the fair Existences of heaven

Came open-eyed to guess what we would speak –
That was before our brows were taught to frown,
Before our lips knew else but solemn sounds;   340
That was before we knew the wingèd thing,
Victory, might be lost, or might be won.
And be ye mindful that Hyperion,
Our brightest brother, still is undisgraced –
Hyperion, lo! his radiance is here!'

    All eyes were on Enceladus's face,
And they beheld, while still Hyperion's name
Flew from his lips up to the vaulted rocks,
A pallid gleam across his features stern –
Not savage, for he saw full many a God   350
Wroth as himself. He looked upon them all,
And in each face he saw a gleam of light,
But splendider in Saturn's, whose hoar locks
Shone like the bubbling foam about a keel
When the prow sweeps into a midnight cove.
In pale and silver silence they remained,
Till suddenly a splendour, like the morn,
Pervaded all the beetling gloomy steeps,
All the sad spaces of oblivion,
And every gulf, and every chasm old,   360
And every height, and every sullen depth,
Voiceless, or hoarse with loud tormented streams;
And all the everlasting cataracts,
And all the headlong torrents far and near,
Mantled before in darkness and huge shade,
Now saw the light and made it terrible.
It was Hyperion: a granite peak
His bright feet touched, and there he stayed to view
The misery his brilliance had betrayed
To the most hateful seeing of itself.   370
Golden his hair of short Numidian curl,
Regal his shape majestic, a vast shade
In midst of his own brightness, like the bulk
Of Memnon's image at the set of sun

To one who travels from the dusking East:
Sighs, too, as mournful as that Memnon's harp,
He uttered, while his hands contemplative
He pressed together, and in silence stood.
Despondence seized again the fallen Gods
380 At sight of the dejected King of Day,
And many hid their faces from the light:
But fierce Enceladus sent forth his eyes
Among the brotherhood; and, at their glare,
Uprose Iäpetus, and Creüs too,
And Phorcus, sea-born, and together strode
To where he towered on his eminence.
There those four shouted forth old Saturn's name;
Hyperion from the peak loud answered, 'Saturn!'
Saturn sat near the Mother of the Gods,
390 In whose face was no joy, though all the Gods
Gave from their hollow throats the name of 'Saturn!'

BOOK III

Thus in alternate uproar and sad peace,
Amazèd were those Titans utterly.
O leave them, Muse! O leave them to their woes;
For thou art weak to sing such tumults dire:
A solitary sorrow best befits
Thy lips, and antheming a lonely grief.
Leave them, O Muse! for thou anon wilt find
Many a fallen old Divinity
Wandering in vain about bewildered shores.
10   Meantime touch piously the Delphic harp,
And not a wind of heaven but will breathe
In aid soft warble from the Dorian flute;
For lo! 'tis for the Father of all verse.
Flush every thing that hath a vermeil hue,
Let the rose glow intense and warm the air,
And let the clouds of even and of morn
Float in voluptuous fleeces o'er the hills;
Let the red wine within the goblet boil,

Cold as a bubbling well; let faint-lipped shells,
On sands, or in great deeps, vermilion turn   20
Through all their labyrinths; and let the maid
Blush keenly, as with some warm kiss surprised.
Chief isle of the embowered Cyclades,
Rejoice, O Delos, with thine olives green,
And poplars, and lawn-shading palms, and beech,
In which the Zephyr breathes the loudest song,
And hazels thick, dark-stemmed beneath the shade:
Apollo is once more the golden theme!
Where was he, when the Giant of the Sun
Stood bright, amid the sorrow of his peers?   30
Together had he left his mother fair
And his twin-sister sleeping in their bower,
And in the morning twilight wandered forth
Beside the osiers of a rivulet,
Full ankle-deep in lilies of the vale.
The nightingale had ceased, and a few stars
Were lingering in the heavens, while the thrush
Began calm-throated. Throughout all the isle
There was no covert, no retirèd cave
Unhaunted by the murmurous noise of waves,   40
Though scarcely heard in many a green recess.
He listened, and he wept, and his bright tears
Went trickling down the golden bow he held.
Thus with half-shut suffusèd eyes he stood,
While from beneath some cumbrous boughs hard by
With solemn step an awful Goddess came,
And there was purport in her looks for him,
Which he with eager guess began to read
Perplexed, the while melodiously he said:
'How cam'st thou over the unfooted sea?   50
Or hath that antique mien and robèd form
Moved in these vales invisible till now?
Sure I have heard those vestments sweeping o'er
The fallen leaves, when I have sat alone
In cool mid-forest. Surely I have traced
The rustle of those ample skirts about

These grassy solitudes, and seen the flowers
Lift up their heads, as still the whisper passed.
Goddess! I have beheld those eyes before,
60   And their eternal calm, and all that face,
Or I have dreamed.' – 'Yes,' said the supreme shape,
Thou hast dreamed of me; and awaking up
Didst find a lyre all golden by thy side,
Whose strings touched by thy fingers, all the vast
Unwearied ear of the whole universe
Listened in pain and pleasure at the birth
Of such new tuneful wonder. Is't not strange
That thou shouldst weep, so gifted? Tell me, youth,
What sorrow thou canst feel; for I am sad
70   When thou dost shed a tear. Explain thy griefs
To one who in this lonely isle hath been
The watcher of thy sleep and hours of life,
From the young day when first thy infant hand
Plucked witless the weak flowers, till thine arm
Could bend that bow heroic to all times.
Show thy heart's secret to an ancient Power
Who hath forsaken old and sacred thrones
For prophecies of thee, and for the sake
Of loveliness new born.' – Apollo then,
80   With sudden scrutiny and gloomless eyes,
Thus answered, while his white melodious throat
Throbbed with the syllables: 'Mnemosyne!
Thy name is on my tongue, I know not how;
Why should I tell thee what thou so well seest?
Why should I strive to show what from thy lips
Would come no mystery? For me, dark, dark,
And painful vile oblivion seals my eyes:
I strive to search wherefore I am so sad,
Until a melancholy numbs my limbs;
90   And then upon the grass I sit, and moan,
Like one who once had wings. O why should I
Feel cursed and thwarted, when the liegeless air
Yields to my step aspirant? Why should I

Spurn the green turf as hateful to my feet?
Goddess benign, point forth some unknown thing:
Are there not other regions than this isle?
What are the stars? There is the sun, the sun!
And the most patient brilliance of the moon!
And stars by thousands! Point me out the way
To any one particular beauteous star,   100
And I will flit into it with my lyre,
And make its silvery splendour pant with bliss.
I have heard the cloudy thunder. Where is power?
Whose hand, whose essence, what Divinity
Makes this alarum in the elements,
While I here idle listen on the shores
In fearless yet in aching ignorance?
O tell me, lonely Goddess, by thy harp,
That waileth every morn and eventide,
Tell me why thus I rave, about these groves!   110
Mute thou remainest – mute! yet I can read
A wondrous lesson in thy silent face:
Knowledge enormous makes a God of me.
Names, deeds, grey legends, dire events, rebellions,
Majesties, sovran voices, agonies,
Creations and destroyings, all at once
Pour into the wide hollows of my brain,
And deify me, as if some blithe wine
Or bright elixir peerless I had drunk,
And so become immortal.' – Thus the God,   120
While his enkindlèd eyes, with level glance
Beneath his white soft temples, steadfast kept
Trembling with light upon Mnemosyne.
Soon wild commotions shook him, and made flush
All the immortal fairness of his limbs –
Most like the struggle at the gate of death;
Or liker still to one who should take leave
Of pale immortal death, and with a pang
As hot as death's is chill, with fierce convulse
Die into life: so young Apollo anguished.   130

His very hair, his golden tresses famed
Kept undulation round his eager neck.
During the pain Mnemosyne upheld
Her arms as one who prophesied. – At length
Apollo shrieked – and lo! From all his limbs
Celestial . . .

(Published against Keats's wishes)

'Hush, hush! tread softly! hush, hush my dear!'

I

Hush, hush! tread softly! hush, hush my dear!
  All the house is asleep, but we know very well
That the jealous, the jealous old bald-pate may hear,
    Though you've padded his night-cap – O sweet Isabel!
     Though your feet are more light than a faery's feet,
     Who dances on bubbles where brooklets meet –
Hush, hush! tread softly! hush, hush my dear!
For less than a nothing the jealous can hear.

II

No leaf doth tremble, no ripple is there
10   On the river – all's still, and the night's sleepy eye
Closes up, and forgets all its Lethean care,
    Charmed to death by the drone of the humming
         mayfly;
     And the moon, whether prudish or complaisant,
     Hath fled to her bower, well knowing I want
No light in the darkness, no torch in the gloom,
But my Isabel's eyes, and her lips pulped with bloom.

III

Lift the latch! Ah gently! Ah tenderly – sweet!
  We are dead if that latchet gives one little clink!
Well done – now those lips, and a flowery seat –
    The old man may dream, and the planets may
20   wink;

The shut rose may dream of our loves, and awake
Full-blown, and such warmth for the morning take,
The stock-dove shall hatch her soft brace and shall coo,
While I kiss to the melody, aching all through!

(Not published by Keats)

The Eve of St Agnes

I

St Agnes' Eve – Ah, bitter chill it was!
The owl, for all his feathers, was a-cold;
The hare limped trembling through the frozen grass,
And silent was the flock in woolly fold:
Numb were the Beadsman's fingers, while he told
His rosary, and while his frosted breath,
Like pious incense from a censer old,
Seemed taking flight for heaven, without a death,
Past the sweet Virgin's picture, while his prayer he
        saith.

II

His prayer he saith, this patient, holy man;   10
Then takes his lamp, and riseth from his knees,
And back returneth, meagre, barefoot, wan,
Along the chapel aisle by slow degrees:
The sculptured dead, on each side, seem to freeze,
Emprisoned in black, purgatorial rails;
Knights, ladies, praying in dumb orat'ries,
He passeth by; and his weak spirit fails
To think how they may ache in icy hoods and mails.

III

Northward he turneth through a little door,
And scarce three steps, ere Music's golden tongue   20
Flattered to tears this agèd man and poor;
But no – already had his deathbell rung:

The joys of all his life were said and sung:
His was harsh penance on St Agnes' Eve.
Another way he went, and soon among
    Rough ashes sat he for his soul's reprieve,
And all night kept awake, for sinners' sake to grieve.

IV

That ancient Beadsman heard the prelude soft;
And so it chanced, for many a door was wide,
From hurry to and fro. Soon, up aloft,
The silver, snarling trumpets 'gan to chide:
The level chambers, ready with their pride,
Were glowing to receive a thousand guests:
    The carvèd angels, ever eager-eyed,
    Stared, where upon their heads the cornice rests,
With hair blown back, and wings put cross-wise on their
        breasts.

V

At length burst in the argent revelry,
With plume, tiara, and all rich array,
Numerous as shadows haunting faerily
The brain, new-stuffed, in youth, with triumphs gay
Of old romance. These let us wish away,
And turn, sole-thoughted, to one Lady there,
    Whose heart had brooded, all that wintry day,
    On love, and winged St Agnes' saintly care,
As she had heard old dames full many times declare.

VI

They told her how, upon St Agnes' Eve,
Young virgins might have visions of delight,
And soft adorings from their loves receive
Upon the honeyed middle of the night,

If ceremonies due they did aright;   50
As, supperless to bed they must retire,
And couch supine their beauties, lily white;
Nor look behind, nor sideways, but require
Of Heaven with upward eyes for all that they desire.

VII

Full of this whim was thoughtful Madeline:
The music, yearning like a God in pain,
She scarcely heard: her maiden eyes divine,
Fixed on the floor, saw many a sweeping train
Pass by – she heeded not at all: in vain
Came many a tip-toe, amorous cavalier,   60
And back retired – not cooled by high disdain,
But she saw not: her heart was otherwhere.
She sighed for Agnes' dreams, the sweetest of the
      year.

VIII

She danced along with vague, regardless eyes,
Anxious her lips, her breathing quick and short:
The hallowed hour was near at hand: she sighs
Amid the timbrels, and the thronged resort
Of whisperers in anger, or in sport;
'Mid looks of love, defiance, hate, and scorn,
Hoodwinked with faery fancy – all amort,   70
Save to St Agnes and her lambs unshorn,
And all the bliss to be before to-morrow morn.

IX

So, purposing each moment to retire,
She lingered still. Meantime, across the moors,
Had come young Porphyro, with heart on fire
For Madeline. Beside the portal doors,

Buttressed from moonlight, stands he, and implores
All saints to give him sight of Madeline
But for one moment in the tedious hours,
80   That he might gaze and worship all unseen;
Perchance speak, kneel, touch, kiss – in sooth such
      things have been.

X

He ventures in – let no buzzed whisper tell,
All eyes be muffled, or a hundred swords
Will storm his heart, Love's fev'rous citadel:
For him, those chambers held barbarian hordes,
Hyena foemen, and hot-blooded lords,
Whose very dogs would execrations howl
Against his lineage: not one breast affords
Him any mercy, in that mansion foul,
90   Save one old beldame, weak in body and in soul.

XI

Ah, happy chance! the agèd creature came,
Shuffling along with ivory-headed wand,
To where he stood, hid from the torch's flame,
Behind a broad hall-pillar, far beyond
The sound of merriment and chorus bland:
He startled her; but soon she knew his face,
And grasped his fingers in her palsied hand,
Saying, 'Mercy, Porphyro! hie thee from this place:
They are all here to-night, the whole blood-thirsty race!

XII

100   'Get hence! get hence! there's dwarfish Hildebrand –
He had a fever late, and in the fit
He cursèd thee and thine, both house and land:
Then there's that old Lord Maurice, not a whit
More tame for his grey hairs – Alas me! flit!

Flit like a ghost away.' 'Ah, gossip dear,
We're safe enough; here in this arm-chair sit,
And tell me how –' 'Good Saints! not here, not here;
Follow me, child, or else these stones will be thy bier.'

XIII

He followed through a lowly archèd way,
Brushing the cobwebs with his lofty plume,   110
And as she muttered, 'Well-a – well-a-day!'
He found him in a little moonlight room,
Pale, latticed, chill, and silent as a tomb.
'Now tell me where is Madeline,' said he,
'O tell me, Angela, by the holy loom
Which none but secret sisterhood may see,
When they St Agnes' wool are weaving piously.'

XIV

'St Agnes? Ah! it is St Agnes' Eve –
Yet men will murder upon holy days:
Thou must hold water in a witch's sieve,   120
And be liege-lord of all the Elves and Fays,
To venture so: it fills me with amaze
To see thee, Porphyro! – St Agnes' Eve!
God's help! my lady fair the conjuror plays
This very night. Good angels her deceive!
But let me laugh awhile, I've mickle time to grieve.'

XV

Feebly she laugheth in the languid moon,
While Porphyro upon her face doth look,
Like puzzled urchin on an agèd crone
Who keepeth closed a wondrous riddle-book,   130
As spectacled she sits in chimney nook.
But soon his eyes grew brilliant, when she told
His lady's purpose; and he scarce could brook
Tears, at the thought of those enchantments cold,
And Madeline asleep in lap of legends old.

XVI

Sudden a thought came like a full-blown rose,
Flushing his brow, and in his painèd heart
Made purple riot; then doth he propose
A stratagem, that makes the beldame start:
140   'A cruel man and impious thou art:
Sweet lady, let her pray, and sleep, and dream
Alone with her good angels, far apart
From wicked men like thee. Go, go! – I deem
Thou canst not surely be the same that thou didst seem.'

XVII

'I will not harm her, by all saints I swear,'
Quoth Porphyro: 'O may I ne'er find grace
When my weak voice shall whisper its last prayer,
If one of her soft ringlets I displace,
Or look with ruffian passion in her face:
150   Good Angela, believe me by these tears,
Or I will, even in a moment's space,
Awake, with horrid shout, my foeman's ears,
And beard them, though they be more fanged than
      wolves and bears.'

XVIII

'Ah! why wilt thou affright a feeble soul?
A poor, weak, palsy-stricken, churchyard thing,
Whose passing-bell may ere the midnight toll;
Whose prayers for thee, each morn and evening,
Were never missed.' – Thus plaining, doth she bring
A gentler speech from burning Porphyro,
160   So woeful, and of such deep sorrowing,
That Angela gives promise she will do
Whatever he shall wish, betide her weal or woe.

XIX

Which was, to lead him, in close secrecy,
Even to Madeline's chamber, and there hide
Him in a closet, of such privacy
That he might see her beauty unespied,
And win perhaps that night a peerless bride,
While legioned faeries paced the coverlet,
And pale enchantment held her sleepy-eyed.
Never on such a night have lovers met,   170
Since Merlin paid his Demon all the monstrous debt.

XX

'It shall be as thou wishest,' said the Dame:
'All cates and dainties shall be storèd there
Quickly on this feast-night; by the tambour frame
Her own lute thou wilt see. No time to spare,
For I am slow and feeble, and scarce dare
On such a catering trust my dizzy head.
Wait here, my child, with patience; kneel in prayer
The while. Ah! thou must needs the lady wed,
Or may I never leave my grave among the dead.'   180

XXI

So saying, she hobbled off with busy fear.
The lover's endless minutes slowly passed;
The dame returned, and whispered in his ear
To follow her; with agèd eyes aghast
From fright of dim espial. Safe at last,
Through many a dusky gallery, they gain
The maiden's chamber, silken, hushed, and chaste;
Where Porphyro took covert, pleased amain.
His poor guide hurried back with agues in her brain.

XXII

Her faltering hand upon the balustrade,   190
Old Angela was feeling for the stair,
When Madeline, St Agnes' charmèd maid,
Rose, like a missioned spirit, unaware:

With silver taper's light, and pious care,
She turned, and down the agèd gossip led
To a safe level matting. Now prepare,
Young Porphyro, for gazing on that bed –
She comes, she comes again, like ring-dove frayed and
        fled.

XXIII

Out went the taper as she hurried in;
Its little smoke, in pallid moonshine, died:
She closed the door, she panted, all akin
To spirits of the air, and visions wide –
No uttered syllable, or, woe betide!
But to her heart, her heart was voluble,
Paining with eloquence her balmy side;
As though a tongueless nightingale should swell
Her throat in vain, and die, heart-stiflèd, in her dell.

XXIV

A casement high and triple-arched there was,
All garlanded with carven imag'ries
Of fruits, and flowers, and bunches of knot-grass,
And diamonded with panes of quaint device,
Innumerable of stains and splendid dyes,
As are the tiger-moth's deep-damasked wings;
And in the midst, 'mong thousand heraldries,
And twilight saints, and dim emblazonings,
A shielded scutcheon blushed with blood of queens and
        kings.

XXV

Full on this casement shone the wintry moon,
And threw warm gules on Madeline's fair breast,
As down she knelt for heaven's grace and boon;
Rose-bloom fell on her hands, together pressed,

200

210

220

And on her silver cross soft amethyst,
And on her hair a glory, like a saint:
She seemed a splendid angel, newly dressed,
Save wings, for Heaven – Porphyro grew faint;
She knelt, so pure a thing, so free from mortal taint.

XXVI

Anon his heart revives; her vespers done,
Of all its wreathèd pearls her hair she frees;
Unclasps her warmèd jewels one by one;
Loosens her fragrant bodice; by degrees
Her rich attire creeps rustling to her knees: 230
Half-hidden, like a mermaid in sea-weed,
Pensive awhile she dreams awake, and sees,
In fancy, fair St Agnes in her bed,
But dares not look behind, or all the charm is fled.

XXVII

Soon, trembling in her soft and chilly nest,
In sort of wakeful swoon, perplexed she lay,
Until the poppied warmth of sleep oppressed
Her soothèd limbs, and soul fatigued away –
Flown, like a thought, until the morrow-day;
Blissfully havened both from joy and pain;   240
Clasped like a missal where swart Paynims pray;
Blinded alike from sunshine and from rain,
As though a rose should shut, and be a bud again.

XXVIII

Stolen to this paradise, and so entranced,
Porphyro gazed upon her empty dress,
And listened to her breathing, if it chanced
To wake into a slumbrous tenderness;
Which when he heard, that minute did he bless,

And breathed himself: then from the closet crept,
250   Noiseless as fear in a wide wilderness,
And over the hushed carpet, silent, stepped,
And 'tween the curtains peeped, where, lo! – how fast
    she slept.

XXIX

Then by the bed-side, where the faded moon
Made a dim, silver twilight, soft he set
A table, and, half anguished, threw thereon
A cloth of woven crimson, gold, and jet –
O for some drowsy Morphean amulet!
The boisterous, midnight, festive clarion,
The kettle-drum, and far-heard clarinet,
260   Affray his ears, though but in dying tone;
The hall door shuts again, and all the noise is gone.

XXX

And still she slept an azure-lidded sleep,
In blanchèd linen, smooth, and lavendered,
While he from forth the closet brought a heap
Of candied apple, quince, and plum, and gourd,
With jellies soother than the creamy curd,
And lucent syrups, tinct with cinnamon;
Manna and dates, in argosy transferred
From Fez; and spicèd dainties, every one,
270 From silken Samarkand to cedared Lebanon.

XXXI

These delicates he heaped with glowing hand
On golden dishes and in baskets bright
Of wreathèd silver; sumptuous they stand
In the retirèd quiet of the night,
Filling the chilly room with perfume light.
'And now, my love, my seraph fair, awake!
Thou art my heaven, and I thine eremite:
Open thine eyes, for meek St Agnes' sake,
Or I shall drowse beside thee, so my soul doth ache.'

XXXII

Thus whispering, his warm, unnervèd arm   280
Sank in her pillow. Shaded was her dream
By the dusk curtains – 'twas a midnight charm
Impossible to melt as icèd stream:
The lustrous salvers in the moonlight gleam;
Broad golden fringe upon the carpet lies.
It seemed he never, never could redeem
From such a steadfast spell his lady's eyes;
So mused awhile, entoiled in woofèd fantasies.

XXXIII

Awakening up, he took her hollow lute,
Tumultuous, and, in chords that tenderest be,   290
He played an ancient ditty, long since mute,
In Provence called, 'La belle dame sans mercy',
Close to her ear touching the melody –
Wherewith disturbed, she uttered a soft moan:
He ceased – she panted quick – and suddenly
Her blue affrayèd eyes wide open shone.
Upon his knees he sank, pale as smooth-sculptured
        stone.

XXXIV

Her eyes were open, but she still beheld,
Now wide awake, the vision of her sleep –
There was a painful change, that nigh expelled   300
The blisses of her dream so pure and deep.
At which fair Madeline began to weep,
And moan forth witless words with many a sigh,
While still her gaze on Porphyro would keep;
Who knelt, with joinèd hands and piteous eye,
Fearing to move or speak, she looked so dreamingly.

XXXV

'Ah, Porphyro!' said she, 'but even now
Thy voice was at sweet tremble in mine ear,
Made tuneable with every sweetest vow,
And those sad eyes were spiritual and clear:
How changed thou art! How pallid, chill, and drear!
Give me that voice again, my Porphyro,
Those looks immortal, those complainings dear!
O leave me not in this eternal woe,
For if thou diest, my Love, I know not where to go.'

XXXVI

Beyond a mortal man impassioned far
At these voluptuous accents, he arose,
Ethereal, flushed, and like a throbbing star
Seen mid the sapphire heaven's deep repose;
Into her dream he melted, as the rose
Blendeth its odour with the violet –
Solution sweet. Meantime the frost-wind blows
Like Love's alarum pattering the sharp sleet
Against the window-panes; St Agnes' moon hath set.

XXXVII

'Tis dark: quick pattereth the flaw-blown sleet.
'This is no dream, my bride, my Madeline!'
'Tis dark: the icèd gusts still rave and beat.
'No dream, alas! alas! and woe is mine!
Porphyro will leave me here to fade and pine. –
Cruel! what traitor could thee hither bring?
I curse not, for my heart is lost in thine,
Though thou forsakest a deceivèd thing –
A dove forlorn and lost with sick unprunèd wing.'

XXXVIII

'My Madeline! sweet dreamer! lovely bride!
Say, may I be for aye thy vassal blessed?
Thy beauty's shield, heart-shaped and vermeil dyed?
Ah, silver shrine, here will I take my rest

After so many hours of toil and quest,
A famished pilgrim – saved by miracle.
Though I have found, I will not rob thy nest   340
Saving of thy sweet self; if thou think'st well
To trust, fair Madeline, to no rude infidel.

XXXIX

'Hark! 'tis an elfin-storm from faery land,
Of haggard seeming, but a boon indeed:
Arise – arise! the morning is at hand.
The bloated wassaillers will never heed –
Let us away, my love, with happy speed –
There are no ears to hear, or eyes to see,
Drowned all in Rhenish and the sleepy mead;
Awake! arise! my love, and fearless be,   350
For o'er the southern moors I have a home for thee.'

XL

She hurried at his words, beset with fears,
For there were sleeping dragons all around,
At glaring watch, perhaps, with ready spears –
Down the wide stairs a darkling way they found.
In all the house was heard no human sound.
A chain-drooped lamp was flickering by each door;
The arras, rich with horseman, hawk, and hound,
Fluttered in the besieging wind's uproar;
And the long carpets rose along the gusty floor.   360

XLI

They glide, like phantoms, into the wide hall;
Like phantoms, to the iron porch, they glide;
Where lay the Porter, in uneasy sprawl,
With a huge empty flaggon by his side:
The wakeful bloodhound rose, and shook his hide,
But his sagacious eye an inmate owns.
By one, and one, the bolts full easy slide –
The chains lie silent on the footworn stones –
The key turns, and the door upon its hinges groans.

XLII

370   And they are gone – ay, ages long ago
        These lovers fled away into the storm.
        That night the Baron dreamt of many a woe,
        And all his warrior-guests, with shade and form
        Of witch, and demon, and large coffin-worm,
        Were long be-nightmared. Angela the old
        Died palsy-twitched, with meagre face deform;
        The Beadsman, after thousand aves told,
For aye unsought for slept among his ashes cold.

The Eve of St Mark

        Upon a Sabbath-day it fell;
        Twice holy was the Sabbath bell,
        That called the folk to evening prayer;
        The city streets were clean and fair
        From wholesome drench of April rains;
        And, on the western window panes,
        The chilly sunset faintly told
        Of unmatured green valleys cold,
        Of the green thorny bloomless hedge,
10   Of rivers new with spring-tide sedge,
        Of primroses by sheltered rills,
        And daisies on the aguish hills.
        Twice holy was the Sabbath bell:
        The silent streets were crowded well
        With staid and pious companies,
        Warm from their fireside orat'ries,
        And moving, with demurest air,
        To even-song, and vesper prayer.
        Each archèd porch, and entry low,
20   Was filled with patient folk and slow,
        With whispers hush, and shuffling feet,
        While played the organs loud and sweet.

The bells had ceased, the prayers begun,
And Bertha had not yet half done
A curious volume, patched and torn,
That all day long, from earliest morn,
Had taken captive her two eyes,
Among its golden broideries;
Perplexed her with a thousand things –
The stars of Heaven, and angels' wings,   30
Martyrs in a fiery blaze,
Azure saints 'mid silver rays,
Aaron's breastplate, and the seven
Candlesticks John saw in Heaven,
The wingèd Lion of Saint Mark,
And the Covenantal Ark,
With its many mysteries,
Cherubim and golden mice.

Bertha was a maiden fair,
Dwelling in the old Minster Square;   40
From her fireside she could see,
Sidelong, its rich antiquity,
Far as the Bishop's garden wall,
Where sycamores and elm trees tall,
Full-leaved, the forest had outstripped,
By no sharp north-wind ever nipped,
So sheltered by the mighty pile.
Bertha arose, and read awhile,
With forehead 'gainst the window-pane.
Again she tried, and then again,   50
Until the dusk eve left her dark
Upon the legend of St Mark.
From pleated lawn-frill, fine and thin,
She lifted up her soft warm chin,
With aching neck and swimming eyes,
And dazed with saintly imageries.

All was gloom, and silent all,
Save now and then the still foot-fall
Of one returning townwards late,
Past the echoing Minster gate.
The clamorous daws, that all the day
Above tree-tops and towers play,
Pair by pair had gone to rest,
Each in its ancient belfry-nest,
Where asleep they fall betimes,
To music of the drowsy chimes.

All was silent, all was gloom,
Abroad and in the homely room:
Down she sat, poor cheated soul!
And struck a lamp from the dismal coal,
Leaned forward, with bright drooping hair,
And slant book full against the glare.
Her shadow, in uneasy guise,
Hovered about, a giant size,
On ceiling beam and old oak chair,
The parrot's cage, and panel square;
And the warm angled winter screen,
On which were many monsters seen,
Called doves of Siam, Lima mice,
And legless birds of Paradise,
Macaw, and tender Av'davat,
And silken-furred Angora cat.
Untired she read, her shadow still
Glowered about, as it would fill
The room with wildest forms and shades,
As though some ghostly Queen of Spades
Had come to mock behind her back,
And dance, and ruffle her garments black.
Untired she read the legend page,
Of holy Mark, from youth to age,
On land, on sea, in pagan chains,
Rejoicing for his many pains.

Sometimes the learned eremite,
With golden star, or dagger bright,
Referred to pious poesies
Written in smallest crow-quill size
Beneath the text; and thus the rhyme
Was parcelled out from time to time:
'– Als writith he of swevenis
Men han beforne they wake in bliss,   100
Whanne that hir friendès thinke hem bound
In crimpid shroude farre under grounde;
And how a litling child mote be
A saint er its nativitie,
Gif that the modre (God her blesse!)
Kepen in solitarinesse,
And kissen devoute the holy croce.
Of Goddis love, and Sathan's force,
He writith; and thinges many mo:
Of swichè thinges I may not show.   110
Bot I must tellen verilie
Somdel of Saintè Cicilie,
And chieflie what he auctorith
Of Saintè Markis life and death.'

At length her constant eyelids come
Upon the fervent martyrdom;
Then lastly to his holy shrine,
Exalt amid the tapers' shine
At Venice . . .

                              (Not published by Keats)

'Why did I laugh tonight? No voice will tell'

Why did I laugh tonight? No voice will tell:
  No God, no Demon of severe response,
Deigns to reply from Heaven or from Hell.
  Then to my human heart I turn at once –

Heart! thou and I are here sad and alone;
    Say, wherefore did I laugh! O mortal pain!
O Darkness! Darkness! ever must I moan,
    To question Heaven and Hell and Heart in vain.
Why did I laugh? I know this being's lease –
10   My fancy to its utmost blisses spreads;
Yet could I on this very midnight cease,
    And the world's gaudy ensigns see in shreds.
Verse, Fame, and Beauty are intense indeed,
    But Death intenser – Death is Life's high meed.

                    (Not published by Keats)

Character of Charles Brown

I

He is to weet a melancholy carle:
Thin in the waist, with bushy head of hair,
As hath the seeded thistle when in parle
It holds the Zephyr, ere it sendeth fair
Its light balloons into the summer air;
Thereto his beard had not begun to bloom,
No brush had touched his chin or razor sheer;
No care had touched his cheek with mortal doom,
But new he was and bright as scarf from Persian loom.

II

10   Ne cared he for wine, or half-and-half,
Ne cared he for fish or flesh or fowl,
And sauces held he worthless as the chaff;
He 'sdained the swine-herd at the wassail-bowl,
Ne with lewd ribbalds sat he cheek by jowl,
Ne with sly Lemans in the scorner's chair,
But after water-brooks this Pilgrim's soul
Panted, and all his food was woodland air
Though he would oft-times feast on gillyflowers rare.

III

The slang of cities in no wise he knew,
Tipping the wink to him was heathen Greek.   20
He sipped no olden Tom or ruin blue,
Or Nantz or cheery-brandy drank full meek
By many a damsel hoarse and rouge of cheek.
Nor did he know each agèd watchman's beat,
Nor in obscurèd purlieus would he seek
For curlèd Jewesses, with ankles neat,
Who as they walk abroad make tinkling with their
    feet.

                                    (Not published by Keats)

A Dream, after reading Dante's Episode of Paolo and Francesca

As Hermes once took to his feathers light,
   When lullèd Argus, baffled, swooned and slept,
So on a Delphic reed, my idle spright
   So played, so charmed, so conquered, so bereft
The dragon-world of all its hundred eyes;
   And, seeing it asleep, so fled away –
Not to pure Ida with its snow-cold skies,
   Nor unto Tempe where Jove grieved that day;
But to that second circle of sad hell,
   Where in the gust, the whirlwind, and the flaw   10
Of rain and hail-stones, lovers need not tell
   Their sorrows. Pale were the sweet lips I saw,
Pale were the lips I kissed, and fair the form
I floated with, about that melancholy storm.

La Belle Dame sans Merci. A Ballad

I

O what can ail thee, knight-at-arms,
　　Alone and palely loitering?
The sedge has withered from the lake,
　　And no birds sing.

II

O what can ail thee, knight-at-arms,
　　So haggard and so woe-begone?
The squirrel's granary is full,
　　And the harvest's done.

III

I see a lily on thy brow,
10　　With anguish moist and fever-dew,
And on thy cheeks a fading rose
　　Fast withereth too.

IV

I met a lady in the meads,
　　Full beautiful – a faery's child,
Her hair was long, her foot was light,
　　And her eyes were wild.

V

I made a garland for her head,
　　And bracelets too, and fragrant zone;
She looked at me as she did love,
20　　And made sweet moan.

VI

I set her on my pacing steed,
　　And nothing else saw all day long,
For sidelong would she bend, and sing
　　A faery's song.

VII

She found me roots of relish sweet,
    And honey wild, and manna-dew,
And sure in language strange she said –
    'I love thee true'.

VIII

She took me to her elfin grot,
    And there she wept and sighed full sore,   30
And there I shut her wild wild eyes
    With kisses four.

IX

And there she lullèd me asleep
    And there I dreamed – Ah! woe betide! –
The latest dream I ever dreamt
    On the cold hill side.

X

I saw pale kings and princes too,
    Pale warriors, death-pale were they all;
They cried – 'La Belle Dame sans Merci
    Thee hath in thrall!'   40

XI

I saw their starved lips in the gloam,
    With horrid warning gapèd wide,
And I awoke and found me here,
    On the cold hill's side.

XII

And this is why I sojourn here
    Alone and palely loitering,
Though the sedge is withered from the lake,
    And no birds sing.

To Sleep

O soft embalmer of the still midnight,
    Shutting, with careful fingers and benign,
Our gloom-pleased eyes, embowered from the light,
    Enshaded in forgetfulness divine:
O soothest Sleep! if so it please thee, close
    In midst of this thine hymn, my willing eyes,
Or wait the 'Amen', ere thy poppy throws
    Around my bed its lulling charities.
Then save me, or the passèd day will shine
Upon my pillow, breeding many woes;
    Save me from curious conscience, that still hoards
Its strength for darkness, burrowing like the mole;
    Turn the key deftly in the oilèd wards,
And seal the hushèd casket of my soul.

                                  (Not published by Keats)

'If by dull rhymes our English must be chained'

If by dull rhymes our English must be chained,
And, like Andromeda, the Sonnet sweet
Fettered, in spite of painèd loveliness,
Let us find out, if we must be constrained,
Sandals more interwoven and complete
To fit the naked foot of Poesy:
Let us inspect the lyre, and weigh the stress
Of every chord, and see what may be gained
By ear industrious, and attention meet;
Misers of sound and syllable, no less
Than Midas of his coinage, let us be
Jealous of dead leaves in the bay wreath crown;
So, if we may not let the Muse be free,
She will be bound with garlands of her own.

                                  (Not published by Keats)

Ode to Psyche

O Goddess! hear these tuneless numbers, wrung
  By sweet enforcement and remembrance dear,
And pardon that thy secrets should be sung
  Even into thine own soft-conchèd ear:
Surely I dreamt to-day, or did I see
  The wingèd Psyche with awakened eyes?
I wandered in a forest thoughtlessly,
  And, on the sudden, fainting with surprise,
Saw two fair creatures, couchèd side by side
  In deepest grass, beneath the whispering roof   10
  Of leaves and tremblèd blossoms, where there ran
    A brooklet, scarce espied:
'Mid hushed, cool-rooted flowers, fragrant-eyed,
  Blue, silver-white, and budded Tyrian,
They lay calm-breathing on the bedded grass;
  Their arms embraced, and their pinions too:
  Their lips touched not, but had not bade adieu,
As if disjoined by soft-handed slumber,
And ready still past kisses to outnumber
  At tender eye-dawn of aurorean love: 20
    The wingèd boy I knew;
  But who wast thou, O happy, happy dove?
    His Psyche true!

O latest born and loveliest vision far
  Of all Olympus' faded hierarchy!
Fairer than Phoebe's sapphire-regioned star,
  Or Vesper, amorous glow-worm of the sky;
Fairer than these, though temple thou hast none,
  Nor altar heaped with flowers;
Nor virgin-choir to make delicious moan   30
  Upon the midnight hours;

No voice, no lute, no pipe, no incense sweet
    From chain-swung censer teeming;
No shrine, no grove, no oracle, no heat
    Of pale-mouthed prophet dreaming.

O brightest! though too late for antique vows,
    Too, too late for the fond believing lyre,
When holy were the haunted forest boughs,
    Holy the air, the water, and the fire;
40 Yet even in these days so far retired
    From happy pieties, thy lucent fans,
    Fluttering among the faint Olympians,
I see, and sing, by my own eyes inspired.
So let me be thy choir, and make a moan
        Upon the midnight hours;
Thy voice, thy lute, thy pipe, thy incense sweet
    From swingèd censer teeming –
Thy shrine, thy grove, thy oracle, thy heat
    Of pale-mouthed prophet dreaming.

50 Yes, I will be thy priest, and build a fane
    In some untrodden region of my mind,
Where branchèd thoughts, new grown with pleasant
        pain,
    Instead of pines shall murmur in the wind:
Far, far around shall those dark-clustered trees
    Fledge the wild-ridgèd mountains steep by steep;
And there by zephyrs, streams, and birds, and bees,
    The moss-lain Dryads shall be lulled to sleep;
And in the midst of this wide quietness
A rosy sanctuary will I dress
60 With the wreathed trellis of a working brain,
    With buds, and bells, and stars without a name,
With all the gardener Fancy e'er could feign,
    Who breeding flowers, will never breed the same:

And there shall be for thee all soft delight
   That shadowy thought can win,
A bright torch, and a casement ope at night,
   To let the warm Love in!

On Fame (I)

Fame, like a wayward girl, will still be coy
   To those who woo her with too slavish knees,
But makes surrender to some thoughtless boy,
   And dotes the more upon a heart at ease;
She is gipsy, will not speak to those
   Who have not learnt to be content without her;
A jilt, whose ear was never whispered close,
   Who thinks they scandal her who talk about her –
A very gipsy is she, Nilus-born,
   Sister-in-law to jealous Potiphar.   10
Ye love-sick bards! repay her scorn for scorn;
   Ye artists lovelorn! madmen that ye are,
Make your best bow to her and bid adieu
Then, if she likes it, she will follow you.

                                        (Not published by Keats)

On Fame (II)

   'You cannot eat your cake and have it too.'
                                        Proverb

How fevered is the man who cannot look
   Upon his mortal days with temperate blood,
Who vexes all the leaves of his life's book,
   And robs his fair name of its maidenhood;
It is as if the rose should pluck herself,
   Or the ripe plum finger its misty bloom,

As if a Naiad, like a meddling elf,
Should darken her pure grot with muddy gloom:
But the rose leaves herself upon the briar,
For winds to kiss and grateful bees to feed,
And the ripe plum still wears its dim attire,
The undisturbèd lake has crystal space;
Why then should man, teasing the world for grace,
Spoil his salvation for a fierce miscreed?

(Not published by Keats)

'Two or three posies'

Two or three posies
With two or three simples –
Two or three noses
With two or three pimples –
Two or three wise men
And two or three ninnies –
Two or three purses
And two or three guineas –
Two or three raps
At two or three doors –
Two or three naps
Of two or three hours –
Two or three cats
And two or three mice –
Two or three sprats
At a very great price –
Two or three sandies
And two or three tabbies –
Two or three dandies
And two Mrs – mum!
Two or three smiles
And two or three frowns –
Two or three miles
To two or three towns –

Two or three pegs
For two or three bonnets –
Two or three dove's eggs
To hatch into sonnets.
(Not published by Keats)

Ode on a Grecian Urn

I

Thou still unravished bride of quietness,
    Thou foster-child of silence and slow time,
Sylvan historian, who canst thus express
    A flowery tale more sweetly than our rhyme:
What leaf-fringed legend haunts about thy shape
    Of deities or mortals, or of both,
        In Tempe or the dales of Arcady?
    What men or gods are these? What maidens loth?
What mad pursuit? What struggle to escape?
        What pipes and timbrels? What wild ecstasy?   10

II

Heard melodies are sweet, but those unheard
    Are sweeter; therefore, ye soft pipes, play on;
Not to the sensual ear, but, more endeared,
    Pipe to the spirit ditties of no tone:
Fair youth, beneath the trees, thou canst not leave
    Thy song, nor ever can those trees be bare;
        Bold Lover, never, never canst thou kiss,
Though winning near the goal – yet, do not grieve:
    She cannot fade, though thou hast not thy bliss,
        For ever wilt thou love, and she be fair!   20

III

Ah, happy, happy boughs! that cannot shed
   Your leaves, nor ever bid the Spring adieu;
And, happy melodist, unwearièd,
   For ever piping songs for ever new;
More happy love! more happy, happy love!
   For ever warm and still to be enjoyed,
     For ever panting, and for ever young –
All breathing human passion far above,
   That leaves a heart high-sorrowful and cloyed,
30   A burning forehead, and a parching tongue.

IV

Who are these coming to the sacrifice?
   To what green altar, O mysterious priest,
Lead'st thou that heifer lowing at the skies,
   And all her silken flanks with garlands dressed?
What little town by river or sea shore,
   Or mountain-built with peaceful citadel,
     Is emptied of this folk, this pious morn?
And, little town, thy streets for evermore
   Will silent be; and not a soul to tell
40   Why thou art desolate, can e'er return.

V

O Attic shape! Fair attitude! with brede
   Of marble men and maidens overwrought,
With forest branches and the trodden weed;
   Thou, silent form, dost tease us out of thought
As doth eternity: Cold Pastoral!
   When old age shall this generation waste,
     Thou shalt remain, in midst of other woe
Than ours, a friend to man, to whom thou say'st,
   'Beauty is truth, truth beauty, – that is all
50   Ye know on earth, and all ye need to know.'

Ode to a Nightingale

I

My heart aches, and a drowsy numbness pains
  My sense, as though of hemlock I had drunk,
Or emptied some dull opiate to the drains
  One minute past, and Lethe-wards had sunk:
'Tis not through envy of thy happy lot,
  But being too happy in thine happiness –
    That thou, light-wingèd Dryad of the trees,
      In some melodious plot
  Of beechen green, and shadows numberless,
    Singest of summer in full-throated ease.   10

II

O, for a draught of vintage! that hath been
  Cooled a long age in the deep-delvèd earth,
Tasting of Flora and the country green,
  Dance, and Provençal song, and sunburnt mirth!
O for a beaker full of the warm South,
  Full of the true, the blushful Hippocrene,
    With beaded bubbles winking at the brim,
      And purple-stainèd mouth,
  That I might drink, and leave the world unseen,
    And with thee fade away into the forest dim –   20

III

Fade far away, dissolve, and quite forget
  What thou among the leaves hast never known,
The weariness, the fever, and the fret
  Here, where men sit and hear each other groan;
Where palsy shakes a few, sad, last grey hairs,
  Where youth grows pale, and spectre-thin, and dies;
    Where but to think is to be full of sorrow
      And leaden-eyed despairs;
  Where Beauty cannot keep her lustrous eyes,
    Or new Love pine at them beyond to-morrow.   30

IV

Away! away! for I will fly to thee,
  Not charioted by Bacchus and his pards,
But on the viewless wings of Poesy,
  Though the dull brain perplexes and retards.
Already with thee! tender is the night,
    And haply the Queen-Moon is on her throne,
      Clustered around by all her starry Fays;
        But here there is no light,
    Save what from heaven is with the breezes blown
      Through verdurous glooms and winding mossy
40   ways.

V

I cannot see what flowers are at my feet,
  Nor what soft incense hangs upon the boughs,
But, in embalmèd darkness, guess each sweet
  Wherewith the seasonable month endows
The grass, the thicket, and the fruit-tree wild –
    White hawthorn, and the pastoral eglantine;
      Fast fading violets covered up in leaves;
        And mid-May's eldest child,
    The coming musk-rose, full of dewy wine,
50   The murmurous haunt of flies on summer eves.

VI

Darkling I listen; and, for many a time
  I have been half in love with easeful Death,
Called him soft names in many a musèd rhyme,
  To take into the air my quiet breath;
Now more than ever seems it rich to die,
    To cease upon the midnight with no pain,
      While thou art pouring forth thy soul abroad
        In such an ecstasy!
    Still wouldst thou sing, and I have ears in vain –
60   To thy high requiem become a sod.

VII

Thou wast not born for death, immortal Bird!
  No hungry generations tread thee down;
The voice I hear this passing night was heard
  In ancient days by emperor and clown:
Perhaps the self-same song that found a path
    Through the sad heart of Ruth, when, sick for home,
      She stood in tears amid the alien corn;
        The same that oft-times hath
      Charmed magic casements, opening on the foam
        Of perilous seas, in faery lands forlorn.   70

VIII

Forlorn! the very word is like a bell
  To toll me back from thee to my sole self!
Adieu! the fancy cannot cheat so well
  As she is famed to do, deceiving elf.
Adieu! adieu! thy plaintive anthem fades
    Past the near meadows, over the still stream,
      Up the hill-side; and now 'tis buried deep
        In the next valley-glades:
      Was it a vision, or a waking dream?
        Fled is that music – Do I wake or sleep?   80

Ode on Melancholy

I

No, no, go not to Lethe, neither twist
  Wolf's-bane, tight-rooted, for its poisonous wine:
Nor suffer thy pale forehead to be kissed
  By nightshade, ruby grape of Proserpine;
Make not your rosary of yew-berries,
    Nor let the beetle, nor the death-moth be
      Your mournful Psyche, nor the downy owl
A partner in your sorrow's mysteries;
    For shade to shade will come too drowsily,
      And drown the wakeful anguish of the soul.   10

II

But when the melancholy fit shall fall
   Sudden from heaven like a weeping cloud,
That fosters the droop-headed flowers all,
   And hides the green hill in an April shroud;
Then glut thy sorrow on a morning rose,
    Or on the rainbow of the salt sand-wave,
     Or on the wealth of globèd peonies;
Or if thy mistress some rich anger shows,
    Emprison her soft hand, and let her rave,
20   And feed deep, deep upon her peerless eyes.

III

She dwells with Beauty – Beauty that must die;
   And Joy, whose hand is ever at his lips
Bidding adieu; and aching Pleasure nigh,
   Turning to poison while the bee-mouth sips:
Ay, in the very temple of Delight
   Veiled Melancholy has her sovran shrine,
    Though seen of none save him whose strenuous
      tongue
  Can burst Joy's grape against his palate fine;
His soul shall taste the sadness of her might,
30   And be among her cloudy trophies hung.

Ode on Indolence

'They toil not, neither do they spin.'

I

One morn before me were three figures seen,
   With bowèd necks, and joinèd hands, side-faced;
And one behind the other stepped serene,
   In placid sandals, and in white robes graced;
They passed, like figures on a marble urn,

When shifted round to see the other side;
    They came again; as when the urn once more
Is shifted round, the first seen shades return;
    And they were strange to me, as may betide
      With vases, to one deep in Phidian lore.   10

II

How is it, Shadows! that I knew ye not?
    How came ye muffled in so hush a masque?
Was it a silent deep-disguisèd plot
    To steal away, and leave without a task
My idle days? Ripe was the drowsy hour;
    The blissful cloud of summer-indolence
      Benumbed my eyes; my pulse grew less and less;
Pain had no sting, and pleasure's wreath no flower:
    O, why did ye not melt, and leave my sense
      Unhaunted quite of all but – nothingness?   20

III

A third time passed they by, and, passing, turned
    Each one the face a moment whiles to me;
Then faded, and to follow them I burned
    And ached for wings because I knew the three;
The first was a fair Maid, and Love her name;
    The second was Ambition, pale of cheek,
      And ever watchful with fatiguèd eye;
The last, whom I love more, the more of blame
    Is heaped upon her, maiden most unmeek –
      I knew to be my demon Poesy.   30

IV

They faded, and, forsooth! I wanted wings.
    O folly! What is love! and where is it?
And, for that poor Ambition – it springs
    From a man's little heart's short fever-fit.

For Poesy! – no, she has not a joy –
   At least for me – so sweet as drowsy noons,
     And evenings steeped in honeyed indolence.
O, for an age so sheltered from annoy,
   That I may never know how change the moons,
40   Or hear the voice of busy common-sense!

V

A third time came they by – alas! wherefore?
   My sleep had been embroidered with dim dreams:
My soul had been a lawn besprinkled o'er
   With flowers, and stirring shades, and baffled
       beams:
The morn was clouded, but no shower fell,
   Though in her lids hung the sweet tears of May;
     The open casement pressed a new-leaved vine,
   Let in the budding warmth and throstle's lay;
O Shadows! 'twas a time to bid farewell!
50   Upon your skirts had fallen no tears of mine.

VI

So, ye three Ghosts, adieu! Ye cannot raise
   My head cool-bedded in the flowery grass;
For I would not be dieted with praise,
   A pet-lamb in a sentimental farce!
Fade softly from my eyes, and be once more
   In masque-like figures on the dreamy urn.
     Farewell! I yet have visions for the night,
And for the day faint visions there is store.
     Vanish, ye Phantoms! from my idle sprite,
60   Into the clouds, and never more return!

(Not published by Keats)

Lamia

PART I

Upon a time, before the faery broods
Drove Nymph and Satyr from the prosperous woods,
Before King Oberon's bright diadem,
Sceptre, and mantle, clasped with dewy gem,
Frighted away the Dryads and the Fauns
From rushes green, and brakes, and cowslipped lawns,
The ever-smitten Hermes empty left
His golden throne, bent warm on amorous theft:
From high Olympus had he stolen light,
On this side of Jove's clouds, to escape the sight   10
Of his great summoner, and made retreat
Into a forest on the shores of Crete.
For somewhere in that sacred island dwelt
A nymph, to whom all hoofèd Satyrs knelt;
At whose white feet the languid Tritons poured
Pearls, while on land they withered and adored.
Fast by the springs where she to bathe was wont,
And in those meads where sometime she might haunt,
Were strewn rich gifts, unknown to any Muse,
Though Fancy's casket were unlocked to choose.   20
Ah, what a world of love was at her feet!
So Hermes thought, and a celestial heat
Burnt from his wingèd heels to either ear,
That from a whiteness, as the lily clear,
Blushed into roses 'mid his golden hair,
Fallen in jealous curls about his shoulders bare.

    From vale to vale, from wood to wood, he flew,
Breathing upon the flowers his passion new,
And wound with many a river to its head
To find where this sweet nymph prepared her secret
        bed.   30

In vain; the sweet nymph might nowhere be found,
And so he rested, on the lonely ground,
Pensive, and full of painful jealousies
Of the Wood-Gods, and even the very trees.
There as he stood, he heard a mournful voice,
Such as, once heard, in gentle heart destroys
All pain but pity; thus the lone voice spake:
'When from this wreathèd tomb shall I awake!
When move in a sweet body fit for life,
40   And love, and pleasure, and the ruddy strife
Of hearts and lips! Ah, miserable me!'
The God, dove-footed, glided silently
Round bush and tree, soft-brushing, in his speed,
The taller grasses and full-flowering weed,
Until he found a palpitating snake,
Bright, and cirque-couchant in a dusky brake.

   She was a gordian shape of dazzling hue,
Vermilion-spotted, golden, green, and blue;
Striped like a zebra, freckled like a pard,
50   Eyed like a peacock, and all crimson barred;
And full of silver moons, that, as she breathed,
Dissolved, or brighter shone, or interwreathed
Their lustres with the gloomier tapestries –
So rainbow-sided, touched with miseries,
She seemed, at once, some penanced lady elf,
Some demon's mistress, or the demon's self.
Upon her crest she wore a wannish fire
Sprinkled with stars, like Ariadne's tiar;
Her head was serpent, but ah, bitter-sweet!
60   She had a woman's mouth with all its pearls complete;
And for her eyes – what could such eyes do there
But weep, and weep, that they were born so fair,
As Proserpine still weeps for her Sicilian air?
Her throat was serpent, but the words she spake
Came, as through bubbling honey, for Love's sake,
And thus – while Hermes on his pinions lay,
Like a stooped falcon ere he takes his prey –

'Fair Hermes, crowned with feathers, fluttering light,
I had a splendid dream of thee last night:
I saw thee sitting, on a throne of gold,   70
Among the Gods, upon Olympus old,
The only sad one; for thou didst not hear
The soft, lute-fingered Muses chanting clear,
Nor even Apollo when he sang alone,
Deaf to his throbbing throat's long, long melodious
      moan.
I dreamt I saw thee, robed in purple flakes,
Break amorous through the clouds, as morning
      breaks,
And, swiftly as a bright Phoebean dart,
Strike for the Cretan isle; and here thou art!
Too gentle Hermes, hast thou found the maid?'   80
Whereat the star of Lethe not delayed
His rosy eloquence, and thus inquired:
'Thou smooth-lipped serpent, surely high inspired!
Thou beauteous wreath, with melancholy eyes,
Possess whatever bliss thou canst devise,
Telling me only where my nymph is fled –
Where she doth breathe!' 'Bright planet, thou hast
      said,'
Returned the snake, 'but seal with oaths, fair God!'
'I swear,' said Hermes, 'by my serpent rod,
And by thine eyes, and by thy starry crown!'   90
Light flew his earnest words, among the blossoms
      blown.
Then thus again the brilliance feminine:
'Too frail of heart! for this lost nymph of thine,
Free as the air, invisibly, she strays
About these thornless wilds; her pleasant days
She tastes unseen; unseen her nimble feet
Leave traces in the grass and flowers sweet;
From weary tendrils, and bowed branches green,
She plucks the fruit unseen, she bathes unseen;
And by my power is her beauty veiled   100
To keep it unaffronted, unassailed

By the love-glances of unlovely eyes
Of Satyrs, Fauns, and bleared Silenus' sighs.
Pale grew her immortality, for woe
Of all these lovers, and she grievèd so
I took compassion on her, bade her steep
Her hair in weïrd syrops, that would keep
Her loveliness invisible, yet free
To wander as she loves, in liberty.
110 Thou shalt behold her, Hermes, thou alone,
If thou wilt, as thou swearest, grant my boon!'
Then, once again, the charmèd God began
An oath, and through the serpent's ears it ran
Warm, tremulous, devout, psalterian.
Ravished, she lifted her Circean head,
Blushed a live damask, and swift-lisping said,
'I was a woman, let me have once more
A woman's shape, and charming as before.
I love a youth of Corinth – O the bliss!
120 Give me my woman's form, and place me where he is.
Stoop, Hermes, let me breathe upon thy brow,
And thou shalt see thy sweet nymph even now.'
The God on half-shut feathers sank serene,
She breathed upon his eyes, and swift was seen
Of both the guarded nymph near-smiling on the green.
It was no dream; or say a dream it was,
Real are the dreams of Gods, and smoothly pass
Their pleasures in a long immortal dream.
One warm, flushed moment, hovering, it might seem
130 Dashed by the wood-nymph's beauty, so he burned;
Then, lighting on the printless verdure, turned
To the swooned serpent, and with languid arm,
Delicate, put to proof the lithe Caducean charm.
So done, upon the nymph his eyes he bent
Full of adoring tears and blandishment,
And towards her stepped: she, like a moon in wane,
Faded before him, cowered, nor could restrain
Her fearful sobs, self-folding like a flower
That faints into itself at evening hour:

But the God fostering her chillèd hand,   140
She felt the warmth, her eyelids opened bland,
And, like new flowers at morning song of bees,
Bloomed, and gave up her honey to the lees.
Into the green-recessèd woods they flew;
Nor grew they pale, as mortal lovers do.

   Left to herself, the serpent now began
To change; her elfin blood in madness ran,
Her mouth foamed, and the grass, therewith
     besprent,
Withered at dew so sweet and virulent;
Her eyes in torture fixed, and anguish drear,   150
Hot, glazed, and wide, with lid-lashes all sear,
Flashed phosphor and sharp sparks, without one
     cooling tear.
The colours all inflamed throughout her train,
She writhed about, convulsed with scarlet pain:
A deep volcanian yellow took the place
Of all her milder-moonèd body's grace;
And, as the lava ravishes the mead,
Spoilt all her silver mail, and golden brede;
Made gloom of all her frecklings, streaks and bars,
Eclipsed her crescents, and licked up her stars.   160
So that, in moments few, she was undressed
Of all her sapphires, greens, and amethyst,
And rubious-argent; of all these bereft,
Nothing but pain and ugliness were left.
Still shone her crown; that vanished, also she
Melted and disappeared as suddenly;
And in the air, her new voice luting soft,
Cried, 'Lycius! gentle Lycius!' – Borne aloft
With the bright mists about the mountains hoar
These words dissolved: Crete's forests heard no
     more.   170

Whither fled Lamia, now a lady bright,
A full-born beauty new and exquisite?
She fled into that valley they pass o'er
Who go to Corinth from Cenchreas' shore;
And rested at the foot of those wild hills,
The rugged founts of the Peræan rills,
And of that other ridge whose barren back
Stretches, with all its mist and cloudy rack,
South-westward to Cleone. There she stood
180   About a young bird's flutter from a wood,
Fair, on a sloping green of mossy tread,
By a clear pool, wherein she passionèd
To see herself escaped from so sore ills,
While her robes flaunted with the daffodils.

Ah, happy Lycius! – for she was a maid
More beautiful than ever twisted braid,
Or sighed, or blushed, or on spring-flowered lea
Spread a green kirtle to the minstrelsy:
A virgin purest lipped, yet in the lore
190   Of love deep learnèd to the red heart's core;
Not one hour old, yet of sciential brain
To unperplex bliss from its neighbour pain,
Define their pettish limits, and estrange
Their points of contact, and swift counterchange;
Intrigue with the specious chaos, and dispart
Its most ambiguous atoms with sure art;
As though in Cupid's college she had spent
Sweet days a lovely graduate, still unshent,
And kept his rosy terms in idle languishment.

200   Why this fair creature chose so faerily
By the wayside to linger, we shall see;
But first 'tis fit to tell how she could muse
And dream, when in the serpent prison-house,
Of all she list, strange or magnificent:
How, ever, where she willed, her spirit went;

Whether to faint Elysium, or where
Down through tress-lifting waves the Nereids fair
Wind into Thetis' bower by many a pearly stair;
Or where God Bacchus drains his cups divine,
Stretched out, at ease, beneath a glutinous pine;   210
Or where in Pluto's gardens palatine
Mulciber's columns gleam in far piazzian line.
And sometimes into cities she would send
Her dream, with feast and rioting to blend;
And once, while among mortals dreaming thus,
She saw the young Corinthian Lycius
Charioting foremost in the envious race,
Like a young Jove with calm uneager face,
And fell into a swooning love of him.
Now on the moth-time of that evening dim   220
He would return that way, as well she knew,
To Corinth from the shore; for freshly blew
The eastern soft wind, and his galley now
Grated the quaystones with her brazen prow
In port Cenchreas, from Egina isle
Fresh anchored; whither he had been awhile
To sacrifice to Jove, whose temple there
Waits with high marble doors for blood and incense
        rare.
Jove heard his vows, and bettered his desire;
For by some freakful chance he made retire   230
From his companions, and set forth to walk,
Perhaps grown wearied of their Corinth talk:
Over the solitary hills he fared,
Thoughtless at first, but ere eve's star appeared
His fantasy was lost, where reason fades,
In the calmed twilight of Platonic shades.
Lamia beheld him coming, near, more near –
Close to her passing, in indifference drear,
His silent sandals swept the mossy green;
So neighboured to him, and yet so unseen   240
She stood: he passed, shut up in mysteries,
His mind wrapped like his mantle, while her eyes

Followed his steps, and her neck regal white
Turned – syllabling thus, 'Ah, Lycius bright,
And will you leave me on the hills alone?
Lycius, look back! and be some pity shown.'
He did – not with cold wonder fearingly,
But Orpheus-like at an Eurydice –
For so delicious were the words she sung,
250   It seemed he had loved them a whole summer long.
And soon his eyes had drunk her beauty up,
Leaving no drop in the bewildering cup,
And still the cup was full – while he, afraid
Lest she should vanish ere his lip had paid
Due adoration, thus began to adore
(Her soft look growing coy, she saw his chain so sure):
'Leave thee alone! Look back! Ah, Goddess, see
Whether my eyes can ever turn from thee!
For pity do not this sad heart belie –
260   Even as thou vanishest so I shall die.
Stay! though a Naiad of the rivers, stay!
To thy far wishes will thy streams obey.
Stay! though the greenest woods by thy domain,
Alone they can drink up the morning rain:
Though a descended Pleiad, will not one
Of thine harmonious sisters keep in tune
Thy spheres, and as thy silver proxy shine?
So sweetly to these ravished ears of mine
Came thy sweet greeting, that if thou shouldst fade
270   Thy memory will waste me to a shade –
For pity do not melt!' – 'If I should stay,'
Said Lamia, 'here, upon this floor of clay,
And pain my steps upon these flowers too rough,
What canst thou say or do of charm enough
To dull the nice remembrance of my home?
Thou canst not ask me with thee here to roam
Over these hills and vales, where no joy is –
Empty of immortality and bliss!
Thou art a scholar, Lycius, and must know
280   That finer spirits cannot breathe below

In human climes, and live. Alas! poor youth,
What taste of purer air hast thou to soothe
My essence? What serener palaces,
Where I may all my many senses please,
And by mysterious sleights a hundred thirsts appease?
It cannot be – Adieu!' So said, she rose
Tip-toe with white arms spread. He, sick to lose
The amorous promise of her lone complain,
Swooned, murmuring of love, and pale with pain.
The cruel lady, without any show   290
Of sorrow for her tender favourite's woe,
But rather, if her eyes could brighter be,
With brighter eyes and slow amenity,
Put her new lips to his, and gave afresh
The life she had so tangled in her mesh;
And as he from one trance was wakening
Into another, she began to sing,
Happy in beauty, life, and love, and every thing,
A song of love, too sweet for earthly lyres,
While, like held breath, the stars drew in their panting
      fires.   300
And then she whispered in such trembling tone,
As those who, safe together met alone
For the first time through many anguished days,
Use other speech than looks; bidding him raise
His drooping head, and clear his soul of doubt,
For that she was a woman, and without
Any more subtle fluid in her veins
Than throbbing blood, and that the self-same pains
Inhabited her frail-strung heart as his.
And next she wondered how his eyes could miss   310
Her face so long in Corinth, where, she said,
She dwelt but half retired, and there had led
Days happy as the gold coin could invent
Without the aid of love; yet in content
Till she saw him, as once she passed him by,
Where 'gainst a column he leant thoughtfully

At Venus' temple porch, 'mid baskets heaped
Of amorous herbs and flowers, newly reaped
Late on that eve, as 'twas the night before
320   The Adonian feast; where of she saw no more,
But wept alone those days, for why should she adore?
Lycius from death awoke into amaze,
To see her still, and singing so sweet lays;
Then from amaze into delight he fell
To hear her whisper woman's lore so well;
And every word she spake enticed him on
To unperplexed delight and pleasure known.
Let the mad poets say whate'er they please
Of the sweets of Faeries, Peris, Goddesses,
330   There is not such a treat among them all,
Haunters of cavern, lake, and waterfall,
As a real woman, lineal indeed
From Pyrrha's pebbles or old Adam's seed.
Thus gentle Lamia judged, and judged aright,
That Lycius could not love in half a fright,
So threw the goddess off, and won his heart
More pleasantly by playing woman's part,
With no more awe than what her beauty gave,
That, while it smote, still guaranteed to save.
340   Lycius to all made eloquent reply,
Marrying to every word a twinborn sigh;
And last, pointing to Corinth, asked her sweet,
If 'twas was too far that night for her soft feet.
The way was short, for Lamia's eagerness
Made, by a spell, the triple league decrease
To a few paces; not at all surmised
By blinded Lycius, so in her comprised.
They passed the city gates, he knew not how,
So noiseless, and he never thought to know.

350   As men talk in a dream, so Corinth all,
Throughout her palaces imperial,
And all her populous streets and temples lewd,
Muttered, like tempest in the distance brewed,

To the wide-spreaded night above her towers.
Men, women, rich and poor, in the cool hours,
Shuffled their sandals o'er the pavement white,
Companioned or alone; while many a light
Flared, here and there, from wealthy festivals,
And threw their moving shadows on the walls,
Or found them clustered in the corniced shade   360
Of some arched temple door, or dusky colonnade.

　　Muffling his face, of greeting friends in fear,
Her fingers he pressed hard, as one came near
With curled grey beard, sharp eyes, and smooth bald
　　crown,
Slow-stepped, and robed in philosophic gown:
Lycius shrank closer, as they met and passed,
Into his mantle, adding wings to haste,
While hurried Lamia trembled: 'Ah,' said he,
'Why do you shudder, love, so ruefully?
Why does your tender palm dissolve in dew?' –   370
'I'm wearied,' said fair Lamia, 'tell me who
Is that old man? I cannot bring to mind
His features – Lycius! wherefore did you blind
Yourself from his quick eyes?' Lycius replied,
''Tis Apollonius sage, my trusty guide
And good instructor; but tonight he seems
The ghost of folly haunting my sweet dreams.'

　　While yet he spake they had arrived before
A pillared porch, with lofty portal door,
Where hung a silver lamp, whose phosphor glow   380
Reflected in the slabbèd steps below,
Mild as a star in water; for so new,
And so unsullied was the marble hue,
So through the crystal polish, liquid fine,
Ran the dark veins, that none but feet divine
Could e'er have touched there. Sounds Aeolian
Breathed from the hinges, as the ample span

Of the wide doors disclosed a place unknown
Some time to any, but those two alone,
And a few Persian mutes, who that same year
Were seen about the markets: none knew where
They could inhabit; the most curious
Were foiled, who watched to trace them to their
            house.
And but the flitter-wingèd verse must tell,
For truth's sake, what woe afterwards befell,
'Twould humour many a heart to leave them thus,
Shut from the busy world, of more incredulous.

PART II

Love in a hut, with water and a crust,
Is – Love, forgive us! – cinder, ashes, dust;
Love in a palace is perhaps at last
More grievous torment than a hermit's fast.
That is a doubtful tale from faery land,
Hard for the non-elect to understand.
Had Lycius lived to hand his story down,
He might have given the moral a fresh frown,
Or clenched it quite: but too short was their bliss
To breed distrust and hate, that make the soft voice
            hiss.
Besides, there, nightly, with terrific glare,
Love, jealous grown of so complete a pair,
Hovered and buzzed his wings, with fearful roar,
Above the lintel of their chamber door,
And down the passage cast a glow upon the floor.

    For all this came a ruin: side by side
They were enthronèd, in the eventide,
Upon a couch, near to a curtaining
Whose airy texture, from a golden string,
Floated into the room, and let appear
Unveiled the summer heaven, blue and clear,

Betwixt two marble shafts. There they reposed,
Where use had made it sweet, with eyelids closed,
Saving a tithe which love still open kept,
That they might see each other while they almost slept;
When from the slope side of a suburb hill,
Deafening the swallow's twitter, came a thrill
Of trumpets – Lycius started – the sounds fled,
But left a thought, a buzzing in his head.
For the first time, since first he harboured in   30
That purple-linèd palace of sweet sin,
His spirit passed beyond its golden bourne
Into the noisy world almost forsworn.
The lady, ever watchful, penetrant,
Saw this with pain, so arguing a want
Of something more, more than her empery
Of joys; and she began to moan and sigh
Because he mused beyond her, knowing well
That but a moment's thought is passion's passing-bell.
'Why do you sigh, fair creature?' whispered he: 40
'Why do you think?' returned she tenderly,
'You have deserted me – where am I now?
Not in your heart while care weighs on your brow:
No, no, you have dismissed me; and I go
From your breast houseless – ay, it must be so.'
He answered, bending to her open eyes,
Where he was mirrored small in paradise,
'My silver planet, both of eve and morn!
Why will you plead yourself so sad forlorn,
While I am striving how to fill my heart   50
With deeper crimson, and a double smart?
How to entangle, trammel up and snare
Your soul in mine, and labyrinth you there
Like the hid scent in an unbudded rose?
Ay, a sweet kiss – you see your mighty woes.
My thoughts! shall I unveil them? Listen then!
What mortal hath a prize, that other men
May be confounded and abashed withal,
But lets it sometimes pace abroad majestical,

60 And triumph, as in thee I should rejoice
    Amid the hoarse alarm of Corinth's voice.
    Let my foes choke, and my friends shout afar,
    While through the throngèd streets your bridal car
    Wheels round its dazzling spokes.' – The lady's cheek
    Trembled; she nothing said, but, pale and meek,
    Arose and knelt before him, wept a rain
    Of sorrows at his words; at last with pain
    Beseeching him, the while his hand she wrung,
    To change his purpose. He thereat was stung,
70 Perverse, with stronger fancy to reclaim
    Her wild and timid nature to his aim:
    Besides, for all his love, in self-despite,
    Against his better self, he took delight
    Luxurious in her sorrows, soft and new.
    His passion, cruel grown, took on a hue
    Fierce and sanguineous as 'twas possible
    In one whose brow had no dark veins to swell.
    Fine was the mitigated fury, like
    Apollo's presence when in act to strike
80 The serpent – Ha, the serpent! Certes, she
    Was none. She burnt, she loved the tyranny,
    And, all subdued, consented to the hour
    When to the bridal he should lead his paramour.
    Whispering in midnight silence, said the youth,
    'Sure some sweet name thou hast, though, by my
                truth,
    I have not asked it, ever thinking thee
    Not mortal, but of heavenly progeny,
    As still I do. Hast any mortal name,
    Fit appellation for this dazzling frame?
90 Or friends or kinsfolk on the cited earth,
    To share our marriage feast and nuptial mirth?'
    'I have no friends,' said Lamia, 'no, not one;
    My presence in wide Corinth hardly known:
    My parents' bones are in their dusty urns
    Sepulchred, where no kindled incense burns,

Seeing all their luckless race are dead, save me,
And I neglect the holy rite for thee.
Even as you list invite your many guests;
But if, as now it seems, your vision rests
With any pleasure on me, do not bid   100
Old Apollonius – from him keep me hid.'
Lycius, perplexed at words so blind and blank,
Made close inquiry; from whose touch she shrank,
Feigning a sleep; and he to the dull shade
Of deep sleep in a moment was betrayed.

    It was the custom then to bring away
The bride from home at blushing shut of day,
Veiled, in a chariot, heralded along
By strewn flowers, torches, and a marriage song,
With other pageants: but this fair unknown   110
Had not a friend. So being left alone,
(Lycius was gone to summon all his kin)
And knowing surely she could never win
His foolish heart from its mad pompousness,
She set herself, high-thoughted, how to dress
The misery in fit magnificence.
She did so, but 'tis doubtful how and whence
Came, and who were her subtle servitors.
About the halls, and to and from the doors,
There was a noise of wings, till in short space   120
The glowing banquet-room shone with wide-archèd
        grace.
A haunting music, sole perhaps and lone
Supportress of the faery-roof, made moan
Throughout, as fearful the whole charm might fade.
Fresh carvèd cedar, mimicking a glade
Of palm and plantain, met from either side,
High in the midst, in honour of the bride;
Two palms and then two plantains, and so on,
From either side their stems branched one to one
All down the aislèd place; and beneath all   130
There ran a stream of lamps straight on from wall to wall.

So canopied, lay an untasted feast
Teeming with odours. Lamia, regal dressed,
Silently paced about, and as she went,
In pale contented sort of discontent,
Missioned her viewless servants to enrich
The fretted splendour of each nook and niche.
Between the tree-stems, marbled plain at first,
Came jasper panels; then anon, there burst
140 Forth creeping imagery of slighter trees,
And with the larger wove in small intricacies.
Approving all, she faded at self-will,
And shut the chamber up, close, hushed and still,
Complete and ready for the revels rude,
When dreadful guests would come to spoil her
          solitude.

The day appeared, and all the gossip rout.
O senseless Lycius! Madman! wherefore flout
The silent-blessing fate, warm cloistered hours,
And show to common eyes these secret bowers?
150 The herd approached; each guest, with busy brain,
Arriving at the portal, gazed amain,
And entered marvelling – for they knew the street,
Remembered it from childhood all complete
Without a gap, yet ne'er before had seen
That royal porch, that high-built fair demesne.
So in they hurried all, mazed, curious and keen –
Save one, who looked thereon with eye severe,
And with calm-planted steps walked in austere.
'Twas Apollonius: something too he laughed,
160 As though some knotty problem, that had daffed
His patient thought, had now begun to thaw,
And solve and melt – 'twas just as he foresaw.

He met within the murmurous vestibule
His young disciple. ' 'Tis no common rule,
Lycius,' said he, 'for uninvited guest
To force himself upon you, and infest

With an unbidden presence the bright throng
Of younger friends; yet must I do this wrong,
And you forgive me.' Lycius blushed, and led
The old man through the inner doors broad-
    spread;   170
With reconciling words and courteous mien
Turning into sweet milk the sophist's spleen.

Of wealthy lustre was the banquet-room,
Filled with pervading brilliance and perfume:
Before each lucid panel fuming stood
A censer fed with myrrh and spicèd wood,
Each by a sacred tripod held aloft,
Whose slender feet wide-swerved upon the soft
Wool-woofèd carpets; fifty wreaths of smoke
From fifty censers their light voyage took   180
To the high roof, still mimicked as they rose
Along the mirrored walls by twin-clouds odorous.
Twelve spherèd tables, by silk seats ensphered,
High as the level of a man's breast reared
On libbard's paws, upheld the heavy gold
Of cups and goblets, and the store thrice told
Of Ceres' horn, and in huge vessels, wine
Come from the gloomy tun with merry shine.
Thus loaded with a feast the tables stood,
Each shrining in the midst the image of a God.   190

When in an antechamber every guest
Had felt the cold full sponge to pleasure pressed,
By ministering slaves, upon his hands and feet,
And fragrant oils with ceremony meet
Poured on his hair, they all moved to the feast
In white robes, and themselves in order placed
Around the silken couches, wondering
    Whence all this mighty cost and blaze of wealth
        could spring.

Soft went the music the soft air along,
200   While fluent Greek a vowelled undersong
Kept up among the guests, discoursing low
At first, for scarcely was the wine at flow;
But when the happy vintage touched their brains,
Louder they talk, and louder come the strains
Of powerful instruments. The gorgeous dyes,
The space, the splendour of the draperies,
The roof of awful richness, nectarous cheer,
Beautiful slaves, and Lamia's self, appear,
Now, when the wine has done its rosy deed,
210   And every soul from human trammels freed,
No more so strange; for merry wine, sweet wine,
Will make Elysian shades not too fair, too divine.

Soon was God Bacchus at meridian height;
Flushed were their cheeks, and bright eyes double
        bright:
Garlands of every green, and every scent
From vales deflowered, or forest-trees branch-rent,
In baskets of bright osiered gold were brought
High as the handles heaped, to suit the thought
Of every guest – that each, as he did please,
220   Might fancy-fit his brows, silk-pillowed at his ease.

What wreath for Lamia? What for Lycius?
What for the sage, old Apollonius?
Upon her aching forehead be there hung
The leaves of willow and of adder's tongue;
And for the youth, quick, let us strip for him
The thyrsus, that his watching eyes may swim
Into forgetfulness; and, for the sage,
Let spear-grass and the spiteful thistle wage
War on his temples. Do not all charms fly
230   At the mere touch of cold philosophy?
There was an awful rainbow once in heaven:
We know her woof, her texture; she is given

In the dull catalogue of common things.
Philosophy will clip an Angel's wings,
Conquer all mysteries by rule and line,
Empty the haunted air, and gnoměd mine –
Unweave a rainbow, as it erewhile made
The tender-personed Lamia melt into a shade.

    By her glad Lycius sitting, in chief place,
Scarce saw in all the room another face,   240
Till, checking his love trance, a cup he took
Full brimmed, and opposite sent forth a look
'Cross the broad table, to beseech a glance
From his old teacher's wrinkled countenance,
And pledge him. The bald-head philosopher
Had fixed his eye, without a twinkle or stir
Full on the alarměd beauty of the bride,
Brow-beating her fair form, and troubling her sweet
        pride.
Lycius then pressed her hand, with devout touch,
As pale it lay upon the rosy couch: 250
'Twas icy, and the cold ran through his veins;
Then sudden it grew hot, and all the pains
Of an unnatural heat shot to his heart.
'Lamia, what means this? Wherefore dost thou start?
Know'st thou that man?' Poor Lamia answered not.
He gazed into her eyes, and not a jot
Owned they the lovelorn piteous appeal;
More, more he gazed; his human senses reel;
Some hungry spell that loveliness absorbs;
There was no recognition in those orbs.   260
'Lamia!' he cried – and no soft-toned reply.
The many heard, and the loud revelry
Grew hush; the stately music no more breathes;
The myrtle sickened in a thousand wreaths.
By faint degrees, voice, lute, and pleasure ceased;
A deadly silence step by step increased,
Until it seemed a horrid presence there,
And not a man but felt the terror in his hair.

'Lamia!' he shrieked; and nothing but the shriek
270   With its sad echo did the silence break.
'Begone, foul dream!' he cried, gazing again
In the bride's face, where now no azure vein
Wandered on fair-spaced temples; no soft bloom
Misted the cheek; no passion to illume
The deep-recessèd vision. All was blight;
Lamia, no longer fair, there sat a deadly white.
'Shut, shut those juggling eyes, thou ruthless man!
Turn them aside, wretch! or the righteous ban
Of all the Gods, whose dreadful images
280   Here represent their shadowy presences,
May pierce them on the sudden with the thorn
Of painful blindness; leaving thee forlorn,
In trembling dotage to the feeblest fright
Of conscience, for their long offended might,
For all thine impious proud-heart sophistries,
Unlawful magic, and enticing lies.
Corinthians! look upon that grey-beard wretch!
Mark how, possessed, his lashless eyelids stretch
Around his demon eyes! Corinthians, see!
290   My sweet bride withers at their potency.'
'Fool!' said the sophist, in an undertone
Gruff with contempt; which a death-nighing moan
From Lycius answered, as heart-struck and lost,
He sank supine beside the aching ghost.
'Fool! Fool!' repeated he, while his eyes still
Relented not, nor moved: 'From every ill
Of life have I preserved thee to this day,
And shall I see thee made a serpent's prey?'
Then Lamia breathed death-breath; the sophist's eye,
300   Like a sharp spear, went through her utterly,
Keen, cruel, perceant, stinging: she, as well
As her weak hand could any meaning tell,
Motioned him to be silent; vainly so,
He looked and looked again a level – *No!*

'A Serpent!' echoed he; no sooner said,
Than with a frightful scream she vanishèd:
And Lycius' arms were empty of delight,
As were his limbs of life, from that same night.
On the high couch he lay! – his friends came round –
Supported him – no pulse, or breath they found,   310
And, in its marriage robe, the heavy body wound.

'Bright star! would I were steadfast as thou art'

Bright star! would I were steadfast as thou art –
    Not in lone splendour hung aloft the night
And watching, with eternal lids apart,
    Like nature's patient, sleepless Eremite,
The moving waters at their priestlike task
    Of pure ablution round earth's human shores,
Or gazing on the new soft-fallen mask
    Of snow upon the mountains and the moors –
No – yet still steadfast, still unchangeable,
    Pillowed upon my fair love's ripening breast,   10
To feel for ever its soft swell and fall,
    Awake for ever in a sweet unrest,
Still, still to hear her tender-taken breath,
And so live ever – or else swoon to death.
                              (Not published by Keats)

To Autumn

I

Season of mists and mellow fruitfulness,
    Close bosom-friend of the maturing sun,
Conspiring with him how to load and bless
    With fruit the vines that round the thatch-eves run;
To bend with apples the mossed cottage-trees,

And fill all fruit with ripeness to the core;
    To swell the gourd, and plump the hazel shells
    With a sweet kernel; to set budding more,
And still more, later flowers for the bees,
Until they think warm days will never cease,
    For Summer has o'er-brimmed their clammy cells.

II

Who hath not seen thee oft amid thy store?
    Sometimes whoever seeks abroad may find
Thee sitting careless on a granary floor,
    Thy hair soft-lifted by the winnowing wind;
Or on a half-reaped furrow sound asleep,
    Drowsed with the fume of poppies, while thy hook
        Spares the next swath and all its twinèd flowers;
And sometimes like a gleaner thou dost keep
    Steady thy laden head across a brook;
    Or by a cider-press, with patient look,
        Thou watchest the last oozings hours by hours.

III

Where are the songs of Spring? Ay, where are they?
    Think not of them, thou hast thy music too –
While barrèd clouds bloom the soft-dying day,
    And touch the stubble-plains with rosy hue:
Then in a wailful choir the small gnats mourn
    Among the river sallows, borne aloft
        Or sinking as the light wind lives or dies;
And full-grown lambs loud bleat from hilly bourn;
    Hedge-crickets sing; and now with treble soft
    The red-breast whistles from a garden-croft;
        And gathering swallows twitter in the skies.

The Fall of Hyperion. A Dream

CANTO I

Fanatics have their dreams, wherewith they weave
A paradise for a sect; the savage too
From forth the loftiest fashion of his sleep
Guesses at Heaven: pity these have not
Traced upon vellum or wild Indian leaf
The shadows of melodious utterance.
But bare of laurel they live, dream, and die;
For Poesy alone can tell her dreams,
With the fine spell of words alone can save
Imagination from the sable charm   10
And dumb enchantment. Who alive can say,
'Thou art no Poet – mayst not tell thy dreams'?
Since every man whose soul is not a clod
Hath visions, and would speak, if he had loved,
And been well nurtured in his mother tongue.
Whether the dream now purposed to rehearse
Be Poet's or Fanatic's will be known
When this warm scribe my hand is in the grave.

    Methought I stood where trees of every clime,
Palm, myrtle, oak, and sycamore, and beech,   20
With plantain, and spice-blossoms, made a screen –
In neighbourhood of fountains, by the noise
Soft-showering in mine ears, and, by the touch
Of scent, not far from roses. Turning round,
I saw an arbour with a drooping roof
Of trellis vines, and bells, and larger blooms,
Like floral censers, swinging light in air;
Before its wreathèd doorway, on a mound
Of moss, was spread a feast of summer fruits,
Which, nearer seen, seemed refuse of a meal   30
By angel tasted, or our Mother Eve;
For empty shells were scattered on the grass,

And grape-stalks but half bare, and remnants more,
Sweet-smelling, whose pure kinds I could not know.
Still was more plenty than the fabled horn
Thrice emptied could pour forth at banqueting
For Proserpine returned to her own fields,
Where the white heifers low. And appetite
More yearning than on earth I ever felt
40 Growing within, I ate deliciously;
And, after not long, thirsted, for thereby
Stood a cool vessel of transparent juice,
Sipped by the wandered bee, the which I took,
And, pledging all the mortals of the world,
And all the dead whose names are in our lips,
Drank. That full draught is parent of my theme.
No Asian poppy, nor elixir fine
Of the soon-fading jealous Caliphat;
No poison gendered in close monkish cell,
50 To thin the scarlet conclave of old men,
Could so have rapt unwilling life away.
Among the fragrant husks and berries crushed,
Upon the grass I struggled hard against
The domineering potion; but in vain –
The cloudy swoon came on, and down I sunk,
Like a Silenus on an antique vase.
How long I slumbered 'tis a chance to guess.
When sense of life returned, I started up
60 As if with wings; but the fair trees were gone,
The mossy mound and arbour were no more.
I looked around upon the carvèd sides
Of an old sanctuary with roof august,
Builded so high, it seemed that filmèd clouds
Might spread beneath, as o'er the stars of heaven.
So old the place was, I remembered none
The like upon the earth: what I had seen
Of grey cathedrals, buttressed walls, rent towers,
The superannuations of sunk realms,
Or Nature's rocks toiled hard in waves and winds,
70 Seemed but the faulture of decrepit things

To that eternal domèd monument.
Upon the marble at my feet there lay
Store of strange vessels and large draperies,
Which needs had been of dyed asbestos wove,
Or in that place the moth could not corrupt,
So white the linen; so, in some, distinct
Ran imageries from a sombre loom.
All in a mingled heap confused there lay
Robes, golden tongs, censer and chafing-dish,
Girdles, and chains, and holy jewelleries –   80

　　Turning from these with awe, once more I raised
My eyes to fathom the space every way –
The embossèd roof, the silent massy range
Of columns north and south, ending in mist
Of nothing, then to eastward, where black gates
Were shut against the sunrise evermore.
Then to the west I looked, and saw far off
An Image, huge of feature as a cloud,
At level of whose feet an altar slept,
To be approached on either side by steps,   90
And marble balustrade, and patient travail
To count with toil the innumerable degrees.
Towards the altar sober-paced I went,
Repressing haste, as too unholy there;
And, coming nearer, saw beside the shrine
One ministering; and there arose a flame.
When in mid-May the sickening East wind
Shifts sudden to the south, the small warm rain
Melts out the frozen incense from all flowers,
And fills the air with so much pleasant health   100
That even the dying man forgets his shroud –
Even so that lofty sacrificial fire,
Sending forth Maian incense, spread around
Forgetfulness of everything but bliss,
And clouded all the altar with soft smoke,
From whose white fragrant curtains thus I heard
Language pronounced: 'If thou canst not ascend

Those steps, die on that marble where thou art.
They flesh, near cousin to the common dust,
110 Will parch for lack of nutriment – thy bones
Will wither in few years, and vanish so
That not the quickest eye could find a grain
Of what thou now art on that pavement cold.
The sands of thy short life are spent this hour,
And no hand in the universe can turn
Thy hourglass, if these gummèd leaves be burnt
Ere thou canst mount up these immortal steps.'
I heard, I looked: two senses both at once,
So fine, so subtle, felt the tyranny
120 Of that fierce threat, and the hard task proposed.
Prodigious seemed the toil; the leaves were yet
Burning – when suddenly a palsied chill
Struck from the pavèd level up my limbs,
And was ascending quick to put cold grasp
Upon those streams that pulse beside the throat.
I shrieked; and the sharp anguish of my shriek
Stung my own ears – I strove hard to escape
The numbness, strove to gain the lowest step.
Slow, heavy, deadly was my pace: the cold
130 Grew stifling, suffocating, at the heart;
And when I clasped my hands I felt them not.
One minute before death, my iced foot touched
The lowest stair; and as it touched, life seemed
To pour in at the toes: I mounted up,
As once fair Angels on a ladder flew
From the green turf to Heaven. 'Holy Power,'
Cried I, approaching near the hornèd shrine,
'What am I that should so be saved from death?
What am I that another death come not
140 To choke my utterance sacrilegious, here?'
Then said the veilèd shadow: 'Thou hast felt
What 'tis to die and live again before
Thy fated hour. That thou hadst power to do so
Is thy own safety; thou hast dated on
Thy doom.' 'High Prophetess,' said I, 'purge off,

Benign, if so it please thee, my mind's film.'
'None can usurp this height,' returned that shade,
'But those to whom the miseries of the world
Are misery, and will not let them rest.
All else who find a haven in the world,   150
Where they may thoughtless sleep away their days,
If by a chance into this fane they come,
Rot on the pavement where thou rotted'st half.'
'Are there not thousands in the world,' said I,
Encouraged by the sooth voice of the shade,
'Who love their fellows even to the death;
Who feel the giant agony of the world;
And more, like slaves to poor humanity,
Labour for mortal good? I sure should see
Other men here: but I am here alone.'   160
'They whom thou spak'st of are no visionaries,'
Rejoined that voice – 'They are no dreamers weak,
They seek no wonder but the human face;
No music but a happy-noted voice –
They come not here, they have no thought to come –
And thou art here, for thou art less than they –
What benefit canst thou do, or all thy tribe,
To the great world? Thou art a dreaming thing,
A fever of thyself. Think of the Earth;
What bliss even in hope is there for thee?   170
What haven? Every creature hath its home;
Every sole man hath days of joy and pain,
Whether his labours be sublime or low –
The pain alone; the joy alone; distinct:
Only the dreamer venoms all his days,
Bearing more woe than all his sins deserve.
Therefore, that happiness be somewhat shared,
Such things as thou art are admitted oft
Into like gardens thou didst pass erewhile,
And suffered in these temples; for that cause   180
Thou standest safe beneath this statue's knees.'
'That I am favoured for unworthiness,
By such propitious parley medicined

In sickness not ignoble, I rejoice –
Ay, and could weep for love of such award.'
So answered I, continuing, 'If it please,
Majestic shadow, tell me: sure not all
Those melodies sung into the world's ear
Are useless: sure a poet is a sage,
190   A humanist, physician to all men.
That I am none I feel, as vultures feel
They are no birds when eagles are abroad.
What am I then? Thou spakest of my tribe:
What tribe?' – The tall shade veiled in drooping white
Then spake, so much more earnest, that the breath
Moved the thin linen folds that drooping hung
About a golden censer from the hand
Pendant. – 'Art thou not of the dreamer tribe?
The poet and the dreamer are distinct,
200   Diverse, sheer opposite, antipodes.
The one pours out a balm upon the world,
The other vexes it.' Then shouted I,
Spite of myself, and with a Pythia's spleen,
'Apollo! faded, far-flown Apollo!
Where is thy misty pestilence to creep
Into the dwellings, through the door crannies,
Of all mock lyrists, large self-worshippers
And careless hectorers in proud bad verse.
Though I breathe death with them it will be life
210   To see them sprawl before me into graves.
Majestic shadow, tell me where I am,
Whose altar this; for whom this incense curls;
What image this, whose face I cannot see,
For the broad marble knees; and who thou art,
Of accent feminine so courteous?'

Then the tall shade, in drooping linens veiled,
Spake out, so much more earnest, that her breath
Stirred the thin folds of gauze that drooping hung
About a golden censer from her hand
220   Pendant; and by her voice I knew she shed

Long-treasured tears. 'This temple, sad and lone,
Is all spared from the thunder of a war
Foughten long since by giant hierarchy
Against rebellion; this old image here,
Whose carvèd features wrinkled as he fell,
Is Saturn's; I Moneta, left supreme
Sole priestess of his desolation.'
I had no words to answer, for my tongue,
Useless, could find about its roofèd home
No syllable of a fit majesty   230
To make rejoinder to Moneta's mourn.
There was a silence, while the altar's blaze
Was fainting for sweet food: I looked thereon,
And on the pavèd floor, where nigh were piled
Faggots of cinnamon, and many heaps
Of other crispèd spice-wood – then again
I looked upon the altar, and its horns
Whitened with ashes, and its languorous flame,
And then upon the offerings again;
And so by turns – till sad Moneta cried: 240
'The sacrifice is done, but not the less
Will I be kind to thee for thy goodwill.
My power, which to me is still a curse,
Shall be to thee a wonder; for the scenes
Still swooning vivid through my globèd brain,
With an electral changing misery,
Thou shalt with those dull mortal eyes behold,
Free from all pain, if wonder pain thee not.'
As near as an immortal's spherèd words
Could to a mother's soften, were these last: 250
But yet I had a terror of her robes,
And chiefly of the veils, that from her brow
Hung pale, and curtained her in mysteries
That made my heart too small to hold its blood.
This saw that Goddess, and with sacred hand
Parted the veils. Then saw I a wan face,
Not pined by human sorrows, but bright-blanched
By an immortal sickness which kills not;

It works a constant change, which happy death
260   Can put no end to; deathwards progressing
To no death was that visage; it had passed
The lily and the snow; and beyond these
I must not think now, though I saw that face –
But for her eyes I should have fled away.
They held me back, with a benignant light,
Soft-mitigated by divinest lids
Half-closed, and visionless entire they seemed
Of all external things – they saw me not,
But in blank splendour beamed like the mild moon,
270   Who comforts those she sees not, who knows not
What eyes are upward cast. As I had found
A grain of gold upon a mountain's side,
And twinged with avarice strained out my eyes
To search its sullen entrails rich with ore,
So at the view of sad Moneta's brow
I ached to see what things the hollow brain
Behind enwombèd; what high tragedy
In the dark secret chambers of her skull
Was acting, that could give so dread a stress
280   To her cold lips, and fill with such a light
Her planetary eyes; and touch her voice
With such a sorrow – 'Shade of Memory!'
Cried I, with act adorant at her feet,
'By all the gloom hung round thy fallen house,
By this last temple, by the golden age,
By great Apollo, thy dear foster child,
And by thyself, forlorn divinity,
The pale Omega of a withered race,
Let me behold, according as thou said'st,
290   What in thy brain so ferments to and fro.'
No sooner had this conjuration passed
My devout lips, than side by side we stood
(Like a stunt bramble by a solemn pine)
Deep in the shady sadness of a vale,
Far sunken from the healthy breath of morn,

Far from the fiery noon and eve's one star.
Onward I looked beneath the gloomy boughs,
And saw, what first I thought an image huge,
Like to the image pedestalled so high
In Saturn's temple. Then Moneta's voice   300
Came brief upon mine ear: 'So Saturn sat
When he had lost his realms.' Whereon there grew
A power within me of enormous ken
To see as a God sees, and take the depth
Of things as nimbly as the outward eye
Can size and shape pervade. The lofty theme
At those few words hung vast before my mind,
With half-unravelled web. I set myself
Upon an eagle's watch, that I might see,
And seeing ne'er forget. No stir of life   310
Was in this shrouded vale, not so much air
As in zoning of a summer's day
Robs not one light seed from the feathered grass,
But where the dead leaf fell there did it rest.
A stream went voiceless by, still deadened more
By reason of the fallen divinity
Spreading more shade; the Naiad 'mid her reeds
Pressed her cold finger closer to her lips.
Along the margin-sand large footmarks went
No farther than to where old Saturn's feet   320
Had rested, and there slept – how long a sleep!
Degraded, cold, upon the sodden ground
His old right hand lay nerveless, listless, dead,
Unsceptred; and his realmless eyes were closed,
While his bowed head seemed listening to the Earth,
His ancient mother, for some comfort yet.

It seemed no force could wake him from his place;
But there came one who, with a kindred hand
Touched his wide shoulders, after bending low
With reverence, though to one who knew it not.   330
Then came the grieved voice of Mnemosyne,

And grieved I hearkened. 'That divinity
Whom thou saw'st step from yon forlornest wood,
And with slow pace approach our fallen King,
Is Thea, softest-natured of our brood.'
I marked the goddess in fair statuary
Surpassing wan Moneta by the head,
And in her sorrow nearer woman's tears.
There was a listening fear in her regard,
As if calamity had but begun;
As if the vanward clouds of evil days
Had spent their malice, and the sullen rear
Was with its storèd thunder labouring up.
One hand she pressed upon that aching spot
Where beats the human heart, as if just there,
Though an immortal, she felt cruel pain;
The other upon Saturn's bended neck
She laid, and to the level of his hollow ear
Leaning with parted lips, some words she spake
In solemn tenor and deep organ tune,
Some mourning words, which in our feeble tongue
Would come in this-like accenting – how frail
To that large utterance of the early Gods! –
'Saturn! look up – and for what, poor lost King?
I have no comfort for thee, no – not one;
I cannot cry, *Wherefore thus sleepest thou?*
For Heaven is parted from thee, and the Earth
Knows thee not, so afflicted, for a God;
And Ocean too, with all its solemn noise,
Has from thy sceptre passed, and all the air
Is emptied of thine hoary Majesty.
Thy thunder, captious at the new command,
Rumbles reluctant o'er our fallen house;
And thy sharp lightning, in unpractised hands,
Scorches and burns our once serene domain.
With such remorseless speed still come new woes
That unbelief has not a space to breathe.
Saturn! sleep on. Me thoughtless, why should I

340

350

360

Thus violate thy slumbrous solitude?
Why should I ope thy melancholy eyes?   370
Saturn, sleep on, while at thy feet I weep.'

    As when, upon a t.-.icèd summer-night,
Forests, branch-charmèd by the earnest stars,
Dream, and so dream all night without a noise,
Save from one gradual solitary gust,
Swelling upon the silence; dying off;
As if the ebbing air had but one wave –
So came these words, and went; the while in tears
She pressed her fair large forehead to the earth,
Just where her fallen hair might spread in curls,   380
A soft and silken mat for Saturn's feet.
Long, long those two were postured motionless,
Like sculpture builded-up upon the grave
Of their own power. A long awful time
I looked upon them: still they were the same;
The frozen God still bending to the earth,
And the sad Goddess weeping at his feet;
Moneta silent. Without stay or prop,
But my own weak mortality, I bore
The load of this eternal quietude,   390
The unchanging gloom, and the three fixèd shapes
Ponderous upon my senses a whole moon.
For by my burning brain I measured sure
Her silver seasons shedded on the night,
And every day by day methought I grew
More gaunt and ghostly. Oftentimes I prayed
Intense, that death would take me from the vale
And all its burthens. Gasping with despair
Of change, hour after hour I cursed myself –
Until old Saturn raised his faded eyes,   400
And looked around and saw his kingdom gone,
And all the gloom and sorrow of the place,
And that fair kneeling Goddess at his feet.
As the moist scent of flowers, and grass, and leaves,

Fills forest dells with a pervading air
Known to the woodland nostril, so the words
Of Saturn filled the mossy glooms around,
Even to the hollows of time-eaten oaks,
And to the windings in the foxes' hole,
410   With sad low tones, while thus he spake, and sent
Strange musings to the solitary Pan.

     'Moan, brethren, moan; for we are swallowed up
And buried from all godlike exercise
Of influence benign on planets pale,
And peaceful sway above man's harvesting,
And all those acts which deity supreme
Doth ease its heart of love in. Moan and wail.
Moan, brethren, moan; for lo! the rebel spheres
Spin round, the stars their ancient courses keep,
420   Clouds still with shadowy moisture haunt the earth,
Still suck their fill of light from sun and moon,
Still buds the tree, and still the sea-shores murmur.
There is no death in all the universe,
No smell of death – there shall be death – moan,
          moan,
Moan, Cybele, moan; for thy pernicious babes
Have changed a God into a shaking palsy.
Moan, brethren, moan, for I have no strength left,
Weak as the reed – weak – feeble as my voice –
O, O, the pain, the pain of feebleness.
430   Moan, moan, for still I thaw – or give me help:
Throw down those imps, and give me victory.
Let me hear other groans, and trumpets blown
Of triumph calm, and hymns of festival,
From the gold peaks of heaven's high-pilèd clouds –
Voices of soft proclaim, and silver stir
Of strings in hollow shells; and let there be
Beautiful things made new for the surprise
Of the sky-children –' So he feebly ceased,
With such a poor and sickly sounding pause,
440   Methought I heard some old man of the earth

Bewailing earthly loss; nor could my eyes
And ears act with that pleasant unison of sense
Which marries sweet sound with the grace of form
And dolorous accent from a tragic harp
With large-limbed visions. More I scrutinized:
Still fixed he sat beneath the sable trees,
Whose arms spread straggling in wild serpent forms,
With leaves all hushed; his awful presence there
(Now all was silent) gave a deadly lie
To what I erewhile heard – only his lips   450
Trembled amid the white curls of his beard.
They told the truth, though, round, the snowy locks
Hung nobly, as upon the face of heaven
A midday fleece of clouds. Thea arose,
And stretched her white arm through the hollow dark,
Pointing some whither; whereat he too rose
Like a vast giant, seen by men at sea
To grow pale from the waves at dull midnight.
They melted from my sight into the woods;
Ere I could turn, Moneta cried: 'These twain   460
Are speeding to the families of grief,
Where roofed in by black rocks they waste, in pain
And darkness, for no hope.' – And she spake on,
As ye may read who can unwearied pass
Onward from the antechamber of this dream,
Where even at the open doors awhile
I must delay, and glean my memory
Of her high phrase – perhaps no further dare.

CANTO II

'Mortal, that thou mayst understand aright,
I humanize my sayings to thine ear,
Making comparisons of earthly things;
Or thou mightst better listen to the wind,
Whose language is to thee a barren noise,
Though it blows legend-laden through the trees –
In melancholy realms big tears are shed,

More sorrow like to this, and such-like woe,
Too huge for mortal tongue, or pen of scribe.
The Titans fierce, self-hid or prison-bound,
Groan for the old allegiance once more,
Listening in their doom for Saturn's voice.
But one of our whole eagle-brood still keeps
His sovereignty, and rule, and majesty;
Blazing Hyperion on his orbèd fire
Still sits, still snuffs the incense teeming up
From man to the sun's God – yet unsecure.
For as upon the earth dire prodigies
Fright and perplex, so also shudders he:
Nor at dog's howl or gloom-bird's even screech,
Or the familiar visitings of one
Upon the first toll of his passing-bell:
But horrors, portioned to a giant nerve,
Make great Hyperion ache. His palace bright,
Bastioned with pyramids of glowing gold,
And touched with shade of bronzèd obelisks,
Glares a blood-red through all the thousand courts,
Arches, and domes, and fiery galleries;
And all its curtains of Aurorian clouds
Flush angerly: when he would taste the wreaths
Of incense breathed aloft from sacred hills,
Instead of sweets, his ample palate takes
Savour of poisonous brass and metals sick.
Wherefore, when harboured in the sleepy West,
After the full completion of fair day,
For rest divine upon exalted couch
And slumber in the arms of melody,
He paces through the pleasant hours of ease
With strides colossal, on from hall to hall;
While far within each aisle and deep recess
His wingèd minions in close clusters stand
Amazed, and full of fear; like anxious men,
Who on a wide plain gather in sad troops,
When earthquakes jar their battlements and towers.
Even now, while Saturn, roused from icy trance,

Goes, step for step, with Thea from yon woods,
Hyperion, leaving twilight in the rear,
Is sloping to the threshold of the West –
Thither we tend.' – Now in clear light I stood,
Relieved from the dusk vale. Mnemosyne   50
Was sitting on a square-edged polished stone,
That in its lucid depth reflected pure
Her priestess-garments. My quick eyes ran on
From stately nave to nave, from vault to vault,
Through bowers of fragrant and enwreathèd light
And diamond-pavèd lustrous long arcades.
Anon rushed by the bright Hyperion;
His flaming robes streamed out beyond his heels,
And gave a roar, as if of earthly fire,
That scared away the meek ethereal Hours,   60
And made their dove-wings tremble. On he flared . . .

(Not published by Keats)

'What can I do to drive away'

What can I do to drive away
Remembrance from my eyes? for they have seen,
Ay, an hour ago, my brilliant Queen!
Touch has a memory. O say, love, say,
What can I do to kill it and be free
In my old liberty?
When every fair one that I saw was fair,
Enough to catch me in but half a snare,
Not keep me there;
When, howe'er poor or parti-coloured things,   10
My muse had wings,
And ever ready was to take her course
Whither I bent her force,
Unintellectual, yet divine to me –
Divine, I say! What sea-bird o'er the sea
Is a philosopher the while he goes
Winging along where the great water throes?

How shall I do
To get anew
Those moulted feathers, and so mount once more
   Above, above
   The reach of fluttering Love,
And make him cower lowly while I soar?
Shall I gulp wine? No, that is vulgarism,
A heresy and schism,
   Foisted into the canon law of love;
No – wine is only sweet to happy men;
   More dismal cares
   Seize on me unawares –
Where shall I learn to get my peace again?
To banish thoughts of that most hateful land,
Dungeoner of my friends, that wicked strand
Where they were wrecked and live a wreckèd life;
That monstrous region, whose dull rivers pour,
Ever from their sordid urns into the shore,
Unowned of any weedy-hairèd gods;
Whose winds, all zephyrless, hold scourging rods,
Iced in the great lakes, to afflict mankind;
Whose rank-grown forests, frosted, black, and blind,
Would fright a Dryad; whose harsh-herbaged meads
Make lean and lank the starved ox while he feeds;
There flowers have no scent, birds no sweet song,
And great unerring Nature once seems wrong.

O, for some sunny spell
To dissipate the shadows of this hell!
Say they are gone – with the new dawning light
Steps forth my lady bright!
O, let me once more rest
My soul upon that dazzling breast!
Let once again these aching arms be placed,
The tender gaolers of thy waist!
And let me feel that warm breath here and there
To spread a rapture in my very hair –

20

30

40

50

O, the sweetness of the pain!
Give me those lips again!
Enough! Enough! It is enough for me
To dream of thee!

(Not published by Keats)

'*I cry your mercy, pity, love – ay, love!*'

I cry your mercy, pity, love – ay, love!
   Merciful love that tantalises not,
One-thoughted, never-wandering, guileless love,
   Unmasked, and being seen – without a blot!
O! let me have thee whole, – all, all, be mine!
   That shape, that fairness, that sweet minor zest
Of love, your kiss – those hands, those eyes divine,
   That warm, white, lucent, million-pleasured
      breast –
Yourself – your soul – in pity give me all,
   Withhold no atom's atom or I die;   10
Or living on perhaps, your wretched thrall,
   Forget, in the mist of idle ecstasy,
Life's purposes – the palate of my mind
Losing its gust, and my ambition blind!

(Not published by Keats)

'*This living hand, now warm and capable*'

This living hand, now warm and capable
Of earnest grasping, would, if it were cold
And in the icy silence of the tomb,
So haunt thy days and chill thy dreaming nights
That thou would wish thine own heart dry of blood
So in my veins red life might stream again,
And thou be conscience-calmed – see here it is –
I hold it towards you.

(Not published by Keats)

To Fanny

I

Physician Nature! let my spirit blood!
  O ease my heart of verse and let me rest;
Throw me upon thy tripod till the flood
  Of stifling numbers ebbs from my full breast.
A theme! a theme! Great Nature! give a theme;
  Let me begin my dream.
I come – I see thee, as thou standest there,
Beckon me out into the wintry air.

II

Ah! dearest love, sweet home of all my fears,
  And hopes, and joys, and panting miseries,
Tonight, if I may guess, thy beauty wears
    A smile of such delight,
    As brilliant and as bright,
  As when with ravished, aching, vassal eyes,
    Lost in a soft amaze,
    I gaze, I gaze!

III

Who now, with greedy looks, eats up my feast?
  What stare outfaces now my silver moon!
Ah! keep that hand unravished at the least;
    Let, let, the amorous burn –
    But, prithee, do not turn
The current of your heart from me so soon.
    O save, in charity,
    The quickest pulse for me!

IV

Save it for me, sweet love! though music breathe
  Voluptuous visions into the warm air,
Though swimming through the dance's dangerous
      wreath,

Be like an April day,
Smiling and cold and gay,
A temperate lily, temperate as fair,   30
    Then Heaven, there will be
    A warmer June for me.

V

Why, this – you'll say, my Fanny! – is not true:
    Put your soft hand upon your snowy side,
Where the heart beats; confess – 'tis nothing new –
    Must not a woman be
    A feather on the sea,
Swayed to and fro by every wind and tide?
    Of as uncertain speed
    As blow-ball from the mead?   40

VI

I know it – and to know it is despair
    To one who loves you as I love, sweet Fanny!
Whose heart goes fluttering for you everywhere,
    Nor, when away you roam,
    Dare keep its wretched home.
Love, Love alone, has pains severe and many:
    Then, loveliest! keep me free
    From torturing jealousy.

VII

Ah! if you prize my subdued soul above
    The poor, the fading, brief, pride of an hour,   50
Let none profane my Holy See of Love,
    Or with a rude hand break
    The sacramental cake;
Let none else touch the just new-budded flower;
    If not – may my eyes close,
    Love! on their last repose.
                        (Not published by Keats)

'In after-time, a sage of mickle lore'

In after-time, a sage of mickle lore
Y-cleped Typographus, the Giant took,
And did refit his limbs as heretofore,
And made him read in many a learned book,
And into many a lively legend look;
Thereby in goodly themes so training him,
That all his brutishness he quite forsook,
When, meeting Artegall and Talus grim,
The one he struck stone-blind, the other's eyes wox
      dim.

(Not published by Keats)

Notes

ABBREVIATIONS

1817	*Poems* (1817)
1818	*Endymion: A Poetic Romance* (1818)
1820	*Lamia, Isabella, The Eve of St Agnes, and Other Poems* (1820)
1848	*Life, Letters, and Literary Remains*, ed. R. M. Milnes, 2 vols. (London, 1848)
Cowden Clarke	Charles and Mary Cowden Clarke, *Recollections of Writers* (London, 1878)
Forman (1883)	*The Poetical Works and Other Writings of John Keats*, ed. H. B. Forman, 4 vols. (London, 1883)
L	*The Letters of John Keats*, ed. H. E. Rollins, 2 vols. (Cambridge, Mass., 1958)
Texts	Jack Stillinger, *The Texts of Keats's Poems* (Cambridge, Mass., 1974)
W1–3	Richard Woodhouse's transcripts of Keats's poem. W1–2 are at Harvard, W3 is in the Morgan Library.

For classical references in the poems the reader should consult the Dictionary of Classical Names.

Imitation of Spenser

Written 1814. Published *1817*. Keats's first extant poem. Charles Brown reported, 'It was the "Faery Queen" that awakened his genius.'

On Peace

Perhaps written in April 1814. Published *Notes and Queries*, 4 February 1905: text based on W3 (in l. 14 'honours' emended to 'horrors'). Napoleon had surrendered on 11 April. This irregular Shakespearean sonnet echoes the tone of Leigh Hunt's editorials in the *Examiner*, which hoped that victory would lead to constitutional monarchies in Europe.

Lines Written on 29 May, the Anniversary of the Restoration of Charles II, on Hearing the Bells Ringing

Probably written 29 May 1814, a month after Napoleon's abdication, or possibly the following year. Published A. Lowell, *John Keats* (1925): text from W3. On 29 May bells were rung all over England to commemorate Charles II's restoration.

5.   Algernon Sidney, Lord William Russell and Sir Henry Vane, all executed for treason against Charles II, were regarded by the Whigs as heroes who opposed royal tyranny.

'O Solitude! if I must with thee dwell'

Probably written in October or November 1815, shortly after Keats entered Guy's Hospital as a student. Published *Examiner*, 5 May 1816 (titled 'To Solitude'), and *1817*.

14.   *two kindred spirits*: The poet and probably George Keats.

'Give me Women, Wine, and Snuff'

Written in autumn 1815 or the first half of 1816, as Keats wrote it on the cover of the lecture notebook of Henry Stephens, a fellow medical student. Published H. B. Forman, *The Poetical Works of John Keats* (1884): text from Keats's MS.

'I am as brisk'

Probably written in 1816 (*Texts*, p. 109). Published H. W. Garrod, *The Poetical Works of John Keats* (1939): text from Keats's MS.

Specimen of an Induction to a Poem

Probably written late spring 1816. Published *1817*. Influenced by Leigh Hunt's *The Story of Rimini* (1816): Hunt admired lines and passages of Keats's poem (*Texts*, p. 110).
6.   *Archimago*: The magician in Spencer's *The Faerie Queene* I and II.
61.   *Libertas*: Leigh Hunt, imprisoned for his liberal views in 1813.

To Charles Cowden Clarke

Written as a verse epistle in September 1816 while at Margate. Published *1817*. Clarke (1787–1877) taught Keats at Enfield School and encouraged his interest in poetry, music and liberal politics (see 52–75, 109–end). He had recently moved to London.
6. *Naiad Zephyr*: Keats's invention, a composite deity: Naiads are female water deities, Zephyrs are male wind deities.
29–30. *Baiae*: On the Bay of Naples, the home of the Italian poet Tasso (1544–95).
31–7. *Armida ... Mulla ... Belphoebe ... Una ... Archimago*: all Spenserian references.
46–7. These two lines refer to Hunt's *The Story of Rimini*.
70–71. *Alfred ... Tell ... Brutus*: Here Keats mentions three Whig heroes: Alfred the Great, vanquisher of the Danes, the Swiss patriot William Tell, and Brutus, who helped assassinate Julius Caesar after he had made himself dictator.

On First Looking into Chapman's Homer

Dated October in the *Examiner*. Published *Examiner*, 1 December 1816, and *1817*. Cowden Clarke and Keats read a borrowed copy of Chapman's translation of Homer one evening: Keats departed 'at day-spring, yet he contrived that I should receive the poem from the

distance of, may be, two miles by ten o'clock' (*Cowden Clarke*, p. 130).
11.   *Cortez*: The Spanish conquistador, more usually spelt Cortés.
      Tennyson pointed out that Keats was wrong: 'History requires
      here *Balbóa*' (the explorer Vasco de Balbóa).

To my Brothers

Written on 18 November 1816, Tom Keats's seventeenth birthday.
Published *1817*. The sonnet probably celebrates the brothers' coming
together in their new lodgings, 76 Cheapside.

Addressed to [Haydon]

Written 19 or 20 November 1816. Published *1817*. The three '*spirits*'
celebrated are Wordsworth (2–4), Leigh Hunt (5–6), and the painter,
Benjamin Robert Haydon (7–8). Keats had recently met the older
Haydon: they were for a while mutually supportive friends.
13.   *Of mighty workings?* –: The version Keats sent Haydon on
      20 November read 'Of mighty Workings in a distant Mart?' (*L*,
      I, 117); altered at Haydon's suggestion.

'I stood tip-toe upon a little hill'

Completed 1816, after 17 December. Published *1817*. Leigh Hunt
said this poem 'was suggested . . . by a delightful summer-day, as he
stood beside the gate that leads from the Battery on Hampstead Heath,
into a field by Caen Wood' (*Lord Byron and some of his Contempor-
aries*, 2nd edn. (1828), I, 413). Printed here before 'Sleep and Poetry'
because it was begun before that poem. Keats's ideas on the origin and
nature of poetry are probably indebted to his reading of Wordsworth's
Excursion (1814), IV, 687–765, 840–81, which describes Classical
deities as originating in man's pantheistic response to natural phenom-
ena. Compare Keats's treatment of the story of Psyche here (141–50)
with that in 'Ode to Psyche'. The passage on the love of Diana and
Endymion (192–end) is the imaginative start of Keats's long poem,
Endymion, begun the following March.
Epigraph: Leigh Hunt, *The Story of Rimini* (1816), III, 430.
61–80. Keats 'himself told me [this passage] was the recollection of
      having frequently loitered over the rail of a footbridge that

spanned . . . a little brook in the last field on entering Edmonton'
(*Cowden Clarke*, p. 138).

Sleep and Poetry

Written after meeting Hunt in October 1816, completed by December.
Published *1817*. 'It was in the library at Hunt's cottage, where an
extemporary bed had been made up for him on the sofa, that he
composed the frame-work and many lines of the poem . . . the last
sixty or seventy being an inventory of the art garniture of the room'
(*Cowden Clarke*, pp. 133–4).
Epigraph: *The Floure and the Leafe*, 17–21. The poem is no longer
attributed to Chaucer.

89. *Montmorenci*: River in Quebec with a waterfall.

96–154. Keats's account of the development of the artist.

101–21. *the realm . . ./Of Flora, and old Pan*: the pre-Fall world of
pastoral innocence.

162–229. A brief history of the development of English poetry. The
Elizabethan and seventeenth-century poets (171–80) were
betrayed by the formalism of Alexander Pope (1688–1744) and
his school (181–206). The conclusion records, with reservations,
the resurgence of contemporary poetry (221–9).

202. *Lyrist*: Apollo.

206. *Boileau*: Nicolas Boileau (1636–1711), French neoclassical poet
and critic.

218. *lone spirits*: Henry Kirke White (1785–1806) and Thomas Chat-
terton (1752–70), both neglected poets who died young.

226. *swan's ebon bill*: Possibly a reference to Wordsworth.

231–5, 241–5. An obscure attack on some contemporary poets; it
probably includes aspects of the poetry of Wordsworth, Cole-
ridge and Byron.

354. *a poet's house*: Hunt's cottage (see headnote).

385. *Alfred*: See 'To Charles Cowden Clarke', note to 70–71.

387. *Kosciusko*: See headnote *To Kosciusko* below.

Written in Disgust of Vulgar Superstition

Written in fifteen minutes on Sunday evening, 22 December 1816.
Published *1876*. An important poem for an understanding of Keats's
religious attitudes.

7.   *Lydian airs*: Lydia was an ancient kingdom in West Asia, home
     of the Lydian diatonic scale. Echoes Milton, *L'Allegro* 136.

To Kosciusko

Written December 1816. So dated in *Examiner*, 16 February 1817.
Republished *1817*. Tadeusz Kosciusko (1746–1817), Polish patriot,
fought against Russia and in the American War of Independence. He
died a hero of English liberals: Hunt had a bust of him in his Hamp-
stead cottage (see *Sleep and Poetry* 387–8).

'After dark vapours have oppressed our plains'

Dated 31 January 1817 (W1–2). Published *Examiner*, 23 February
1817, *1848*: text based on MSS.
14. *Poet's death*: perhaps Thomas Chatterton (see *Sleep and Poetry*,
     note to 218).

To Leigh Hunt, Esq.

Probably written February 1817. Published as Dedication to *1817*.
Written in company when Keats received proofs of his first volume.

On Seeing the Elgin Marbles

Written before 3 March 1817, after visiting the British Museum with
Haydon to see the Elgin Marbles from the Parthenon, recently brought
to England by Lord Elgin and purchased by the government in 1816.
Published *Examiner* and *Champion*, 9 March 1817.
14. *magnitude*: Probably used in the scientific sense, which classifies
     stars according to their brightness.

On the Sea

Written on 16 or 17 April 1817 at Carisbrooke, Isle of Wight, and
sent to John Hamilton Reynolds on 17 April (*L*, I, 132). Published
Champion, 17 August 1817, and *1848*. Reynolds (1796–1852), a

close friend of Keats and also a poet, was at that time pursuing a literary career.

3–4. *spell of/ Hecate*: Refers to the moon's control of the tides.

'Hither, hither love –'

Date uncertain; possibly summer 1817. Published *Ladies' Companion*, August 1837: text from Keats's holograph.

'The Gothic looks solemn'

Written September 1817 in a (lost) letter to J. H. Reynolds. Published *Forman (1883)*: text based on *Forman* (see *Texts*, pp. 143–4). Keats was staying with his friend Benjamin Bailey (1791–1853) in Magdalen Hall, Oxford, while working on *Endymion*.

Endymion: A Poetic Romance

Begun *c.* 18 April 1817 on the Isle of Wight, and the first draft completed November 1817 at Burford Bridge, Surrey. Published May 1818.

Endymion is a Romantic quest-poem portraying the poet's search for true imaginative powers. The hero's confusions arise from the decision of Diana, the moon-goddess, to visit the poet-prince first in the form of an unknown goddess (Books I and II), and later in the guise of an Indian Maid (Book IV). In love with all three, Endymion's divided feelings are finally resolved by the discovery that they are one. The romance ends with the deification of Endymion and his union with Diana.

Endymion argues for the interconnectedness of human love and the truth of ideal beauty. In Book I, the hero is set apart from his Latmian subjects by the 'cankering venom' (I, 396) caused by his dream of being visited by a heavenly goddess. He is then initiated into the mysteries of the heavens (Book I), the earth (Book II) and the sea (Book III), before being returned to earth. He is shown progressively learning to sympathize with the joys and sufferings of other lovers – Venus and Adonis (II, 387–587), Alpheus and Arethusa (II, 932–1017) and Glaucus (III, 187–1015, here represented by 314–638). Endymion is variously named as 'the Latmian' and the 'Carian', Diana as 'Cynthia' and 'Phoebe'.

Keats saw the writing of *Endymion* as a 'test, a trial of my Powers of Imagination and chiefly of my Invention ... by which I must make 4000 Lines of one bare circumstance and fill them with Poetry ... Besides a long Poem is a test of Invention which I take to be the Polar Star of Poetry, as Fancy is the Sails, and Imagination the Rudder. Did our great Poets ever write short Pieces?' (*L*, I, 169–70).

Epigraph: Shakespeare, Sonnet xvii, 12.

Preface: Keats's original Preface, which attacked the reading public, met with strong objections from his friend, J. H. Reynolds, and from his publishers, Taylor and Hessey, and was replaced with the present text.

BOOK I

232–306. The stanzaic poem to Pan is indebted to Chapman's Homeric hymns. Wordsworth thought it a 'Very pretty piece of Paganism'.

347–54. The appearance of Apollo's bow in the sky to aid the Argonauts is not found in Keats's usual sources, and was probably drawn from Apollonius Rhodius.

408. *Peona*: Endymion's sister and confidante is Keats's invention.

777–81. On 30 January 1818 Keats sent his publishers an additional passage (777–81), which he believed, together with the following passage (782–842), represented 'a regular stepping of the Imagination towards a Truth. My having written that Argument will perhaps be of the greatest Service to me of any thing I ever did' (*L*, I, 218). In private Benjamin Bailey commented adversely on the 'inclination' of the whole passage towards 'that abominable principle of *Shelley*'s – that *Sensual Love* is the principle of *things*'.

BOOK II

1–43. Keats's defence of human love as the 'chief intensity' (see Book I, 777–81).

31–2. *Hero ... Imogen ... Pastorella*: Heroines of Marlowe's *Hero and Leander*, Shakespeare's *Cymbeline*, and *The Faerie Queene*, VI, xi.

387–587. The wandering Endymion is vouchsafed this vision of the sleeping Adonis and his union with Venus by '*a heavenly guide benignant*' (377). It foreshadows Endymion's later union with Diana.

827–end. The narrator explains how myths are created (827–48) and Endymion awakes to find he has been deserted by an unknown goddess or woman. Book II ends with Endymion overhearing the story of Arethusa and Alpheus, before following them under the ocean.

BOOK III

1–21. Keats is reported as saying, 'It will easily be seen what I think of the present Ministers by the beginning of the 3rd Book [of *Endymion*].' The passage reflects Leigh Hunt's attacks in the *Examiner* on tyrants and the clergy. The references are obscure, but '*idiot blink*' (6) may refer either to the king or the Tory ministry, or both, for keeping the price of corn high in a period of poor harvests and distress.

42. *thy Sister*: Diana, the moon.

314–638. In his journey under the sea Endymion meets an aged man with a mysterious book who has been awaiting the coming of a young man to release him. The old man tells his story, and identifies himself as Glaucus. This excerpt ends with the death of Scylla following Glaucus's entrancement by Circe. The remainder of Book III (639–1032, not included here) is taken up with Endymion and Glaucus releasing 'All lovers, whom fell storms have doomed to die' (702).

414. *Phoebus' daughter*: Circe.

BOOK IV

1–29. Keats's invocation places the British Muse in an historical relationship to Biblical inspiration (10), Greek poetry (11–14), and the Italy of Virgil and of Dante (14–17). Keats seems to make an implicit contrast between modern day '*barren souls*' and the achievements of the Elizabethan poets (17–20).

143–290. Endymion chances on an Indian Maid, with whom, to his consternation, he instantly falls in love. She for pity sings '*this roundelay*', in which she tells the story of Bacchus's progress (to which she apparently attached herself in India) through Egypt, Abyssinia and Asia.

954–61. *This dusk religion ... impious*: This obscure passage may be an attack on conventional moral (and Christian) attitudes to human love.

'In drear-nighted December'

Written December 1817. Published *Literary Gazette*, 19 September 1829: text based on Keats's holograph.

Nebuchadnezzar's Dream

Date uncertain, but probably December 1817: text based on Charles Brown's transcript. Published *Literary Anecdotes of the Nineteenth Century* (1896). This obscure poem appears to satirize the repressive measures taken by the Tory government to silence its critics. Based on Daniel 2–4, Nebuchadnezzar probably stands for George III, the *'valiant crew'*, (10) for his ministry. Daniel (6) probably stands for William Hone (1780–1842), unsuccessfully tried for blasphemous and seditious writings, 18–20 December 1817. Keats, like other liberals, followed the trial with keen interest.

4.   *naumachia*: A 'Serpentine Naumachia' or 'sham naval fight' had been a feature in the peace celebrations of 1814.

To Mrs Reynolds's Cat

Written 21 January 1818. Published Thomas Hood's *The Comic Annual* (1830): text based on Keats's fair copy. Mrs Charlotte Reynolds was the mother of Keats's friend John Hamilton Reynolds. He was a frequent visitor to the Reynolds's house at this time.

On Sitting Down to Read King Lear Once Again

Written 22 January 1818. Published *Plymouth and Devonport Weekly*, 8 November 1838: text based on fair copy made in Keats's copy of the 1808 facsimile of the First Folio. Keats was preparing *Endymion* for the press, which forced upon him the contrast between Shakespearean poetry and *'golden-tongued Romance'*.

'When I have fears that I may cease to be'

Written between 22 and 31 January 1818 and copied in Keats's letter to J. H. Reynolds, 31 January (*L*, I, 222). Published *1848*: text based on *L*.

'O blush not so! O blush not so!'

Probably written on 31 January 1818. Published *Forman (1883)*: text based on Charles Brown's transcript.

To — ('Time's sea hath been five years at its slow ebb')

Written 4 February 1818. Published *Hood's Magazine*, September 1844: text based on W2.

'O thou whose face hath felt the Winter's wind'

Written 19 February 1818 in a letter to J. H. Reynolds (*L*, I, 233). Published *1848*: text based on *L*. Introduced by the explanation, 'I had no Idea but of the Morning and the Thrush said I was right – seeming to say . . .' (*L*, I, 233).

The Human Seasons

Written between 7 and 13 March 1819. Published in Leigh Hunt's *Literary Pocket-Book* for 1819 (1818), with this title but without Keats's name attached.

'For there's Bishop's Teign'

Written in a letter to B. R. Haydon, *c.* 21 March 1818 (*L*, I, 249–50). Published T. Taylor's *Life of Benjamin Robert Haydon* (1853): text based on *L*. Like the next three poems, it was written while Keats was staying in Teignmouth, completing *Endymion* for publication. Virtually all the places mentioned are in the vicinity.

'Where be ye going, you Devon maid'

Written in Keats' letter to Haydon, *c.* 21 March 1818. Published *1848*: text based on *L*.

'Over the hill and over the dale'

Drafted or copied *c.* 23 March 1818 in a letter to his friend, James Rice (*L*, I, 256–7). Published *1848* (first quatrain), A. Lowell, *John Keats* (1925) (complete): text based on *L*.

5. *Rantipole*: 'Wild, disorderly, rakish' (*OED*).

16. *Venus*: A prostitute (colloquial).

To J. H. Reynolds, Esq.

Written 25 March 1818 (*L*, I, 259–63). Published *1848*: text based on *L*. Reynolds was ill when Keats wrote this letter to him from Teignmouth in 'hopes of cheering you through a Minute or two' (*L*, I, 263). However, Keats suddenly turns to the perplexing problem of pain and suffering in nature and the role of the imagination (67–105).

11. *Junius Brutus*: The Shakespearean actor, Junius Brutus Booth (1796–1852).

26. *the Enchanted Castle*: Painting by Claude now in the National Gallery, from which the following description (26–66) is drawn.

29. *Urganda's sword*: Urganda the Unknown, the enchantress in the medieval romance *Amadis of Gaul*.

42. *santon*: European term for a Mohammedan monk or hermit. The ancient Chaldeans controlled southern Babylonia.

72–3. *flag ... admiral staff*: The Athenian general, Alcibiades, flew a flag to identify his role as leader, i.e. Keats has not yet attained maturity.

Isabella; or, The Pot of Basil

Begun before 4 March 1818, completed by 27 April. Subsequently revised for publication in *1820*. Based on the fifth novella of the fourth day in Boccaccio's *Decameron*. Keats heightens the grotesque elements.

95. *Theseus' spouse*: Ariadne.

262. *Hinnom's vale*: A valley into which the Jews cast refuse and the bodies of animals and criminals.

393. *Persèan sword*: The sword Perseus used to cut off the Gorgon's head.

451. *Baälites of pelf*: Worshippers of false gods, in this case, money (pelf).

On Visiting the Tomb of Burns

Written 1 July 1818 at Dumfries in a letter to his brother, Tom (*L*, I, 308–9). Published *1848*: text based on *L*. 'This Sonnet I have written in a strange mood, half asleep. I know not how it is, the Clouds, the sky, the Houses [of Scotland], all seem anti Grecian and anti Charlemagnish' (*L*, I, 309), and hence antipathetic to poetry and the imagination. Written on the day Keats visited Burns's tomb during his walking tour through Scotland with Charles Brown (1787–1842), a firm friend, at whose house in Wentworth Place, Hampstead, Keats later stayed. This and the next six poems were written during their tour.

'Old Meg she was a gipsy'

Written in a letter to his sister, Fanny, 3 July 1818 (*L*, I, 311–12). Published *Plymouth and Devonport Weekly Journal*, 22 November 1838: text based on *L*. As they walked to Kirkcudbright, Brown told the story of Meg Merrilies in Scott's *Guy Mannering* (1814), which Keats had not read.

A Song about Myself

Written 3 July 1818 in Keats's letter to his sister Fanny (*L*, I, 312–15), when he and Brown stayed the night in Kirkcudbright. Published *Forman (1883)*: text based on *L*.

To Ailsa Rock

Written 10 July 1818 at an inn at Girvan in a letter to his brother Tom (*L*, I, 329–30). Published Leigh Hunt's *Literary Pocket-Book* for 1819 (1818) without Keats's name attached: text based on *L*.

Lines Written in the Highlands after a Visit to Burns's Country

Written on or before 22 July 1818 and revised in a letter to his friend. Benjamin Bailey (*L*, I, 344–5). Published *New Monthly Magazine*, March 1822 (in part); first complete text in *Examiner*, 14 July 1822: text based on *L*. Keats had reached Inverary by this time. His employment of fourteeners reflects his reading in the Elizabethan poets.

'Read me a lesson, Muse, and speak it loud'

Written 2 August 1818 on the top of Ben Nevis and sent in a letter to his brother Tom (*L*, I, 357). Published *Plymouth and Devonport Weekly Journal*, 6 September 1838: text based on *L*.

'Upon my life, Sir Nevis, I am piqued'

Written 3 August 1818 in a letter to Tom Keats (*L*, I, 354–7). Published *Forman (1883)*: text based on *L*. Keats reports that a fifty-year-old woman, Mrs Cameron, had climbed Ben Nevis a few years earlier. His poem invents a conversation between her and the mountain once she had reached the top and had a glass of whiskey.

29. *Red Crag*: 'A domestic of Ben's' (Keats's note).
53. *Blockhead*: 'Another domestic of Ben's' (Keats's note).

Fragment: 'Where's the Poet? Show him, show him'

Written in 1818, possibly in October. Published *1848*: text based on Charles Brown's transcript.

'And what is love? It is a doll dressed up'

Written in 1818. Published *1848*: text based on W2. Brown's transcript adds the title 'Modern Love'.

Hyperion. A Fragment.

Mainly written between late September 1818 and the death of Tom Keats, 1 December 1818. Finally abandoned in April 1819. Published *1820*, whose Advertisement says the fragment was printed at the publisher's 'particular request, and contrary to the wish of the poet'. Keats said, '. . . in Endymion I think you may have many bits of a deep and sentimental cast – the nature of *Hyperion* will lead me to treat it in a more naked and Grecian manner – and the march of passion and endeavour will be undeviating . . .'

The poem's style and imagery reflect Keats's recent reading of Dante, Shakespeare and, above all, Milton's *Paradise Lost*. Richard Woodhouse recorded, 'The poem, if completed, would have treated of the dethronement of Hyperion, the former God of the Sun, by Apollo . . . and of the war of the Giants [i.e. Titans] for Saturn's re-establishment, of which we have but very dark hints in the mythological poets of Greece and Rome. In fact, the incidents would have been pure creations of the poet's brain.'

Keats's re-imagining of the epic struggle in which Saturn and the Titans are overthrown by their children, the Olympian gods, begins in mid-action. The Titans have been defeated. Only Hyperion, the Titan god of the sun, is as yet undefeated by his successor, Apollo. Books I and II describe the Titans' sufferings, the unfinished Book III Apollo's apotheosis into godhead. Hyperion's downfall is seen as the tragic consequence of an inevitable historical evolution towards higher forms of beauty. For Keats Apollo was the god of poetry as well as the god of the sun and of healing. Although *Hyperion* is not overtly political, its mythic world puts forward an alternative 'Greek' vision of heroic struggle and human progress, created out of Keats's dissatisfactions with the dominant trends in contemporary politics, religion and government.

BOOK I

145. *Chaos*: Saturn is depicted as the creator of the ordered universe.
274. *colure*: An astronomical term. 'Each of two great circles which intersect each other at right angles at the poles, and divide the equinoctial and the ecliptic into four equal parts' (*OED*).
305–8. Here Keats ignores the hostility between Coelus, father of the Titans, and his sons.

BOOK II

22–8. The eruption of Mount Etna was supposed to be caused by the struggles of the Titans, who had been imprisoned by Jupiter beneath it.

45–8. Iapetus's crushing of the snake seems to be Keats's invention.

167. *God of the Sea*: The Titan deity, Oceanus, who was replaced by Neptune.

181–243. Reflects Keats's view that both personal experience and the history of mankind obey a law of progress. Compare *Sleep and Poetry* 101–21.

374–6. *Memnon's image . . . Memnon's harp*: Memnon was the son of Aurora. His statue, near Thebes in Egypt, made melodious music to welcome the dawn and lamented the passing of the day in the evening. Hyperion, god of the sun, gives way to Apollo, god of sun and music.

BOOK III

113–20. Apollo attains godhead through knowledge of suffering. The relationship between poetic power and this knowledge is central to the meaning of *Hyperion*.

'Hush, hush! tread softly! hush, hush my dear!'

Probably written in December 1818. Published *Hood's Magazine*, April 1845; text based on Fanny Brawne's later transcript in her copy of Hunt's *Literary Pocket-Book* for 1819 (1818). Reportedly composed to an air for Charlotte Reynolds to play at the piano, but possibly connected with Keats's flirtation with Isabella Jones.

The Eve of St Agnes

Written between 18 January and 2 February 1819; revised September 1819. Published *1820*. Keats's alterations in September made the poem more sexually explicit (see note to 314–22 for the most significant alteration), and deeply upset his publishers, Taylor and Hessey. Richard Woodhouse told Taylor that 'tho' there are not improper expressions [in the alterations] but all is left to inference, and tho' profanely speaking, the Interest on the reader's imagination is greatly heightened, yet I do apprehend it will render the poem unfit for ladies,

& indeed scarcely to be mentioned to them among the "things that
are"' (*L*, II, 163). Taylor refused to publish the volume unless the
more innocent version was restored. Keats, who was concerned to
appear manly and not mawkish, is usually judged to have coarsened
the poem's balance and tone. The earlier text is printed here. The
narrative turns on the superstition that if a virgin observed the proper
rites on the eve of St Agnes she would dream of her future husband.
The idea of the poem was possibly suggested by Isabella Jones, whose
brief relationship with Keats was marked by strong sexual overtones.
314–22. Keats's revised draft replaced these lines with: 'See, while
she speaks his arms encroaching slow,/Have zoned her, heart to
heart, – loud, loud the dark winds blow!/For on the midnight
came a tempest fell;/More sooth, for that his quick rejoinder
flows/Into her burning ear; and still the spell/Unbroken guards
her in serene repose./With her wild dream he mingled, as a rose/
Marrieth its odour to a violet./Still, still she dreams, louder the
frost wind blows.'

The Eve of St Mark

Written 13–17 February 1819. Published *1848*: text based on MS
(see *Texts*, pp. 220–2). Unfinished. Possibly begun on a suggestion of
Isabella Jones.

'Why did I laugh tonight? No voice will tell'

Written before 19 March 1819 when Keats copied it in a letter to
George and Georgiana Keats (*L*, II, 81). Published *1848*: text based
on *L*.

Character of Charles Brown

Written 16 April 1819 in letter to George and Georgiana Keats (*L*, II,
89–90). Published *1848*: text based on *L*. This extempore *jeu d'esprit*
is a reply to a skit Brown was writing on Keats and Fanny Brawne.
Brown was anything but melancholy: he was bald, heavily built, in his
thirties and flirtatious. He had a child by his housekeeper, Abigail
O'Donaghue.

A Dream, after reading Dante's Episode of
Paolo and Francesca

Written *c.* 16 April 1819, when Keats copied it out for George and
Georgiana Keats (*L*, II, 91). Published in Leigh Hunt's *Indicator*,
28 June 1820, signed 'Caviare': text based on *L*. Not published in
1820. Keats had been reading Cary's translation of Dante's *Inferno*.
Just as Hermes rescued Io by lulling her hundred-eyed guardian Argus
to sleep with music, so his reading makes the poem's narrator forget
worldly anxieties, and flee to Dante's second circle. Paolo and
Francesca are sinners condemned for their illicit love, but for whom
Dante has compassion because of their innocence and youth. The
dreamer and Paolo are assimilated into one.

10.   *whirlwind*: This is the manuscript reading: the *Indicator* text has
        'world-wind', which would indicate that the world itself is wholly
        inimical to romantic love.

La Belle Dame sans Merci. A Ballad

Written 21 April 1819 in letter to George and Georgiana Keats (*L*,
II, 95–6). Published *Indicator*, 10 May 1820, signed 'Caviare'. Not
published in *1820*. The *Indicator*'s text introduces an ironic tone
absent in the letter version Keats sent to George and Georgiana Keats
and the MSS versions. The text given here follows that in Keats's
letter. The title is that of a ballad by the fifteenth-century French poet
Alain Chartier.

To Sleep

Probably written late April 1819, copied in a letter to George and
Georgiana Keats on 30 April (*L*, II, 104). Published *Plymouth and
Devonport Weekly Journal*, 11 October 1838: text based on Keats's
later album text (*Texts*, pp. 235–7). This experimental sonnet, like
the next, led to the stanzaic structure of the 'Ode to Psyche'.

'If by dull rhymes our English must be chained'

Probably written before 30 April 1819. Published *Plymouth, Devon, and Stonehouse News*, 15 October 1836: text from W2.

Ode to Psyche

Written between 21 and 30 April 1819. Published *1820*. Keats described the ode as '. . . the first and only [poem] with which I have taken even moderate pains . . . You must recollect that Psyche was not embodied as a goddess before the time of Apuleius the Platonist who lived after the Augustan age, and consequently the Goddess was never worshipped or sacrificed to with any of the ancient fervour – and perhaps never thought of in the old religion – I am more orthodox tha[n] to let a he[a]then Goddess be so neglected.' According to Lempriere's *Bibliotheca Classica*, Psyche was 'a nymph whom Cupid married and carried into a place of bliss, where he long enjoyed her company. Venus put her to death because she had robbed the world of her son; but Jupiter, at the request of Cupid, granted immortality to Psyche. The word signifies *the soul*, and this personification is posterior to the Augustan age . . .' Keats names Cupid only as 'the winged boy' and 'the warm Love'. The son of Venus and Jupiter, he is identified with Eros, the Greek god of love, and is usually depicted as a child with a bow and quiver of arrows. Here he is a young man. In the legend he visited Psyche secretly at night.

On Fame (I)

Written 30 April 1819 and copied that day in a letter to George and Georgiana Keats (*L*, II, 105). Published *Ladies' Companion* (New York, August 1837): text based on W1–2.

On Fame II

Written 30 April 1819 in a letter to George and Georgiana Keats (*L*, II, 104–5). Published *1848*: text based on W2. An extempore sonnet written while Charles Brown was transcribing the previous poem.

'Two or three posies'

Written *c.* 1 May 1819 in a letter to his sister, Fanny (*L*, II, 56–7). Published *Forman (1883)*: text based on *L*.

20.   *Mrs* —: Mrs Abbey, wife of Richard Abbey who acted as guardian to the Keats children from 1810. Relations between Abbey and Keats were strained.

Ode on a Grecian Urn

Written in 1819. Date conjectural, but probably early May. Published *Annals of the Fine Arts*, 4 (January 1820), *1820*.

The relation of the final couplet to the rest of the ode has been much debated. Does the speaker endorse the Urn's 'motto' or is the 'motto' that of the Urn itself? *1820* reads ' "Beauty is truth, truth beauty." – that is all/Ye know on earth, and all ye need to know.' The *Annals* and MSS texts, with other punctuation variants, omit the inverted commas round the opening phrase. The present text, which encloses the couplet with speech marks, attributes both lines to the Urn.

Ode to a Nightingale

Dated 'May 1819' in *W1–2*, but exact date conjectural. Published *1820*. Normally believed to precede 'Ode on a Grecian Urn', but the internal references suggest a date in mid-May.

16.   *the true, the blushful Hippocrene*: A periphrasis for wine. 'Hippocrene' was a fountain sacred to the Muses.

Ode on Melancholy

Date conjectural, but probably May 1819. Published *1820*.

Ode on Indolence

Probably written late May or early June 1819, though possibly written earlier in spring before the major odes. Published *1848*: text from W2.

Lamia

Written *c.* 28 June and 11 July 1819, 12 August and *c.* 5 September 1819, revised March 1820. Published *1820*. Keats printed his prime source at the end of the poem in *1820*, quoting Robert Burton's *Anatomy of Melancholy* III.2.i.1:

> Philostratus, in his fourth book *de Vita Apollonii*, hath a memorable instance in this kind, which I may not omit, of one Menippus Lycius, a young man twenty-five years of age, that going betwixt Cenchreas and Corinth met such a phantasm in the habit of a fair gentlewoman, which taking him by the hand, carried him home to her house, in the suburbs of Corinth, and told him she was a Phoenician by birth, and if he would tarry with her, he should hear her sing and play, and drink such wine as never any drank, and no man should molest him; but she, being fair and lovely, would live and die with him, that was fair and lovely to behold. The young man, a philosopher, otherwise staid and discreet, able to moderate his passions, though not this of love, tarried with her a while to his great content, and at last married her, to whose wedding, amongst other guests, came Apollonius; who, by some probable conjectures, found her out to be a serpent, a lamia; and that all her furniture was, like Tantalus' gold, described by Homer, no substance but mere illusions. When she saw herself descried, she wept, and desired Apollonius to be silent, but he would not be moved, and thereupon she, plate, house, and all that was in it, vanished in an instant: many thousands took notice of this fact, for it was in the midst of Greece.

PART I

1–6. Keats takes from Elizabethan literature the idea that the classical nymphs, satyrs and gods were displaced by the fairies of English folk-lore.

81. *star of Lethe*: I.e. Hermes (Mercury) who conducted spirits to the underworld.

229. Jove (Jupiter) was one of the gods who had a care over marriage.

320. *Adonian feast*: Summer festival celebrating Adonis's return to earth from the underworld.

PART II

225–6. *let us strip for him/The thyrsus*: Lycius's wreath is to be made from the ivy and vine leaves twisted round Bacchus's thyrsus (wand).

'Bright star! would I were as steadfast as thou art'

Date conjectural and controversial. Published *Plymouth and Devon-port Weekly Journal*, 27 September 1838: text based on fair copy in a blank leaf of Keats's copy of *Poetical Works of William Shakespeare* (1806). Long thought to be Keats's last poem, written on board the *Maria Crowther*, but in fact written earlier. It has been variously dated 1 October 1818, 25 July 1819, and October–November 1819. A date in late July 1819 now seems to me the most probable.

To Autumn

Written *c.* 19 September 1819. Published *1820*.

The Fall of Hyperion. A Dream

Begun mid-July 1819, 'given up' *c.* 21 September 1819. Published *Biographical and Historical Collections of the Philobiblon Society, 1856–7* (1857): text based on W2.

Keats's second attempt at the Hyperion story looks to Dante rather than Milton. The fragment is a dream vision in which the narrator is initiated into knowledge by Moneta, an admonitory version of Mnemosyne (goddess of memory and foster-mother of Apollo). At Canto I, 294, Keats began to work in material from his earlier poem. The fragment concludes with the appearance of Hyperion in Canto II. Its precise allegorical implications are obscure. It has been read as a rejection of the politics of Coleridge and Wordsworth. However, the dream seems not only to examine the nature of a true poet, but to give a Keatsian version of the origins of myth and religion, as well as a critique of his own poetic career. The evolutionary optimism of *Hyperion* is not sustained in *The Fall of Hyperion*. The syntax and thought of the invocation (I, 1–18) are less than transparent. The *'Fanatics'* (I, 1) seem not to be likened to the *'savages'* (I, 2) but to be their opposite. The savage, an animist *'guess[ing] at Heaven'* from the evidence of the natural world, cannot, without the medium of writing perpetuate his dreams. The *'fanatic'* imprisons his sect in a false paradise. Only *'Poesy'* can give permanent life to the truths perceived by unlettered savages. Keats's poem could itself be either a fanatic's dream or truth.

The reader must decide whether the narrator is a poet or dreamer (I, 198–200).

The '*arbor*' entered by the narrator (I, 19–38) seems to represent the pastoral '*realm of Flora*', embodied in Keats's career by *Endymion*, or what Keats elsewhere calls 'the Chamber of Maiden Thought' (*L*, I, 281). There is probably no precise meaning for the '*full draught*' (I, 42–5). The encounter between the narrator and Moneta in a temple (I, 62–293) is probably in some part a reply to Coleridge's second *Lay Sermon* (1817) with a humanist goddess in place of Coleridge's Christian supernaturalism. Although the speaker's outburst against contemporary false poets (I, 204–10) is deliberately generalized, aspects of Wordsworth, Coleridge and Byron are probably in Keats's sights.

'What can I do to drive away'

Date conjectural. Possibly October 1819. Published *1848*: text from *1848* (but omitting 'bud' in line 42). Text possibly taken from a lost MS possessed by Fanny Brawne (see Introduction, p. xxiv). The poem is an expression of Keats's confused feeling for Fanny Brawne (see Introduction). The '*friends*' dungeoned in '*that most hateful land*' are his brother George, his sister-in-law Georgiana and their new child, who were experiencing difficulties after emigrating to America. Keats depicts the New World as barren of mythology.

'I cry your mercy, pity, love – ay, love!'

Probably written October 1819. Published *1848*. The text of *1848* was taken from Charles Brown's transcript, probably made from a lost MS possessed by Fanny Brawne (see Introduction, p. xxiv).

'This living hand, now warm and capable'

Probably written in November or December 1819. Published H. B. Forman, *The Poetical Works of John Keats*, 6th edn (1893): text based on that written in the MS of *The Caps and Bells: or, The Jealousies*. Formerly thought to be addressed to Fanny Brawne, but possibly a fragment for later use in a poem or play.

To Fanny

Probably written in February 1820. Published *1848*: text incorporates corrections from Keats's fragmentary draft. Text possibly drawn from a lost MS possessed by Fanny Brawne (see Introduction, p. xxiv). Keats's first haemorrhage was on 3 February. He was confined indoors: Fanny Brawne was living next door in Wentworth Place.

1–3. *Physician . . . tripod*: Apollo's priestess, the Pythia, delivered her oracles from a tripod in his temple at Delphi. Apollo was god of medicine as well as poetry.

'In after-time, a sage of mickle lore'

Probably written *c*. July 1820 in the (lost) copy of Spenser Keats gave to Fanny Brawne. Published *Plymouth and Devonport Weekly Journal*, 4 July 1839: text based on Charles Brown's transcript in his copy of Spenser. Keats wrote the lines at the end of *The Faerie Queene*, V.ii. Charles Brown said this was 'the last stanza of any kind that [Keats] wrote before his lamented death'. The stanza inverts Spenser's anti-democratic allegory (V.ii. 29–54). There, Spenser's 'mighty Gyant', who demands equality for all, is opposed by Artegall (Justice, and the English crown's representative in Ireland) and Talus (the executive arm of the government). Keats's '*Giant*' of the future restores the lost wisdom of Typographus (that is, restores a free press), and disables the two oppressors.

Dictionary of Classical Names Used by Keats

This Dictionary draws frequently on John Lempriere's *Bibliotheca Classica* (1797, 3rd edn.) to which Charles Cowden Clarke, his schoolteacher and friend, attributed Keats's 'uncommon familiarity – almost consanguinity with the Greek mythology'. Quotations from this work, or entries drawn from it, are indicated by quotation marks. Keats follows Lempriere in using, for the most part, the Roman names of the classical deities.

Acteon. 'A famous huntsman ... He saw Diana and her attendants bathing ... for which he was changed into a stag, and devoured by his own dogs.' Usually spelt Actaeon.

Adonis. A huntsman beloved by the goddess, Venus. He ignored her advice against hunting and was killed by a wild boar, upon which Venus transformed him into the anemone. Proserpine restored him to life on condition that he spent six months with her in the underworld and six months with Venus. 'This implies the alternate return of summer and winter. Adonis is often taken for Osiris, because the festivals of both' celebrated his return to life.

Aeaea. Island off Sicily, birthplace of Circe.

Aeolus. 'The king of storms and waves.' His kingdom was the islands between Italy and Sicily.

Aethon. One of the horses which drew the chariot of the sun.

Aetna. Mount Etna, Sicily. Jupiter was reputed to have confined the fallen Titans under this mountain, which was also the forge of Vulcan, where he and the Cyclops forged thunderbolts.

Alecto. 'One of the furies ... represented with her head covered with serpents, and breathing vengeance, war, and pestilence.'

Alpheus. God of a river in Arcadia. See Arethusa.

Amalthea. Daughter of the king of Crete. She fed Jupiter with goat's milk and in gratitude he elevated her into a constellation.

Amphion. Son of Jupiter by Antiope, who cultivated poetry and music. In *Endymion*, III. 461, Keats fuses him with Arion who had power over the sea.

Apollo. Also known as Phoebus. Above all for Keats, the god of music and poetry: also the god of medicine. Son of Jupiter and Latona, and twin-brother of Diana, he took over the role of god and charioteer of the sun from Hyperion.

Arcadia, Arcady. Inland country in the Peloponnesus of Greece, celebrated by the poets. A pastoral world inhabited by shepherd-warriors, a main dwelling-place of Pan.

Arethusa. One of Diana's nymphs. She bathed in the river Alpheus in Arcadia, whose river-god fell in love with her. Diana turned her into a fountain to escape his attentions, but when she fled under the sea to another island, she was pursued there by Alpheus, where he mingled with her fountain.

Argonauts. The ancient heroes who sailed with Jason in search of the Golden Fleece.

Argus. A watchman with one hundred eyes. See also Io.

Ariadne. Daughter of the king of Crete, who was abandoned by her lover, Theseus, on the Island of Naxos. Bacchus fell in love with her and 'gave her a crown of seven stars, which after her death, were made into a constellation'.

Asia. Daughter of Oceanus and Tethys according to the poet Hesiod. In *Hyperion*, II, 53–5, Keats invents an alternative parentage for her: there she is the daughter of Tellus (Terra) and Caf, an enormous Caucasian mountain that figured in eastern tales.

Atlas. 'One of the Titans, son of Japetus and Clymene . . . Atlas assisted the giants in their wars against the gods, for which Jupiter compelled him to bear the heavens on his shoulders.'

Aurora. Goddess of dawn.

Bacchus. God of the vine, son of Jupiter and Semele. He was celebrated for his progress to the East with an army of men and women, drawn in a chariot by a lion and tiger and accompanied by Pan, Silenus and the satyrs, spreading the cultivation of the vine. Keats's descriptions of Bacchus were influenced by Titian's painting *Bacchus and Ariadne*, shown at the British Institution in 1816.

Boreas. God of the north wind.

Briareus. A Titan.

Caf. See Asia.

Carian. Alternative name for Endymion: see also Latmos.

Ceres. Goddess of corn and harvests, 'represented with garland of ears of corn on her head, holding in one hand a lighted torch, and in the other a poppy, which was sacred to her.'

Chaos. The original confusion in which earth, sea and air were mixed together: for the Greeks the most ancient of the gods.

Circe. Enchantress celebrated 'for her knowledge of magic and venomous herbs', who 'showed herself cruel towards her rival Scylla'. She was expelled by the inhabitants of Colchis to the island Aeaea. When Ulysses and his men visited the isle, she changed all but Ulysses to swine: Ulysses himself was proof against her magic, but not her charms. See also Glaucus.

Clymene. A Titan, daughter of Oceanus and Tethys, who married Iapetus and bore him Atlas and Prometheus.

Coelus. 'An ancient deity' of the heavens, son of Tellus, whom he afterwards married. Their sons were the Titans who, led by Saturn, rebelled against their father and overthrew him. Also known as Uranus.

Cocus. A Titan.

Cottus. A Titan.

Creus. A Titan.

Cupid. See note to 'Ode to Psyche'.

Cyclades. A cluster of islands in the Aegean.

Cyclops. 'A certain race of man of gigantic stature, supposed to be the sons of Coelus and Terra. They had but one eye in the middle of their forehead; whence their name . . .'

Cynthia. Alternative name for Diana.

Cytherea. Cyprus, birthplace of Venus.

Delos. One of the islands of the Cyclades: birthplace of Apollo and Diana, where the former had a famous temple.

Delphos. Delphi, a place above all sacred to Apollo, who was supposed to have killed the Python there.

Diana. (also called by Keats Cynthia, Phoebe, or Hecate): twin sister of Apollo. In heaven, the moon, on earth the goddess of hunting, of chastity and of child-birth. In her personification as Hecate, she was sometimes confused with Proserpine, goddess of the underworld.

Dis. See Pluto.

Dolor. A Titan.

Dryads. Immortal wood nymphs.

Dryope. (i) Mother of Pan (*Endymion*, I, 290); (ii) nymph ravished by Apollo (*Endymion*, I, 495).

Echo. A nymph punished by Juno for loquacity, and only allowed to answer questions put to her. Spurned by Narcissus, she pined away until only her voice remained.

Elysium. The Elysian Fields, the abode of the virtuous, in the infernal regions.

Enceladus. The 'most powerful' of the Titans. 'He was struck with Jupiter's thunderbolt, and overwhelmed under Mount Aetna. Some suppose he is the same as Typhon.'

Endymion. Shepherd prince of Caria and astronomer, who studied the moon. The goddess Diana fell in love when she saw him on Mount Latmos. She cast him in a deep sleep so that she could visit him undiscovered, and ultimately persuaded Jupiter to give him eternal life. Keats freely elaborates his sources.

Fauns. Alternative name for satyrs.

Flora. 'The Goddess of flowers and gardens among the Romans.'

Ganymede. A beautiful youth taken up to heaven by Jupiter as cup-bearer to the gods.

Glaucus. Keats uses Ovid, *Metamorphoses*, XIII, 898–968 and XIV, 11–74 as a starting point for the story of Glaucus in *Endymion*. According to Ovid, Glaucus, a fisherman and son of Neptune and Nais, leaps into the sea where he wishes to live, and is made a sea deity by Oceanus and Tethys. He falls in love with the Nereid Scylla, who rebuffs him. Glaucus seeks help from Circe who, however, falls in love with him herself, and metamorphoses Scylla into a monster. In horror, Scylla hurls herself into the sea between Italy and Sicily, becoming a legendary rock dangerous to shipping.

Gyges. A Titan.

Hamadryads. Mortal wood nymphs, bound to the tree in which they lived.

Hecate. Goddess associated with magic, witchcraft and the moon, sometimes identified with Diana and hence an alternative name for that goddess.

Helicon. Mountain in Boeotia, source of the Hippocrene fountain. Sacred to the Muses, who had a temple there.

Hercules. Mythological hero who performed Twelve Labours and built his funeral pyre on Mount Oeta.

Hermes. Greek name for Mercury.

Hesperides. Daughters of Hesperus who guarded the golden apples that Juno gave to Jupiter as a wedding gift. The garden of the Hesperides was sited beyond the ocean. It 'abounded with fruits of the most delicious kind'.

Hesperus. (i) Son of Iapetus and father of the preceding; (ii) also the name given to the planet Venus when it appeared after sunset, but called Phosphorus or Lucifer when it preceded sunset.

Hippocrene. See *Ode to a Nightingale*, note to line 16 (p. 260).

Hyacinth(us). Youth beloved by Apollo and Zephyrus, the west wind.
The latter was jealous of Hyacinth's love for Apollo: while the two
were playing quoits, Zephyrus blew one of the stone discs towards
Hyacinth so that it killed him. The disconsolate Apollo changed
Hyacinth's blood into the hyacinth flower and 'placed his body
among the constellations'.

Hyperion. A Titan, son of Coelus and Tellus. 'Hyperion is often taken
by the poets for the sun itself.' Hence, he was Apollo's predecessor
as sun-god, and associated by Keats with the Olympian god's other
roles.

Iapetus. One of the Titan deities, the father of Atlas and Prometheus.

Ida. A mountain near Troy where 'the shepherd Paris adjudged the
price of beauty to the goddess Venus'.

Io. Juno's priestess at Argos, who was loved by Jupiter. He changed
her into a beautiful heifer to avoid Juno's jealousy, but 'the goddess,
who well knew the fraud . . . commanded the hundred-eyed Argus'
to guard her. In revenge Jupiter sent Hermes to destroy Argus and
free her.

Jove. Alternative name for Jupiter.

Jupiter. The most powerful of the Olympian gods, son of Saturn and
Ops. Saturn devoured his children at birth, but Jupiter was secreted
in a cave on Mount Ida. Jupiter rebelled against Saturn, and became
sole master of the universe, reserving heaven for himself, and gave
the empires of the sea and infernal regions to his brothers, Neptune
and Pluto.

Lamia. A serpent; see headnote to *Lamia* (p. 261).

Latmos. Mountain in Caria, seat of Endymion's rule. Hence 'Latmian'
and 'Carian' are alternative names for Endymion.

Latona. Mother of Apollo and Diana by Jupiter.

Leda. Wife of Tyndarus, king of Sparta, visited by Jupiter in the shape
of a swan. She gave birth to two eggs, from which were hatched the
heroes Castor and Pollux, Helen of Troy, and Clytemnestra.

Lethe. A river in hell. When the souls of the dead drank from it they
forgot 'whatever they had done, seen or heard before'.

Lucifer. See Hesperus.

Lycaeus. Mountain in Arcadia sacred to Jupiter and Pan.

Meander. River in Asia Minor celebrated for its windings.

Melpomene. Muse of tragedy.

Mercury. Son of Jupiter by Maia. Messenger of the gods portrayed
with a winged hat and winged feet and carrying a caduceus (a wand,

usually represented with two serpents twisted round it). Conducted spirits to and from the spirit world. Supposed to be the inventor of letters: hence the god of eloquence and trade.

Mnemosyne. Daughter of Coelus and Terra, mother of the Nine Muses by Jupiter. 'The word *Mnemosyne* signifies *memory*, and therefore poets have rightly called memory the mother of the muses . . .' In *Hyperion*, she deserts the Titans to join her foster-child Apollo (III, 76–9). In *The Fall of Hyperion* she is represented as Moneta, who initiates the narrator into knowledge.

Moneta. See previous entry.

Morpheus. God of sleep.

Mulciber. Alternative name for Vulcan.

Naiads. Inferior deities who presided over rivers, springs, wells and fountains.

Narcissus. A youth of Boeotia who fell in love with his own image in a pool. He killed himself thinking it an unattainable nymph, and was transformed into the flower of that name. See also Echo.

Neptune. Son of Saturn, who became Olympian god of the sea.

Nereids. Sea nymphs.

Niobe. Wife of Amphion who had twenty children. She insulted Latona, at whose request Apollo and Diana struck down all her children but one. Niobe 'was changed to a stone' by her misfortunes.

Oceanus. 'A powerful deity of the sea, son of Coelus and Terra . . .'

Olympians. Gods and goddesses who, led by Jupiter, rebelled against the Titans led by Saturn. Lived on Mount Olympus.

Ops. Daughter of Coelus and Tellus. Often identified with Cybele, wife of Saturn and mother of Jupiter, hence known as Mother of the Gods.

Oreads. Nymphs of the mountains.

Orpheus. Thracian shepherd, the son of Calliope and of Apollo, who gave him a lyre on which he could play music with the power to move inanimate things. He followed his dead wife Eurydice to the infernal regions and, by his music, persuaded Pluto to release her, provided Orpheus did not look back until they reached earth. At the last moment Orpheus did so, and Eurydice vanished.

Pan. God of shepherds and country people in Arcadia, player of the pan-pipes. Son of Mercury and Dryope, half man, half goat, he was thought to derive from the Egyptian god of fecundity. The 'name of *Pan* . . . signifies *all* or *every thing*'.

Paphos. Birthplace of Venus in Cyprus.

Peona. Endymion's sister (Keats's invention).

Phoebe. See Diana.

Phoebus. See Apollo.

Phoebus' daughter. The enchantress Circe.

Phorcus. A Titan sea deity. With his sister Ceto, he fathered the Gorgons (three snake-headed monsters) and other monsters.

Pleiades. The 'seven daughters of Atlas . . . They were placed in the heavens after death, where they formed a constellation called Pleiades . . .' In *Lamia* (I, 265–7) Lycius thinks that Lamia is one of these stars descended to earth.

Pluto. Son of Saturn and Ops, he was made 'god of the infernal regions, of death and funerals' following the successful rebellion of the Olympians against the Titans. Also known as Dis.

Pomona. 'Goddess of all sorts of fruit-trees.' See also Vertumnus.

Porphyrion. A Titan.

Prometheus. Son of Iapetus and Clymene, the Titan god who 'made the first man and woman . . . with clay, which animated by . . . fire which he had stolen from heaven.' In the two *Hyperions* he is portrayed as Apollo's predecessor as the god of the sun and poetry.

Proserpine. Daughter of Ceres by Jupiter, carried away to the infernal regions by Pluto where she became queen. Some traditions identify her with Hecate, which may be relevant to her introduction in *Endymion*, I, 944–6.

Psyche. See headnote, *Ode to Psyche* (p. 259).

Pyrrha. Wife of Deucalion. When Jupiter, enraged by mankind's enormities, destroyed the world with a flood, he saved the couple, noted for their virtuous lives. Following an oracle, they cast pebbles over their shoulders; those thrown by Pyrrha turned into women, those by Deucalion into men.

Python. Serpent created by Juno to persecute Latona when pregnant by Jupiter. When her son, Apollo, was born he killed the monster.

Rhadamanthus. Son of Jupiter by Europa, he reigned in the Cyclades 'with so much justice and impartiality' that he became one of the judges in the infernal regions.

Saturn. Son of Coelus by Tellus. Leader of the Titans, he was overthrown by his sons, led by Jupiter, who established the Olympian rule. In the two *Hyperions* Keats passes over the tradition that Saturn devoured his children at birth, and also transposes the Saturnian Golden Age to a period before the Olympian wars.

Satyrs. 'Demigods of the country', half-men, half-goats, attendants on Bacchus.

Scylla. Sea nymph; see Glaucus.

Silenus. 'A demi-god . . . nurse, preceptor, and attendant of the god Bacchus.'

Syrinx. Arcadian nymph who fled to the River Lodon to escape the attentions of Pan, where he metamorphosed her into a reed from which he made his pipes.

Tellus. 'A divinity, the same as the earth, the most antient of all the gods after Chaos.' Mother of the Titans, also known as Cybele or Terra.

Tempe. 'A valley in Thessaly, between mount Olympus in the north, and Ossa at the south . . . The poets have described it as the most delightful spot on earth.'

Terra. See Tellus.

Tethys. 'The greatest of the sea deities, was wife of Oceanus, and daughter of Uranus and Terra.'

Thea. A Titan, daughter of Coelus and Tellus.

Themis. A Titan, daughter of Coelus and Tellus.

Theseus. Greek hero who was a legendary king of Athens. With the help of his lover Ariadne, he killed the Minotaur, but later abandoned her.

Thessaly. Region of northern Greece.

Titans. A race of giant gods led by Saturn who were defeated by the Olympians; the children of Coelus and Tellus.

Triton. 'A sea deity, son of Neptune by Amphitrite', generally represented as half man, half fish.

Typhon. One of the Titans, thought to be the type of ambition, aspiring to rebel against heaven. See also Enceladus.

Urania. (i) Daughter of Jupiter and Mnemosyne, Muse of astronomy and music; (ii) a surname of Venus.

Uranus. See Coelus.

Venus. (i) '. . . the goddess of beauty, the mother of love . . . the mistress of graces and pleasures, and the patroness of courtesans . . .' She was the mother of Cupid and Anteros by Mars. For her love for Adonis, see Adonis; (ii) the evening star (i.e., Venus Urania).

Vertumnus. Roman deity presiding over the spring and gardens. He unsuccessfully tried to gain the affections of Pomona.

Vulcan. 'A god of the antients who presided over fire, and was the patron of artists who worked iron and metals . . . The Cyclops . . . were his ministers and attendants.'

Zephyr(us). The west wind, 'said to produce flowers and fruits by the sweetness of his breath.'

Index of Titles

Index of First Lines

Penguin Classics

DON JUAN
LORD BYRON

'Let us have wine and women's mirth and laughter,
Sermons and soda water the day after'

Byron's exuberant parody involves the adventures of a youth named Don Juan.
His exploits include an adulterous liaison in Spain, an affair on a Greek island
with a pirate's daughter, a stay in a Sultan's harem, a bloody battle in Turkey and
a sojourn in Russia as the lover of Catherine the Great – all described by a
narrator who frequently digresses from his hero in order to converse with his
readers about war, society and convention. A revolutionary experiment in epic,
Don Juan blends high drama with earthy humour, outrageous satire of Byron's
contemporaries (in particular Wordsworth and Southey) and mockery of Western
culture, with England under particular attack.

This edition represents a significant contribution to Byron scholarship and the
editors have drawn on their authoritative edition of the poem published by the
University of Texas Press. Their extensive annotation covers points of interest,
selected variant readings and historical allusions Byron wove into his poem.
This edition also includes an illuminating new introduction by Susan J. Wolfson
and Peter J. Manning, and updated further reading.

Edited by T. G. Steffan, E. Steffan and W. W. Pratt

With a new introduction by Susan J. Wolfson and Peter J. Manning

---

PENGUIN CLASSICS

THE COMPLETE POEMS
ANDREW MARVELL

'Thus, though we cannot make our sun
Stand still, yet we will make him run'

Member of Parliament, tutor to Oliver Cromwell's ward, satirist and friend of
John Milton, Andrew Marvell was one of the most significant poets of the
seventeenth century. *The Complete Poems* demonstrates his unique skill and
immense diversity, and includes lyrical love-poetry, religious works and biting
satire. From the passionately erotic 'To his Coy Mistress', to the astutely political
Cromwellian poems and the prescient 'Garden' and 'Mower' poems, which
consider humankind's relationship with the environment, these works are
masterpieces of clarity and metaphysical imagery. Eloquent and compelling, they
remain among the most vital and profound works of the era – works by a figure
who, in the words of T. S. Eliot, 'speaks clearly and unequivocally with the voice
of his literary age'.

This edition of Marvell's complete poems is based on a detailed study of the extant
manuscripts, with modern translations provided for Marvell's Greek and Latin
poems. This edition also includes a chronology, further reading, appendices, notes
and indexes of titles and first lines, with a new introduction by Jonathan Bate.

Edited by Elizabeth Story Donno

With an introduction by Jonathan Bate

PENGUIN CLASSICS

SELECTED ESSAYS, POEMS AND OTHER WRITINGS
GEORGE ELIOT

'We can often detect a man's deficiencies in what he admires more clearly than in what he condemns'

The works collected in this volume provide an illuminating introduction to George Eliot's incisive views on religion, art and science, and the nature and purpose of fiction. Essays such as 'Evangelical Teaching' show her rejecting her earlier religious beliefs, while 'Woman in France' questions conventional ideas about female virtues and marriage, and 'Notes on Form in Art' sets out theories of idealism and realism that she developed further in *Middlemarch* and *Daniel Deronda*. It also includes selections from Eliot's translations of works by Strauss and Feuerbach that challenged many ideas about Christianity; excerpts from her poems; and reviews of writers such as Wollstonecraft, Goethe and Browning. Wonderfully rich in imagery and observations, these pieces reveal the intellectual development of this most challenging and rewarding of writers.

This volume, the first paperback collection of George Eliot's non-fiction, makes available many works never before published in book form. In her introduction, A. S. Byatt discusses Eliot's place in the literary world of Victorian London and the views expounded in these works.

Edited by A. S. Byatt and Nicholas Warren

With an introduction by A. S. Byatt

PENGUIN CLASSICS

THE NEW PENGUIN BOOK OF ROMANTIC POETRY

'And what if all of animated Nature
Be but organic harps, diversely framed'

The Romanticism that emerged after the American and French revolutions of 1776 and 1789 represented a new flowering of the imagination and the spirit, and a celebration of the soul of humanity with its capacity for love. This extraordinary collection sets the acknowledged genius of poems such as Blake's 'Tyger', Coleridge's 'Khubla Khan' and Shelley's 'Ozymandias' alongside verse from less familiar figures and women poets such as Charlotte Smith and Mary Robinson. We also see familiar poets in an unaccustomed light, as Blake, Wordsworth and Shelley demonstrate their comic skills, while Coleridge, Keats and Clare explore the Gothic and surreal.

This volume is arranged by theme and genre, revealing unexpected connections between the poets. In their introduction Jonathan and Jessica Wordsworth explore Romanticism as a way of responding to the world, and they begin each section with a helpful preface, notes and bibliography.

'An absolutely fascinating selection – notable for its women poets, its intriguing thematic categories and its helpful mini biographies' Richard Holmes

Edited with an introduction by Jonathan and Jessica Wordsworth

PENGUIN CLASSICS

TROILUS AND CRISEYDE
GEOFFREY CHAUCER

The tragedy of *Troilus and Criseyde* is one of the greatest narrative poems in English literature. Set during the siege of Troy, it tells how the young knight Troilus, son of King Priam, falls in love with Criseyde, a beautiful widow. Brought together by Criseyde's uncle, Pandarus, the lovers are then forced apart by the events of war, which test their oaths of fidelity and trust to the limits. The first work in English to depict human passion with such sympathy and understanding, *Troilus and Criseyde* is Chaucer's supreme evocation of the joy and grief inherent in love.

In his critical introduction to this original-spelling edition, Barry Windeatt discusses the traditions, sources and interpretations of *Troilus and Criseyde*. The poem is provided with on-page glosses, explanatory notes and full glossary, and appendices explore topics such as metre and versification.

Edited with an introduction and notes by Barry Windeatt

PENGUIN CLASSICS

DANTE IN ENGLISH

'All in the middle of the road of life
I stood bewildered in a dusky wood'

Dante Alighieri (1265–1321) created poetry of profound force and beauty that
proved influential far beyond the borders of his native Italy. This new collection
brings together translations from all his verse, including the *Vita Nuova*, his tale of
erotic despair and hope, and the *Commedia*, his vast yet intimate poem depicting
one man's journey into the afterlife. It also contains extracts from many English
masterpieces influenced by Dante, including Chaucer's *Canterbury Tales*,
Milton's *Paradise Lost*, Byron's *Don Juan*, T. S. Eliot's *The Waste Land* and
Derek Walcott's *Omeros*.

Edited by Eric Griffiths and Matthew Reynolds, this anthology explores the
variety of encounters between Dante and English-speakers across more than six
centuries. Its detailed notes enable even readers with little or no Italian to
appreciate translations that range from the hilarious to the inspired. Eric Griffiths'
introduction explains how intricately Dante's work is tied to his own time, yet still
speaks across the ages. This edition also includes an account of Dante's life and a
list of further reading.

Edited with an introduction and notes by Eric Griffiths
and Matthew Reynolds

PENGUIN CLASSICS

SELECTED POEMS AND LETTERS
ARTHUR RIMBAUD

'I know dusk
And dawn, rising like a multitude of doves.
What men have only thought they'd seen, I've seen'

Arthur Rimbaud was one of the wildest, most uncompromising poets of his age,
although his brief literary career was over by the time he was twenty-one and he
soon embarked on a new life as a trader in Africa. This edition brings together his
extraordinary poetry and more than a hundred of his letters, most of them written
after he had abandoned literature. A master of French verse forms, the young
Rimbaud set out to transform his art, and language itself, by a systematic
'disordering of all the senses', often with the aid of alcohol and drugs. The result
is a highly innovative, modern body of work, obscene and lyrical by turns – a
rigorous journey to extremes.

Jeremy Harding and John Sturrock's new translation includes Rimbaud's greatest
verse, as well as his record of youthful torment, *A Season in Hell*, while the
African letters unveil a portrait of the man who turned his back on poetry. The
edition also includes an introduction examining Rimbaud's two very different
careers.

Translated with an introduction by Jeremy Harding and John Sturrock

PENGUIN CLASSICS

SELECTED POEMS
RABINDRANATH TAGORE

'It dances today, my heart, like a peacock it dances …
It soars to the sky with delight'

The poems of Rabindranath Tagore (1861–1941) are among the most haunting
and tender in Indian and world literature, expressing a profound and passionate
human yearning. His ceaselessly inventive works deal with such subjects as the
interplay between God and the world, the eternal and transient, and the paradox of
an endlessly changing universe that is in tune with unchanging harmonics. Poems
such as 'Earth' and 'In the Eyes of a Peacock' present a picture of natural
processes unaffected by human concerns, while others, as in 'Recovery – 14',
convey the poet's bewilderment about his place in the world. And exuberant
works such as 'New Rain' and 'Grandfather's Holiday' describe Tagore's sheer
joy at the glories of nature or simply in watching a grandchild play.

William Radice's exquisite translations are accompanied by an introduction
discussing Tagore's Bengali cultural background, his social, political and religious
beliefs, and the lyric metres and verse forms he developed.

'An important book … William Radice's introduction is excellent' *Sunday Times*

Translated with an introduction by William Radice

PENGUIN CLASSICS

IDYLLS OF THE KING   ALFRED LORD TENNYSON

'There likewise I beheld Excalibur
Before him at his crowning borne, the sword
That rose from out the bosom of the lake'

Tennyson had a life-long interest in the legend of King Arthur and after the huge success of his poem 'Morte d'Arthur' he built on the theme with this series of twelve poems, written in two periods of intense creativity over nearly twenty years. *Idylls of the King* traces the story of Arthur's rule, from his first encounter with Guinevere and the quest for the Holy Grail to the adultery of his Queen with Launcelot and the King's death in a final battle that spells the ruin of his kingdom. Told with lyrical and dreamlike eloquence, Tennyson's depiction of the Round Table reflects a longing for a past age of valour and chivalry. And in his depiction of King Arthur he created a hero imbued with the values of the Victorian age – one who embodies the highest ideals of manhood and kingship.

This edition includes an introduction examining the publication history of the *Idylls*, a chronology, suggestions for further reading and explanatory notes.

Edited by J. M. Gray

PENGUIN CLASSICS

THE METAPHYSICAL POETS

'Death be not proud, though some have called thee
Mighty and dreadfull, for, thou art not soe'

With their intricate arguments, startling conceits and dazzling wit, the
seventeenth-century poets who became known as 'metaphysical' brought
a new ingenuity and energy to English verse. John Donne's poems are
some of the most passionate and profound to be written on both secular
and spiritual love, from the playful eroticism of 'To his Mistris Going
to Bed' to the dramatic force of his Holy Sonnets. George Herbert's
religious verse, including 'Easter-wings', drew on unusual images such as
music and money to create works that are intensely personal and
devotional. And Andrew Marvell encompassed love poetry like 'To His
Coy Mistress', philosophical dialogues, public odes and pastoral verse.
All the poets collected here, who also include Henry Vaughan, Thomas
Traherne and Richard Crashaw, can be seen fusing intellect and learning
with powerful emotion to create some of the most individual and original
poetry in the language.

Helen Gardner's acclaimed edition contains an introduction placing works
in their historical context, biographical notes for each poet and indexes of
first lines and authors.

Edited with an introduction by Helen Gardner

PENGUIN CLASSICS

THE COMPLETE POEMS   JOHN MILTON

'I may assert Eternal Providence
And justify the ways of God to men'

John Milton was a master of almost every type of verse, from the classical
to the religious and from the lyrical to the epic. His early poems include
the devotional 'On the Morning of Christ's Nativity', 'Comus', a masque,
and the pastoral elegy 'Lycidas'. After Cromwell's death and the dashing
of Milton's political hopes, he began composing *Paradise Lost*, which
reflects his profound understanding of politics and power. Written when
Milton was at the height of his abilities, this great masterpiece fuses the
Christian with the classical in its description of the Fall of Man. In
Samson Agonistes, Milton's last work, the poet draws a parallel with his
own life in the hero's struggle to renew his faith in God.

In this edition of the *Complete Poems*, John Leonard draws attention
to words coined by Milton and those that have changed their meaning
since his time. He also provides full notes to elucidate biblical, classical
and historical allusions and has modernized spelling, capitalization
and punctuation.

Edited with a preface and notes by John Leonard

PENGUIN CLASSICS

PARADISE LOST   JOHN MILTON

'Better to reign in Hell, than serve in Heav'n ...'

In *Paradise Lost* Milton produced a poem of epic scale, conjuring up a vast, awe-inspiring cosmos and ranging across huge tracts of space and time. And yet, in putting a charismatic Satan and naked Adam and Eve at the centre of this story, he also created an intensely human tragedy on the Fall of Man. Written when Milton was in his fifties – blind, bitterly disappointed by the Restoration and briefly in danger of execution – *Paradise Lost*'s apparent ambivalence towards authority has led to intense debate about whether it manages to 'justify the ways of God to men', or exposes the cruelty of Christianity.

John Leonard's revised edition of *Paradise Lost* contains full notes, elucidating Milton's biblical, classical and historical allusions and discussing his vivid, highly original use of language and blank verse.

'An endless moral maze, introducing literature's first Romantic, Satan'
John Carey

Edited with an introduction and notes by John Leonard

THE STORY OF PENGUIN CLASSICS

Before 1946 ...'Classics' are mainly the domain of academics and students, without readable editions for everyone else. This all changes when a little-known classicist, E. V. Rieu, presents Penguin founder Allen Lane with the translation of Homer's *Odyssey* that he has been working on and reading to his wife Nelly in his spare time.

1946 *The Odyssey* becomes the first Penguin Classic published, and promptly sells three million copies. Suddenly, classic books are no longer for the privileged few.

1950s Rieu, now series editor, turns to professional writers for the best modern, readable translations, including Dorothy L. Sayers's *Inferno* and Robert Graves's *The Twelve Caesars*, which revives the salacious original.

1960s The Classics are given the distinctive black jackets that have remained a constant throughout the series's various looks. Rieu retires in 1964, hailing the Penguin Classics list as 'the greatest educative force of the 20th century'.

1970s A new generation of translators arrives to swell the Penguin Classics ranks, and the list grows to encompass more philosophy, religion, science, history and politics.

1980s The Penguin American Library joins the Classics stable, with titles such as *The Last of the Mohicans* safeguarded. Penguin Classics now offers the most comprehensive library of world literature available.

1990s The launch of Penguin Audiobooks brings the classics to a listening audience for the first time, and in 1999 the launch of the Penguin Classics website takes them online to a larger global readership than ever before.

The 21st Century Penguin Classics are rejacketed for the first time in nearly twenty years. This world famous series now consists of more than 1300 titles, making the widest range of the best books ever written available to millions – and constantly redefining the meaning of what makes a 'classic'.

The Odyssey continues ...

The best books ever written

PENGUIN (🐧) CLASSICS

SINCE 1946